African American Theater

For my parents and their parents

African American Theater

A Cultural Companion

GLENDA DICKER/SUN

polity

First published in 2008 by Polity Press

Polity Press
65 Bridge Street
Cambridge CB2 1UR, UK.

Polity Press
350 Main Street
Malden, MA 02148, USA

ISBN-13: 978-0-7456-3442-5
ISBN-13: 978-0-7456-3443-2(pb)

A catalogue record for this book is available from the British Library.

Typeset in 11/13 pt Adobe Garamond
by Servis Filmsetting Ltd, Stockport, Cheshire
Printed and bound in Great Britain by MPG Printers Ltd, Bodmin, Cornwall

For further information on Polity, visit our website: www.polity.co.uk

Contents

Picture Credits

The publisher would like to thank the following for permission to reproduce the images in this book:

Page 7, © 2007 JupiterImages and its Licensors; Page 8, Shutterstock; Page 9, © 2007 JupiterImages and its Licensors; Page 12, © 2007 JupiterImages and its Licensors; Page 13, © 2007 JupiterImages and its Licensors; Page 25, © CORBIS; Page 33, © 2007 JupiterImages and its Licensors; Page 36, © 2007 JupiterImages and its Licensors; Page 37, © 2007 JupiterImages and its Licensors; Page 38, © 2007 JupiterImages and its Licensors; Page 43, © Bettmann/CORBIS; Page 45, CSU Archives/Everett Collection/Rex Features; Page 64, © 2007 JupiterImages and its Licensors; Page 70, Courtesy Hatch-Billops Collection; Page 77, Shutterstock; Page 78, © 2007 JupiterImages and its Licensors; Page 82, © John Springer Collection/CORBIS; Page 89, Courtesy Kimball and Bolcom; Page 90, Courtesy Kimball and Bolcom; Page 92, Roger-Viollet/Rex Features; Page 98, Mark E. Mitchell Collection of African American History; Page 99, Mark E. Mitchell Collection of African American History; Page 100, Courtesy Kimball and Bolcom; Page 106, Everett Collection/Rex Features; Page 100, Courtesy Kimball and Bolcom; Page 106, Everett Collection/Rex Features; Page 110, CSU Archives/Everett Collection/Rex Features; Page 117, Bettmann/CORBIS; Page 118, Bettmann/CORBIS; Page 120, © Jack Moebes/CORBIS; Page 122, Courtesy Hatch-Billops Collection; Page 125, Bettmann/CORBIS; Page 127, CORBIS; Page 132 CSU Archives/Everett Collection/Rex Features; Page 133, © 2007 JupiterImages and its Licensors; Page 138, © 2007 JupiterImages and its Licensors; Page 140, Shutterstock; Page 141, Star Collection, reprinted by permission of the DC Public Library © Washington Post; Page 142, Shutterstock; Page 144, © Bettmann/CORBIS; Page 178, Courtesy of Ms. Dee; Page 187, Everett Collection/Rex Features; Page 188, Teresa Lee/Everett/Rex Features; Page 191, © 2007 JupiterImages and its Licensors, All Rights Reserved

Every effort has been made to trade all copyright holders, but if any have been inadvertently overlooked the publishers will be pleased to include any necessary credits in any subsequent reprint or edition.

The following images are © Glenda Dicker/sun: pages 19, 23, 27, 35, 54, 68, 81, 104, 108, 130, 148, 151, 154, and 180.

For further information on Polity, visit our website: www.polity.co.uk

Acknowledgements

I want to thank Tayana Hardin for her invaluable research assistance. Without the internet savvy her generation takes for granted, I would never have been able to find much of the information I needed to complete the book. Shanesha Brooks Tatum was also helpful with the tidying up process. Susana Castro-Pollard was a friend in need as I struggled with deciding which images to include. A gifted designer, she patiently helped me sift through hundreds of images from seemingly hundred of books to settle on the 60 that are included here. She also helped prepare the photographs for publication.

Judith Stephens and Freda Scott Giles provided extremely helpful feedback and cogent suggestions throughout the writing process. They both remain highly valued friends and colleagues, Judith for encouraging me to keep on climbing and Freda for her careful attention to all my work. Margaret Wilkerson and Eleanor Traylor will always be the bright shining lights who guide my path.

Andrea Drugan, commissioning editor for Polity, was a pleasure to work with and most helpful to me as I navigated the thorny territory from draft to completion. All at Polity were encouraging and uniformly pleasant and professional.

I must pay homage to my family. My great-grandfather, Madison Kilpatrick (pictured in chapter 3), and his five daughters inspired me to strive for a life of service. On my mother's side my grandmother, Ruth Harris Sanders, and her sister, Mazella Harris Goodson, laid down clear, sturdy footsteps for me to follow. The unwavering support of my parents, Harvey and Gerthyl Dickerson, throughout all my creative endeavors has been a constant source of sustenance. My father in particular was helpful with the research for chapter 5, "War Stories." My brother, Harvey, knows all my secrets. My daughter, Anitra, her husband, Pierre, and my little baby grandson, Julian, give me hope for the future.

About this Book

African American Theater: A Cultural Companion is different from many other books on black theater in the United States and elsewhere. Rather than providing a history of African American theater, which has already been done splendidly, I have tried to capture a story told by people in their own words from slavery days to the first decade of the 21st century and to explore how their realities influenced the theater of their times. Elderly people who still remember slavery speak of the days of bondage. Race men and women who came to prominence in the era of Reconstruction provide admonitions to the newly freed. The "exodusters" of the Great Migration explain why they traveled north. Zora Neale Hurston bridges the gap between the elitist "New Negroes" of the Harlem Renaissance and the rowdy Harlem rent parties. Black soldiers recount their war stories from the Civil War to Vietnam. The "ordinary people" who moved the Black Freedom struggle forward tell their extraordinary tales. The cultural workers of the Black Arts Movement conjure the magic of that moment. Ossie Davis eulogizes Malcolm X and reminisces about Marian Anderson's singing. Nine contemporary African American actors pay homage to Ossie Davis and others of his generation, including Paul Robeson, Lena Horne, Sidney Poitier, Ruby Dee, and Harry Belafonte. Angela Davis praises Gertrude "Ma" Rainey; James Earl Jones remembers August Wilson; and James Baldwin empowers Suzan-Lori Parks.

With this interactive workbook, I hope you will become my companion on an African American cultural journey beginning in the middle of the 19th century and ending in the early 21st. The symbol ♠ introduces exercises to bring the historical subject matter to life and suggestions for further thought. Crucially, the book offers a guide to creating what I call a Black Life Book, in which you can document the important events of your life, stories you heard, important dates, and so on. It can contain such artifacts as newspaper articles that interest you, family photos, advertisements, letters, and playbills. The Black Life Book can also be a way to remember and honor members of your family as far back as you can trace them.

African American Theater: A Cultural Companion has 60 illustrations chosen to enrich the written word. These will enhance your understanding of a mask not yet animated by an inner quality called "Iwa" and African art that resonates with cultural significance. They range from photographs of the legendary Harriet Tubman in old age and Denzel Washington before he became internationally renowned to celebrations of black pride. For reasons that will become clear, I have also included portraits of members of my own family and memorabilia from my work as a writer and director. Throughout, I have aimed to offer mythic reminders of how the past still plays out in the world of African American theater.

Timeline of Significant Events

1847	Frederick Douglass begins publication of the anti-slavery newspaper *North Star*.
1850	The passing of the second Fugitive Slave Act in the United States.
1852	Harriet Beecher Stowe's novel *Uncle Tom's Cabin* is published.
1859	John Brown leads a raid on a weapons arsenal at Harper's Ferry, Virginia.
1861	The American Civil War begins.
1863	The Emancipation Proclamation takes effect on January 1, declaring freedom for slaves in the rebelling territories. Black soldiers are allowed to join the Union army.
1865	The Civil War ends with a northern victory; Reconstruction begins; the 13th Amendment formally ends slavery. President Lincoln is assassinated.
1866–9	Black colleges open throughout the southern states including Fisk (Nashville, Tennessee), Morehouse (Atlanta, Georgia), and Hampton (Virginia), as well as Howard University (Washington, DC).
1870	Black men are given the right to vote.
1877	Reconstruction ends.
1895	Booker T. Washington delivers his "Atlanta Compromise" speech.
1896	*Plessy vs. Ferguson*, the case in which the US Supreme Court establishes the doctrine of "separate but equal."
1896	The National Association of Colored Women is founded.
1896	Poems of Paul Laurence Dunbar are acclaimed by New York critics.
1903	W. E. B. DuBois publishes *Souls of Black Folks*, emerging as the leading opponent to the policies of Booker T. Washington.

1909	The National Association for the Advancement of Colored People (NAACP) is formed.
1914	The beginning of World War I.
1914–15	Black migration from the South to the North slowly increases.
1915	Karamu House is founded as a cultural center in Cleveland, Ohio. It includes a theater, the first specifically African American theater in the US.
1916	Marcus Garvey founds his Universal Negro Improvement Association (UNIA). The *Chicago Defender* calls on southern blacks to migrate to the North.
1920s	A second wave of the Great Migration brings roughly 700,000 more southern blacks to the North.
1921	*Shuffle Along*, the hit musical by Eubie Blake and Noble Sissle, opens on Broadway.
1925	Alain Locke publishes a collection of writings by African Americans, *The New Negro*. Brotherhood of Sleeping Car Porters is formed and selects A. Philip Randolph as its president.
1926	The New York Public Library purchases Arturo Schomburg's collection of books and prints.
1935	National Council of Negro Women is founded by Mary McLeod Bethune.
1939	Marian Anderson, barred from Constitution Hall, gives an Easter concert on the steps of the Lincoln Memorial in Washington, DC.
1942–5	Tuskegee Airmen and 92nd Buffalo Soldiers distinguish themselves in World War II.
1954	*Brown vs. Board of Education of Topeka, Kansas*, the case in which the US Supreme Court overturns that of 1896 by arguing for equal educational opportunities.
1955	Emmett Till is murdered; the Montgomery Bus Boycott is initiated by Rosa Parks and Jo Ann Gibson Robinson.
1957	Thirteen students attempt to integrate Central High School in Little Rock, Arkansas.
1960	The nationwide sit-in movement is sparked by four students in Greensboro, North Carolina.
1961	Integrated teams ride buses from North to South in what came to be known as the Freedom Rides.

1963	Martin Luther King leads the March on Washington for Jobs and Freedom.
1964	Civil Rights Act is passed.
1964	Martin Luther King receives the Nobel Peace Prize.
1965	Malcolm X is assassinated.
1966	Stokely Carmichael coins the phrase "black power" during the James Meredith March from Memphis, Tennessee, to Jackson, Mississippi.
1967	Thurgood Marshall is appointed to the US Supreme Court.
1967	Negro Ensemble Company is established in New York.
1968	Martin Luther King is assassinated. The Black Arts and Black Power Movements gather momentum.
1970	Charles Gordone receives the Pulitzer Prize for his play *No Place to be Somebody*.
1976	Ntozake Shange's *for colored girls* opens on Broadway.
1977	The TV mini-series *Roots* draws record ratings.
1979	Lloyd Richards is named Dean of the Yale University School of Drama at New Haven, Connecticut.
1982	Richards directs premiere of August Wilson's *Ma Rainey's Black Bottom* at Yale (the play is the first in Wilson's series of ten, *The Pittsburgh Cycle*, also known as *Century Cycle*).
1984	Richards directs *Ma Rainey's Black Bottom* at its first season on Broadway.
1986	George C. Wolfe wins the Dramatists Guild Award for his play *Colored Museum*.
1991	Lynn Whitfield receives an Emmy Award for her title role performance in *The Josephine Baker Story*.
1992	Anna Deveare Smith's *Fires in the Mirror* premieres.
1999	Halle Berry appears in *Introducing Dorothy Dandridge*.
2001	Suzan-Lori Parks receives the McArthur Genius Award.
2002	Denzel Washington and Halle Berry receive Academy Awards.
2004	Phylicia Rashad and Audra McDonald receive Tony Awards for the Broadway revival of *A Raisin in the Sun*.
2005	August Wilson dies, having completed *Radio Golf*, the tenth (and last) of his *Century Cycle*.
2006	Voting Rights Act is renewed.

2006	Lloyd Richards dies.
2007	Lynn Nottage receives the McArthur Genius Award.
2007	International celebrations of the bicentenary of the Abolition of the Slave Trade Act in Britain.
2008	Bicentenary (January 1) of the prohibition of importing slaves into the US.

Abbreviations

AFSCME	American Federation of State, County, Municipal Employees
AME	African Methodist Episcopal
ANT	American Negro Theatre
ANTA	American National Theatre and Academy
BAM	Black Arts Movement
CNA	Committee for the Negro in the Arts
CORE	Congress for Racial Equality
HBCU	Historically Black Colleges and Universities
FTP	Federal Theatre Project
MFA	Master of Fine Arts
MFDP	Mississippi Freedom Democratic Party
NAACP	National Association for the Advancement of Colored People
NEC	Negro Ensemble Company
NLT	New Lafayette Theatre
RACCA	Richard Allen Cultural Center
SCLC	Southern Christian Leadership Council
SNCC	Student Nonviolent Coordinating Committee
UCLA	University of California, Los Angeles
UNIA	Universal Negro Improvement Association
WPC	Women's Political Council
YWCA	Young Women's Christian Association

Introduction

A Journey with the People who Forgot how to Fly

What I come through in life, if I go down in meself for it, I could make a book.
(J. W. White, a former slave,
in Mellon, ed., xix)

This book is not a history of black theater. It is not an anthology of black plays. It is not a critical analysis. It is meant to be an interactive cultural companion. If you are a student taking a class in African American theater or a teacher of black theater or someone who enjoys studying the topic on your own, this book can be like a friend with whom you go on a journey. It will provide you with a guide to the cultural landscape that has historically surrounded the writers of plays. *African American Theater: A Cultural Companion* will also provide you with material to create your own monologues and scenes and with acting tips to bring this material alive. It is a combination of history, fiction, drama, and myth.

The metaphor of the people who could fly is the unifying thread of the book. The mythic tale describes the unnaturally suppressed inner lives of Africans brought to the American place to serve as slave labor. African American playwrights searched for ways to uncover, demonstrate, and celebrate that suppressed inner life. The story begins around 1850, when most African people were enslaved in America. The legacy of slavery has historically woven itself throughout African American drama and still plays out on the current landscape in the works of such writers as August Wilson and Suzan-Lori Parks. The dehumanizing effects of slavery and the pernicious stereotypes that denigrated black people have been of particular interest to playwrights since 1850 and have remained equally topical.

Throughout the book, I try to allow ordinary people to tell their own stories in their own voices. In chapter 1, "The People who Could Fly," I offer excerpts of oral histories from people who actually lived through slavery. I also examine derogatory stereotypes made popular by the minstrel show.

Chapter 2, "A Leap for Freedom," introduces the Abolitionist, the Underground Railroad Conductor and the Emancipated Interlocutor. These three mythic figures were instrumental in bringing an end to slavery. Illiteracy was one of the most powerful tools to keep people enslaved. Learning to write provided enslaved people with the means to move about more freely and to communicate with each other and with abolitionists. Many of them taught themselves out of hymnals and the Bible, but the way in which Rebecca Jackson learned to read is unique. I recount her story here as an example of the non-dramatic material included in my book with suggestions for how it could be dramatized.

In July 1830, at the age of 35, Rebecca experienced a religious awakening during a severe thunderstorm. After this revelation, she began having visions, in which she said the presence of a divine inner voice instructed her to use her spiritual gifts. She claimed that in these dreams she could heal the sick, make the sinful holy, speak with angels, and *even fly* [italics mine]. Rebecca was still frustrated by her inability to read and write; but she took solace in her inner voice when it said "the time shall come when you can write." So she continued praying, and one day the inner voice spoke to her about learning to read. She later wrote:

> I laid down my dress, picked up my Bible, ran upstairs, opened it, and kneeled down with it pressed to my breast, prayed earnestly to Almighty God if it was consisting to His holy will, to learn me to read His holy word. And when I looked on the word, I began to read. [. . .] So I done, until I read the chapter.
> (Women in History, online)

The Civil War was fought in part to free the slaves, but it turned out to be only the beginning of African Americans' fight for freedom. Initially, the Union government gave hope to its black citizens. It abolished legal slavery in 1865 through the 13th Amendment to the Constitution. In 1868 it guaranteed African Americans equal rights and equal protection under the law with the 14th Amendment. The 15th Amendment (1870) gave black men the right to vote.

The federal government tried to remake the South into a real democracy during the Radical Reconstruction era (1867–77). US soldiers were posted throughout the former Confederacy to back up the rights of freedmen. Black men functioned as citizens and were elected to office, including two to the Senate and 14 to the House of Representatives. But blacks remained economically enslaved to the large landholders who had once owned them. Now "sharecroppers," the freedmen farmed the fields for a share of the cotton crop, which never produced enough income to pull them out of debt to their masters.

One by one, the benefits of emancipation were wrenched from the freedmen's grasp. Faced with this startling new reality, the emancipated descendants of enslaved Africans called upon the networking and community-building skills honed on the Underground Railroad and in the abolition movement. They banded together in churches, freedmen's bureaus, club movements, and benevolent societies in a concerted effort to achieve collective success, which they believed would protect them from the newly manifested hostility among the post-Reconstruction white society.

In chapter 3, "We are Climbing Jacob's Ladder," I discuss some of the reasons for the Great Migration of southern blacks to the urban areas of the North. During two distinct eras, 1915–18 and the 1930s and '40s, blacks from the rural South migrated north in search of freedom and economic security. These migrations gave rise to a new set of concerns for black dramatists.

During the Harlem Renaissance (1920–39) a New Negro Movement was launched by some of the era's strongest literary voices. As discussed in chapter 4, the elitist philosophy for the movement is credited primarily to Alain Locke and Charles Johnson. In the preface to the volume of African American writings that he edited in 1925, *The New Negro*, Locke opines:

> [. . . F]or the present, more immediate hope rests in the revaluation by white and black alike of the Negro in terms of his artistic endowments and cultural contributions, past and prospective. [. . .] He now becomes a conscious contributor and lays aside the status of a beneficiary and ward for that of a collaborator and participant in American civilization.
>
> (in Emanuel and Gross, eds., 84)

Historian Nathan Irvin Huggins, in critiquing the New Negro Movement and the Renaissance writers, points out the fallacy of ignoring ordinary voices. In his book *Harlem Renaissance* (1971) Huggins said, "the decade of the 1920s seems to have been too early for blacks to have felt the certainty about native culture that would have freed them from crippling self-doubt . . . that is why the art of the Renaissance was so problematic, feckless, not fresh, not real" (309). You can come to your own determination after reading this chapter.

In chapter 5, "War Stories," the voices of black soldiers who fought in America's wars from the American Revolution to the Vietnam War can be heard. The chapter also examines how some playwrights responded to the contradiction of these soldiers fighting for freedoms abroad that they were denied at home.

Chapter 6, "Sitting Down, Sitting In, and Standing Up," introduces some of the ordinary men and women who do not always get the credit they deserve for moving the Civil Rights Movement forward. In her memoir *Warriors Don't Cry* (1994) Melba Pattillo Beals, one of the nine students involved in the integration of Central High School in Little Rock, Arkansas, remembers:

> As I watch videotapes now and think back to that first day at Central High on September 4, 1957, I wonder what possessed my parents and the adults of the NAACP to allow us to go to that school in the face of such violence. When I

ask my mother about it, she says none of them honestly believed Governor Faubus had the unmitigated gall to use the troops to keep us out. She recalls as well that even when a rational voice nudged her to keep me home, there seemed to be that tug to go forward from some divine source.

(Beals, 308)

Bernice Johnson Reagon, founder and lead singer of Sweet Honey in the Rock was active in the movement as a student at Albany State College in Georgia. In an interview conducted in 1986, she describes the crucial role that music played in the movement:

When you ask somebody to lead a song, you're asking them to plant a seed. The minute you start the song, then the song is created by everybody there. It's almost like a musical explosion that takes place. But the singing in the movement was different from the singing in church. The singing is the kind of singing where you disappear. When we did those marches and went to jail, we expanded the space we could operate in, and that was echoed in the singing. It was a bigger, more powerful singing. The voice I have now, I got the first time I sang in a movement meeting, after I got out of jail. . . . I had never been that me before. And once I became that me, I have never let that me go.

(in Carson et al., eds., 143–4)

Chapter 7, "Black is Beautiful," explores the convergence of the Black Power Movement with the Black Arts Movement. Between 1965 and 1975 various forms of cultural expression became the preferred means for moving the struggle for "liberation" forward. The Black Arts Movement proposed a separate symbolism, mythology, critique, and iconology that would celebrate, promote, and preserve black history and culture.

In chapter 8, "Conversations," actors Barbara Montgomery, Lynn Whitfield, S. Epatha Merkerson, Giancarlo Esposito, Vondie Curtis-Hall, Joe Morton, Clifton Powell, Debbie Allen, and Phylicia Rashad talk about their long careers working in black theater.

The concluding chapter, "A Presence of Ancestry," examines the presence of the cultural past in today's black theatrical landscape, stretching from Lorraine Hansberry's *Raisin in the Sun* to Suzan-Lori Parks' *Top Dog/Underdog*. An exploration of August Wilson's cycle of ten plays provides the means to review the major cultural landmarks visited in previous chapters.

The plays I have chosen to include for discussion are not necessarily well known or much produced. But, like the ordinary people who tell extraordinary tales, these sometimes hidden gems reflect the cultural stories I am trying to tell in a particular chapter. They highlight a poignant part of the black experience that is not always revealed in the more popular works of other playwrights.

J. W. White is quoted at the beginning of this introduction as saying, "What I come through in life, if I go down in meself for it, I could make a book." What do you think the phrase "if I go down in meself" means? If you "go down in yourself" could you make a book of your life? At the end of each chapter, I offer exercises to help you create a Black Life Book if you choose. I take that title from *The Black Book* (1974), an invaluable compilation of source material edited by Middleton Harris and others. In the introduction Bill Cosby says:

> Suppose a three-hundred-year-old black man had decided, oh say when he was about ten to keep a scrapbook – a record of what it was like for himself and his people in these United States. He would keep newspaper articles that interested him, old family photos, trading cards, advertisements, letters, handbills, dreambooks and posters. . . . He would remember things too, and put those in: stories he'd heard, rumors, dates.
>
> (Cosby, in Harris et al., eds., n.p.)

If you can find *The Black Book* in the library (it is also available on Amazon.com), it will offer lots of ideas for creating a scrapbook of your own.

As you work your way through this cultural companion to African American theater, you may want to begin to think about what stories you want to tell your children and grandchildren. I hope that the suggestions I give you will inspire you to come up with material for your own Black Life Book.

1   The People who Could Fly
Slavery, Stereotypes, Minstrelsy, and Myth

Alexanduh say he can fly.
Say all his people in Africa could fly.

(Floyd White, 177–8)

My hands are like a history book.
They tell a countless number of sad, sad stories.
Like a flowing river they seem to have no end.
The cost of survival was high. Why I paid it I will never know.

(Charlie H. Wingfield, Jr., in Marsh, ed., 36)

There are persistent tales of black people who could fly. In the 1930s, for example, a story spread about a man who walked faster and faster until he took off, flying faster than an airplane. Another recounts how a group of turn-of-the-century party-goers overtook a man on the road; he then mysteriously appeared at the barn before the group's arrival. There were also rumors about shops where wings could be purchased. The old-time spiritual "I'll Fly Away" was first sung during slavery. Toni Morrison explored this tale in her novel *Song of Solomon* (1977), which features "flying African children" and ends with the modern-day protagonist flying away.

The most popular tale in this genre is called "The People Could Fly." In one version of the story, some people who were brought to America on slave ships knew how to fly but had to shed their wings because the ships were so crowded. A mythic figure called High John the Conqueror is said to have flown alongside the ships to gather up the discarded wings. These people subsequently forgot the secret word that enabled them to fly. For African people brought to the American place to perform slave labor, this tale held particular resonance: the ability to fly symbolized the ability to escape their bondage, to "fly away home." It may now seem like a "dark pre-history," but it is important to remember that African people were captured, brought through the Middle Passage, and enslaved in America. In Alabama, in Mississippi, in Maryland, Virginia, Georgia, and the Carolinas, they lived without citizenship, without any rights at all. They were forced into stoop labor. Stoop labor is work that requires bending your back, like picking cotton or beans.

Whispering the Magic Word

Soon, as the tale goes, the enslaved people grow weary of working long hours in the hot sun. They call on High John to return their wings to them. High John whispers a magic word from their homeland and it is passed down the row. Some people recognized the word and leapt up to High John to reclaim their wings. They flew up and away from the field, flew away to Freedom; but they left behind, sorrowfully left behind, the ones who could not recognize the word. The ones who could not fly had to wait for a chance to run away. The ones who could not fly told their children about the people who flew away to Freedom. And it is from these storytellers and their children that I draw my tale.

Hoping to fly away home

Let me begin with a question: What is a slave? A slave is property, just like your cell phone. Just as you cannot think of your cell phone as having feelings, it was hard for slave owners and others living in the 19th century to think of a slave as a human being. The slave was defined solely by who owned him/her. The owner of the slaves called himself their "master" and thought of them as beasts of burden like a cow or a donkey or a device of convenience like a cell phone. To the Yoruba people in West Africa, a mask is only a piece

Mask unanimated by Iwa

of carved wood until it is animated by Iwa or life essence. The animated mask becomes a powerful tool in rituals of life, death, and rebirth. To the people who called themselves "masters," the slave was like that wooden mask, unanimated by an inner life force:

> It come to de time Old Marster have so many slaves he don't know what to do wid them all. He give some of them off to his chillun. I was give to his grandson, just to wait on him and play wid him. Little Marse John treat me good sometime

and kick me round sometime. I see now dat I was just a little dog or monkey, in his heart and mind, dat it 'mused him to pet or kick, as it pleased him.

(Henry Gladney, in Mellon, ed., 149)

Here is another important question: What is the difference between a slave and an enslaved person? If we imagine the Africans placed in bondage as enslaved *people*, we are forced to see them differently. An enslaved person is a human being who has thoughts, feelings, aspirations, and fears; a human being unwillingly placed in bondage. This is the first distinction it is important to make as we proceed through this cultural companion to African American theater in the US.

As we begin our journey, we stand under the shadow of the Fugitive Slave Act, which was passed in 1850. This diabolical act held that even Africans who had escaped bondage and made it to free states could be captured and returned to their former owners. Under this act, even free-born people, if captured, could be sold into slavery. In the beginning, the English settlers didn't use slaves. They had indentured servants who were usually poor men and women who wanted to leave England and come to America. So a deal was struck: if you pay for my boat trip, I'll work for you for four to seven years, but then I'm free. Soon the settlers realized that it was cheaper to have slaves than indentured servants. Slaves could never leave.

The foreign slave trade which brought people from the west coast of Africa to the southern states and forced them into bondage began in the mid-1790s; the importation of slaves into the US was prohibited in 1808. As many as 450,000 Africans were shipped across. Not all of them were enslaved in the southern states. Northern cities such as New York also have a long history of slavery. In 2005–6 the New York Historical Society held an exhibition with an accompanying volume of essays and illustrations, *Slavery in New York*, edited by Ira Berlin and Leslie M. Harris. At one time there were more slaves in New York than in Charleston, South Carolina. Other enslaved people were left in the Caribbean, South America, and Central America.

Even after 1808, some slave dealers still illegally brought people from Africa to the United States. But a domestic slave trade also sprang up as slaves were sold from the older and more exhausted lands of the upper South to the newer and more fertile areas of the lower South. Furthermore, children born on American soil were automatically owned by the people who owned their mothers, making for a whole new source of free labor. A five-year-old friend of mine, upon hearing these facts, told me in shock: "You can't own people!" – but in 1850, in the United States, sadly you could.

History continues to conceal the humanity of the person trapped in slavery. The story of slavery in this country has been told in many voices, from many vantage points, but rarely from the point of view of those who lived through it. How, then, can one learn about the enslaved person's life in bondage? It is hard to believe, but thousands of ex-slaves were able to tell their stories in their own words before they died. From them, we are able to learn about slavery from the enslaved person's point of view. As John Little, a fugitive slave who had escaped to Canada, said in 1855: "'Tisn't he who has stood and looked on, that can tell you what slavery is – 'tis he who has endured" (in Yetman, ed., repr. 2000, 1). Not everyone found it easy to tell these stories: "Lots of old slaves close the door before they tell the truth about their days of slavery" (Martin Jackson, in Mellon, ed., 225).

During the Great Depression of the 1930s, various government agencies initiated work programs across the country to provide jobs for the unemployed. The Library of Congress supervised the programs conceived for jobless writers. The Federal Writers' Project, for example, culminated in a collection of black folk histories. Field workers were sent out to interview blacks who had lived under slavery. The project yielded first-hand accounts of such experiences on an unprecedented scale. In time, these oral histories came to be published in a wide variety of books by many different authors, extracts of which are quoted below.

The oral histories taken down in the 1930s paint an unbelievable picture. Little children were told that the stork brought the white babies to their mothers, but that the slave children were all hatched out from buzzards' eggs. And the children believed it was true. (Yetman, ed., repr. 2002, 39). Delia Garlic, one of the elderly women who remembered slavery, told of the grief when people were sold like cattle:

> Babies was snatched from their mothers' breast and sold to speculators. Chilluns was separated from sisters and brothers and never saw each other again. 'Course they cry! You think they not cry when they was sold like cattle? I could tell you about it all day, but even then you couldn't guess the awfulness of it.
>
> (in Hurmence, 1994, 99)

Some stories describe where these people lived: *"The slave houses were called the quarters, and the house where Master lived was called the Great House. Our houses had two rooms each, and Marster's house had twelve rooms"* (Mary Anderson, in Yetman, ed., repr. 2000, 15). Others describe food and clothing:

> Didn't have much to eat. Well, they give the colored people an allowance every week. A woman with children would get about a half-bushel of meal a week; a childless woman would get about a peck and a half of meal a week. They get some suet and a slice of bread for breakfast. For dinner they'd eat ashcake baked on the blade of a hoe. The men on the road got one cotton shirt and jacket.

Mourning woman

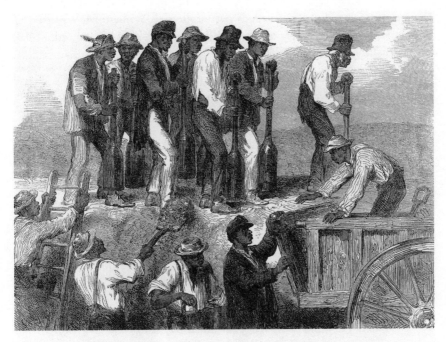

Men going to work in the field

If you was working they'd give you shoes. Children went barefooted the year around.

(Elizabeth Sparks, in Hurmence, 1994, 29)

They tell of the hard work: *"Oh lordy! The way us niggers was treated was awful. Master would beat, knock, kick, kill. He done ever'thing he could cept eat us. We was worked to death"* (Charlie Moses, in Mellon, ed., 80). About the cruel beatings: *"Folks a mile away could hear dem awful whippings. Dey wuz a turrible part of livin"* (Delia Garlic, in Mellon, ed., 244). Of never being able to visit loved ones on other plantations or go anywhere without a pass:

> We had one slave there on the plantation that Maser could not do anything with in the way of keeping him at home. When night come, he had him a girl that lived over on another plantation joining ours, and that Negro would go over there. Just as soon as Maser got to bed, he would get up and slip off over to see his girl. So Maser, he finally got him some chains and put them around that Negro's legs. But then, he would get him a pole to hop around on, and he would get over there some way to see his girl. Maser, he would not be outdone, so he fixed that Negro a shed and bed close to a tree, there on the plantation, and chained his hands and feet to that tree, so he could not slip off to see his Girl.
>
> (Polly Shine, in Mellon, ed., 242)

Among those to tell of the dreaded "patty rollers" is William McWhorter: *"I clare to goodness, patterollers was de devil's own hosses"* (in Mellon, ed., 140). Another is Julia Brown:

> We wasn't allowed to go around and have pleasure as the folks does today. We had to have passes to go wherever we wanted. When we'd get out there was a bunch of white men called the "patty rollers." They'd come in and see if all us had passes, and if they found any who didn't have a pass, he was whipped, give fifty or more lashes – and they'd count them lashes. If they said a hundred, you got a hundred.
>
> (in Yetman, ed., 2000, 47)

The people who could not fly were not only forbidden to speak their own languages, but forbidden to learn to read or write the language of their captors. The slave owners believed that reading and writing makes a person unfit to be a slave forever (Meltzer, ed., 1964, 60). As Jacob Branch put it: *De War comin' on den and us darsn't even pick up a piece of paper. De white folks didn't want us to learn to read for fear us find out things* (in Yetman, ed., 2000, 41).

Many slaves suffered forced marriages and rape:

> Plenty of the colored women have children by the white men. She know better than to not do what he say. They take them very same children what have they own blood and make slaves out of them. If the missus find out she raise revolution. But she hardly find out. The white men not going to tell and the nigger women were always afraid to. So they just go on hopin' that things won't be that way always.
>
> (W. L. Bost, in Hurmence, 1984, 95)

The experience of slavery can be epitomized in two examples: *"Yes, I was a slave. And I'll say this to the whole world: Slavery was the worst curse ever visited on the people of the United States"* (John Rudd, in Mellon, ed., 441); and *"Here's the idea: freedom is worth it all"* (Moses Mitchell, in Mellon, ed., 455).

James De Jongh drew upon some of the recorded memories collected by the Federal Writers' Project and created a play from them. *Do Lord Remember Me* opened at the American Place Theatre in New York in 1983. The play has five characters. Their stories are interspersed with songs and spirituals, creating a collage of song, dance, and dialogue that encapsulates the collective black experience from pre-Civil War days on. De Jongh's play does much to reveal the person hidden in slavery; the person behind the mask of stupidity and servility; the wingless person animated by inner life. *Do Lord* was revived on its 20th anniversary by the New Federal Theatre in New York. Ebony Jo-Ann, Barbara Montgomery, Glynn Turman, Roscoe Orman, and Chuck Patterson – most of them veterans of previous productions – were the accomplished cast directed by Reggie Life. In 2006 another revival was mounted by the Chromolume Theatre company in Los Angeles.

Iwa, Inner Life and Inner Monologue

Victoria Earle Matthews, an author of short stories and essays and a co-founder in 1896 of the National Association of Colored Women, wrote of "the unnaturally suppressed inner lives which our people have been compelled to lead" (in Andrews, ed., xv). The enslaved Africans were forced to live such unnaturally suppressed inner lives. Nonetheless, the people who could not fly developed mythic ways of coping with their bondage.

The Yoruba concept of Iwa or inner essence, mentioned above, can be informative in approaching an acting role. The inner monologue of the actor as he seeks to inhabit a character can be compared to this inner life of the enslaved person. What is said and what is thought are frequently two very different things. The inner monologue of the actor enriches and makes poignant the spoken or unspoken word. Denzel Washington delivers a powerful example of the unspoken, in the film *Glory* (1989) as he prepares for and accepts an undeserved beating. Charles Gordone, in his play *No Place to Be Somebody* (1969), has the character Gabe Gabriel say: "They is mo' to being black than meets the eye" (in Hamalian and Hatch, 20).

The first time that the contemporary media explored slavery in any depth was in the televison mini-series, *Roots*, filmed in 1977. The series was based on Alex Haley's book of the same name, published the previous year (with the subtitle *The Saga of an American Family*). Haley himself recalled how the inner life of the enslaved person and the inner monologue of the actor came together with startling results:

> We were in Savannah, Georgia, getting ready to film a scene where Kunta Kinte refused to call himself by the name his master had given him. The master had decided Kunta's name would be "Toby." The overseer was given the word, and he passed it to the old slave who was training the young Kunta. The old slave was being played by Lou Gossett, and the young slave, of course, by Levar Burton. But no matter what the old slave did, the young one refused to accept another name. Finally, word of his defiance went back via the overseer to the master, who ordered Kunta beaten until he would say his new name was now "Toby." That was the scene to be filmed that day. Levar was brought out and tied with his wrists to a set of crossed poles, much like an Indian tepee. As he hung there, to his right sat the old slave, Lou Gossett. He was being punished for his inability to get the young slave to say the name and would be needed to help remove the young slave after what would surely be a terrible beating. When the director announced "Action!" the overseer came out, dressed in a kind of cloak, proud and furious. He looked at the young one, hanging up there by his wrists, and he said, "What's your name, boy?"
>
> Levar answered quietly, "Kunta."

Smirking, the overseer looked over at a tall, anonymous slave in the background who was holding a whip, and this slave walked out into camera range, raised his arm and began. The whip they were using was made with loosely woven hemp, nothing that would hurt anybody. But a trained actor knows how to jerk the instant it touches his skin, making the force and sting of the blow appear painfully real. Levar took two blows, then a third, which, with the special effects blood capsules breaking, was almost too much to watch. Then, again, the overseer asked, "What your name, boy?"

Again, now weakly, Levar said, "Kunta."

After three more blows, and more blood, the 35 or so of us just out of camera range were so angry we were ready to charge out there and choke somebody.

This time Levar, his head nodding to one side, with no strength left even to lift his chin, said, in a whisper, "Toby, master." And the overseer whirled about, proud, arrogant. "Louder! Let me hear it again. What's your name, boy?"

Barely, Levar whispered, "Toby, master."

Then the tall slave who had done the beating cut Levar down, and Levar slumped into Lou Gossett's lap. Gossett, an experienced veteran actor, was supposed to embrace the young slave, to comfort him. One camera was to slowly slide out of focus, as an optional way to end that two-hour episode. But what happened is something that people who spend their lives around films being made may witness but a few times – when experienced actors or actresses totally forget who they are and become the role they are portraying, letting what's inside them take over. When Levar slumped into Lou Gossett's lap, Lou's own body began convulsing. He curled into a near-fetal position, grasping Levar to his own shaking self – and out of Lou's voice box, through his tears, came a hoarse, guttural cry.

"What difference it make what they calls you? You knows who you is, you's Kunta!" He convulsed again. He let out another, even higher pitched cry: "Dey's gonna be a better day."

"Dey's gonna be a better day!"

He paused. Silence. Then he repeated it. Maybe ten seconds passed, then the last film was clicked through three cameras. The only sound was Lou's weeping. Then he pulled himself back out of the role, into the present.

"I don't know what happened to me," he said. "I forgot about who I am. I was there, a hundred and fifty years ago, and that was my little Guinea boy. I was supposed to teach him how to be a slave and instead he had taught me how to be a man."

(in Marsh, 6)

The Trickster and the Old-time Negro Preacher

No amount of hard labor and suffering could suppress the powers of imagination of the people who could not fly. Two folk heroes of mythic proportion were born during slavery: the Trickster and the Old-Time Negro Preacher. As Charity Moore recalled: "When I remember Pappy, after he was a grown man, he was still telling the tales, and his sides were shaking and he was laughing. He told all us chillun the tales about the fox and the rabbit, the squirrel, brer terrapin, and such like, long before Joel Chandler Harris wrote them in a book. He sure did!" (in Rhyne, 33).

The African trickster tale exalted the triumph of the weak over the strong by means of wit and wile. Drawing upon their memories of trickster tales from Africa, the people who could not fly created new tales in which various animals, such as the rabbit, fox, bear, wolf, turtle, snake, and possum, took on the characteristics of the people found on the plantation. The American hero of the trickster tale became Brer Rabbit (made famous in the US and beyond in the *Uncle Remus* series, compiled by Joel Chandler Harris and first published in 1881). Some of Brer Rabbit's escapades and predicaments are virtually identical with those of Anansi, the West African Ashanti spider trickster.

There are also stories of real survival tricks. Henry Johnson described his experience as follows:

> They raised turkeys in the five hundred lots and never did give us one. So we wanted one so bad once, I put corn underneath the cabin and a turkey, a great big one, would come under our cabin to eat that corn. One day when I got a chance I caught that old gobbler by the neck and him and me went round and round under that old cabin house. He was the biggest, strongest bird I ever see. I was only a boy but finally I beat. I twisted his neck till he died. Then I took out up to the big house, fast as anything, to tell my old mistress one of our finest turkeys dead. She said, "Stop crying, Henry, and throw him under the hill." I was satisfied. I run back, picked that old bird, taken all his feathers to the river, and throwed them in. That night we cooked him, and didn't we eat something good! I had to tell her about that missing bird, because when they check up it all had to tally; so that fixed that.
>
> (in Hurmence, 1994, 37)

A character – usually called Slave John – often took the place of Brer Rabbit in the tales. John became the trickster hero who outwits the slave owner to win his freedom. The trickster looms large in African American cultural mythology. Slave John is named for the mythic figure of High John the Conqueror, who appeared and reappeared in many forms over the next decades. From the trickster come such sly, clever, and innovative characters as "Stagger Lee," made famous in poems and songs, for example:

> The high sheriff told the deputies
> "Get you pistols and come with me.
> We got to go 'rest that badman Stagolee."
> The deputies took their pistols
> And laid them on the shelf.
> "If you want that badman Stagolee
> Go'rest him by yourself!"

The development of these legendary personalities ultimately led to such folk heroes as Harriet Tubman, Huey Newton, Whoopi Goldberg, Moms Mabley, Chris Rock, Richard Pryor, and Malcolm X.

The Old-Time Negro Preacher is another kind of mythic folk hero who "sho could read outen his han" (Mellon, ed., 187). He had never learned to read and write, but he knew his Bible and would hold his hand up as though reading a book and preach the prettiest "preachins you ever heard" (187). He is epitomized in a traditional song:

> Way down yonder by myself,
> Couldn't hear nobody pray.
> Way down yonder in the valley,
> Couldn't hear nobody pray.
> Had to pray myself,
> Jest had to pray myself.

Secret meetings were held in "brush arbors" in the woods, gathered around an overturned pot to hold the sound and keep the meetings secret from the patty rollers. The Old-Time Negro Preacher was an orator of great ability, who could paint apocalyptic portraits and sweep his congregation along to heights of rapture. George McAlilley recalled: "In the summertime, after the crops were laid by, we went to hear one of our color expound on the Word in a brush arbor" (in Rhyne, 31).

There is an introduction to this inspirational figure in James Weldon Johnson's *God's Trombones: Seven Negro Sermons in Verse*, first published in 1927. Based on the Old-Time Negro Preacher's stock sermons, which Johnson put into poetic form, this work celebrates the black preachers whom he recalled from his youth in the South and as a young man in New York. Although these preachers had often been depicted as comic figures in American popular culture, Johnson hoped to give them "the niche in which [they] properly belong":

> It was the old-time preacher who for generations was the mainspring of hope
> and inspiration for the Negro in America. [. . .] This power of the old-time
> preacher, somewhat lessened and changed in his successors, is still a vital force;
> in fact, it is still the greatest single influence among the colored people of the
> United States. (Johnson, repr. 1990, 2)

Flyer for James Weldon Johnson's *God's Trombones*, which I directed in 1988

The excerpt that follows is from Johnson's poem "Let my People Go" and can be performed as a brief monologue. This could be extended by referring to the whole poem. Why do you think this sermon might have had special resonance for the people who could not fly? How would you dramatize this? Would you use a pulpit or imagine that you were in a "brush arbor"?

> And God said to Moses:
> I've seen the awful suffering
> Of my people down in Egypt.
> I've watched their hard oppressors,
> Their overseers and drivers;
> The groans of my people have filled my ears
> And I can't stand it no longer;
> So I'm come down to deliver them
> Out of the land of Egypt,
> And I will bring them out of that land
> Into the land of Canaan;
> Therefore, Moses, go down,
> Go down into Egypt,
> And tell Old Pharaoh
> To let my people go.
>
> Listen! – Listen!
> All you sons of Pharaoh.
> Who do you think can hold God's people
> When the Lord God himself has said,
> Let my people go?
>
> (Johnson, repr. 1990, 45)

Author/director Vinnette Carroll adapted Johnson's *God's Trombones* for the stage at her Urban Arts Corps in New York, calling it *Trumpets of the Lord.* While in 1927 Johnson had drawn public attention to the Old-Time Negro Preacher, Carroll's version of 1963, directed by Donald McKayle and starring Theresa Merritt, Cicely Tyson, and Al Freeman, Jr., captured the critics through its electric gospel singing. The play opened at the Circle in the Square in New York and was revived on Broadway in 1969 at the Brooks Atkinson Theatre.

From the Old-Time Negro Preacher who preached in secret in the woods during slavery times were born such important religious figures as Rebecca

Jackson, Richard Allen, founder of the African Methodist Episcopal Church, Sara Hatcher Duncan, a prominent voice in AME history who paved the way for Vashti McKenzie to become the first woman bishop in 2000. Martin Luther King can be said to be the 20th-century culmination of this spirit. As an anonymous slave once said: *"I've heard 'em pray for freedom. I thought it was foolishness, then, but the old-time folks always felt they was to be free. It must have been something 'vealed unto 'em"* (in Mellon, ed., 190).

Gentlemen be Seated: Enter the Minstrel Show

In additon to storytelling, folktales, riddles, and rhymes, enslaved people often entertained themselves on the plantations with masking rituals imported from their homeland. Through song and dance they poked fun at the habits and mores of the people who owned them. Ultimately the masking ritual was turned on the enslaved people in a cruel and hateful way. An itinerant performer, Thomas C. "Daddy" Rice, saw some of these entertainments and created the character "Jim Crow." This name became a generic term for Negro and later for segregation. When Rice took his farcical buffoon on the road, the African slave became a caricature on the American stage in his "Negro extravaganzas," the precursor of the minstrel show.

In the US, minstrel shows began with working-class white men dressing up as plantation slaves. White performers blackened their faces with burnt cork or greasepaint and performed songs and skits that mocked enslaved Africans. Among the many acts were the African Melodists, the Congo Minstrels, the Buckley Serenaders, the Ethiopian Mountain Singers, and Bryant's Minstrels.

There were three important stock characters in the minstrel show: Mr. Interlocutor, Mr. Tambo, and Mr. Bones. All three kept the action fast and furious. Mr. Interlocutor was the master of ceremonies. As controller of the show, he always sat at center-stage. Mr. Interlocutor represented the white presence on stage. Even though he sometimes performed in blackface, he was better dressed than the others and projected an image that was less ignorant than the rest of the troupe.

"Tam and Bones" sat at either end of a semicircle of blackfaced men and were dressed in outrageous, flashy costumes. Known as the "endmen," they contorted their bodies in exaggerated gestures and twisted their words in endless puns in order to keep the audience laughing. Their make-up gave them large eyes and gaping mouths with huge lips, and they spoke in ludicrous dialect. Mr. Tambo and Mr. Bones were named for the instruments they played: Mr. Tambo played the tambourine, while Mr. Bones clicked together bones with his wrist or sometimes his entire arm. The bones, derived from the ancient use of clapping animal ribs, consisted of two 10-inch pieces of wood carved to the same shape as cow ribs. The tambourine can make a rattling, clacking sound, sometimes like that of a snare drum. Both instruments are used to highlight rhythmical features in musical performance.

Other aspects of the minstrel show included stump speeches and parade skits. Stump speeches made fun of politicians, feminists, abolitionists, slaveholders, health quacks, and the like. A typical line from a stump speech satirizing feminists would be, "We ladies refuse always to be under the men! We want to be on top sometimes!" This was delivered, of course, by a male member of the cast, impersonating an African American impersonating a woman. Parade skits were supposedly set in the office waiting room of a physician, bureaucrat, or theatrical agent. One by one, a series of outlandish characters would make their appearance at stage right. Each one interacted with the gatekeeper in some comedic manner and eventually exited at stage left. Parade skits continue to be popular among comedy troupes because they can easily draw on topical people and issues, and are inexpensive to produce. Each exiting performer can change costume and character, and enter again at stage right.

Such denigrating stereotypes as the Uncle Tom, the Mammy, the Tragic Mulatto, the Coon, and the Buck descend primarily from the minstrel show but also from other sources. The Coon stereotype popularized in the minstrel show is the stupid, malapropism-spouting, grinning, dancing, cowardly character who appeals to white audiences for mere entertainment value. He is the no-account, unreliable, crazy, lazy, subhuman creature, good for nothing more than eating watermelons, stealing chickens, shooting craps, or butchering the English language.

A variant of this insulting stereotype is the picaninny, a harmless, little screwball whose eyes pop and hair stands on end at the slightest provocation. Topsy in Harriet Beecher Stowe's *Uncle Tom's Cabin* (1852) is a quintessential example. This novel about the evils of slavery was a bestseller, translated into 23 languages and distributed around the world. It was also reworked into a popular play. Among the central characters is Eliza Harris, a young woman who learns that her child is to be sold away from her. Eliza runs to the thawing Ohio River, the southern border of the non-slave state of Ohio, with her baby in arms, and jumps from ice floe to ice floe to escape her master, who is in close pursuit. The heart-rending fictional escape is said to be based on the real-life flight of a woman named Mary.

The eponymous (and stereotypical) character of Stowe's narrative has been much maligned. The author's unfamiliarity with more than a handful of former slaves led her inadvertently to depict her characters with minstrel show speech and mannerisms. While her motives were more than worthy,

Advertisement featuring the "picaninny" stereotype

among most African Americans the name "Uncle Tom" has become an epithet for the obsequious lackey who will lay down his life for his "white folks." The defiant Christ-like hero of Stowe's novel and play has been utterly forgotten.

The Tragic Mulatta is of mixed blood. She is irrevocably stained by (as little as) one drop of Negro blood. (The mulatta is half black; the quadroon is one quarter black, and the octoroon is one eighth black.) She is self-sacrificing and sympathetic (because of her white blood). Fair of skin, she often attempts to pass for white. She is a victim of her forbidden love for an heroic white figure and often kills herself when her dark secret is revealed. She is quintessentially presented as the Pecola figure in Fannie Hurst's novel *Imitation of Life* (1933), which was made into a film in 1934, with Claudette Colbert and the ephemeral Fredi Washington; it was refilmed in 1959 with Lana Turner and Susan Kohner, a white woman. Dion Boucicault's play *The Octoroon*, which opened in 1859, portrays a classic version of the story and was followed by numerous turn-of-the-century plays that explored the theme. The Tragic Mulatta is often conflated with the Jezebel stereotype, who supposedly seduced her owners during slavery and must bear the responsibility for her mulatto children. The interpretation of Jezebel as an oversexed and irresistible figure made black women extremely sensitive about how they were portrayed in literature and in life. Black women of the 19th century and the early 20th took great care to protect their virtue and to present a dignified image of the race.

The Mammy is big, fat, dark, cantankerous, fiercely independent, and asexual. She can also be generally sweet, jolly, good-tempered, and completely dedicated to her white family, especially to the children. She is the house servant who runs the white household with a firm hand and keeps other house slaves in line. *Imitation of Life* offers a somewhat refined version of this stereotype; but perhaps the most famous image of Mammy occurs in *Gone with the Wind*, filmed in 1939 as an adaptation of Margaret Mitchell's novel (1936). Hattie McDaniels was the first African American woman to receive an Oscar for her supporting role as Mammy in the film. The Mammy figure may be most familiar to modern audiences in the changing faces of Aunt Jemima on the pancake box as she evolved from sporting a headrag and smiling red lips to having pressed hair and pearl earrings.

The Brutal Black Buck is perhaps the most insidious and lingering stereotype confronting black people. Born of white fear, the Buck entered national consciousness in D. W. Griffith's film *Birth of a Nation* (1915), in which he appears as a lascivious, violent usurper of the virtue of white women, out to raise havoc. Barbaric, subhuman, and feral, he was on a rampage full of black rage. The only solution to the Buck problem was death through hanging (lynching). As late as the Black Power Movement of the 1960s, angry young black men who were willing to fight for equality were often painted with the damaging brush of the Brutal Black Buck.

But to revert to the topic of the minstrel show itself: as Paul Laurence Dunbar put it in the first line of one of his poems, "We wear the mask that grins and lies." Before the Civil War, black men were prohibited from appearing in minstrel shows. Yet there are some bizarre images as early as 1843 of black men putting on minstrel make-up and appearing as white men imitating black men. Dan Emmett's Virginia Minstrels, the first blackface troupe, first appeared at the Bowery Amphitheatre in New York that year. By the early 20th century, several of the most famous minstrels were black men who wore make-up – the most famous being Bert Williams, who performed in blackface into the 1920s. With George Walker, he was part of the famous vaudeville team, Williams and Walker. He joined Flo Ziegfeld's all-white "Follies" in 1910.

Williams met Walker in San Francisco in 1893, and the pair spent the next two years playing in different venues and putting together their act. During this time, they were employed by the Mid-Winter Exposition in Golden Gate Park to participate in an exhibit of a Dahomean village, intended to portray life in "darkest Africa." Because the real Africans were late in arriving,

Bert Williams in one of his Ziegfeld "Follies" sketches. To distinguish themselves from white comedians in blackface, he and George Walker billed themselves as "Two Real Coons"

Williams and Walker played Dahomeans, wearing animal skins in a setting of potted palms. Once the Africans did arrive, the duo took time to study their singing and dancing. This experience was to become an important influence on their work, particularly their popular and groundbreaking *In Dahomey,* the first all-black musical on a major Broadway stage. Will Marion Cook composed the music and Paul Laurence Dunbar and Alex Roger wrote the lyrics. On February 18, 1903, it opened on Broadway at the New York Theater. The show later traveled to England and the cast performed at the Shaftesbury Theatre in London and in November that year at Buckingham Palace in a royal command performance for the 62nd birthday party of Edward, Prince of Wales (later Edward VII).

The legacy of Bert Williams is complex. Intellectuals discuss his blackface "mask" in the same terms as they do the issues explored in Ralph Ellison's classic novel of black identity, *Invisible Man* (1952). Williams' philosophy of comedy was sophisticated, and it influenced the likes of Richard Pryor and Bill Cosby. A later commentator quotes some good acting advice:

> "All the jokes in the world are based on a few elemental ideas," Williams wrote in a 1918 magazine article. "Troubles are funny only when you pin them down to one particular individual. And that individual, the fellow who is the goat, must be the man who is singing the song or telling the story. [. . .] It was not until I could see myself as another person that my sense of humor developed."
>
> (Morgan, online)

Three plays that examine the real people behind the minstrel masks are published in *Colored Contradictions* (1996), a volume edited by Harry J. Elam, Jr., and Robert Alexander. It includes *Re/membering Aunt Jemima: A Menstrual Show*, which I wrote with Breena Clarke. This play, structured like an old-fashioned minstrel show, reclaims the much derided Mammy figure and reimagines her as a hero; Aunt Jemima has 13 daughters who represent both lampooned stereotypes such as Jezebel and important historic figures like Anna Julia Cooper. In the end, Aunt Jemima escapes from the pancake box and goes to live on the moon for ever.

The Little Tommy Parker Colored Minstrel Show, by Carlyle Brown, explores the experiences of black minstrel performers. The characters discuss how they saw one man play Uncle Tom with dignity. One harrowing night, they are attacked by an angry group of townspeople. On stage, the most haunting scene from this play is one in which the actors, who have been established as individual characters, put on blackface make-up and become an anonymous group of masked entertainers, their humanity gone.

I Ain't Yo' Uncle: The New Jack Revisionist Uncle Tom's Cabin (1995), a play by Robert Alexander, puts Harriet Beecher Stowe on trial for her role in the creation and perpetuation of black stereotypes. Alexander revises the stereotypical Topsy and Uncle Tom characters: Topsy appears in 1990s hip-hop attire, while Uncle Tom subverts the self-deprecating, God-loving images associated with Stowe's character.

Costume designer's rendering from my *Re/membering Aunt Jemina: A Menstrual Show*

Many black authors have historically written plays to celebrate the inner life, Iwa, of the people who could not fly. In a never-ending search for black identity, these authors write about the men and women who animate the mask. Collectively their work uncovers a vastly rich and complicated culture. The following chapters explore many avenues for the rest of this journey.

Food for Further Thought

To learn more about African American humor, trickster tales, and folklore, read Lawrence Levine's *Black Culture and Black Consciousness* (1977), Harold Courlander's *Treasury of Afro-American Folklore* (1976), and *On the Real Side* (1994) by Mel Watkins.

By reviewing the recollections of the people quoted in the first part of this chapter, can you write a first-person narrative describing what your life would be like living on a plantation? Starting at sun-up and ending at midnight, what specific experiences and interactions with other people would you have? What causes would there be for sorrow? For joy? Would your day end by sharing a trickster tale with others or might you play a trick during the day? Does the following quote help?

> Everybody except chillun had a task. If you were cleaning, mashing, and leveling the ground where the rice would be planted, your task was a half or a quarter of an acre a day, depending on how old you were. You had to chop the big sods and mash the ground, then fill up the holes and level the whole field. After that, you dug trenches where the rice seed would be planted and you sowed the seeds in the trench. Old Marse Joshua John Ward was king of the rice planters. He owned 1,092 Africans, and his fields yielded nearly four million pounds of rice a year.
>
> (Ben Horry, in Rhyne, 29)

The imaginary first-person narrative that you write can be coupled with a real story or stories that your grandmother or another elderly person in your family told you, a story that you don't want to forget. If you write it down and perhaps include some family photos, these two entries can begin your Black Life Book.

Devote as much time as you can to reading the newspaper and listening to the news. What stories would be good fodder for a parade skit or a stump speech? Clip them for inclusion in your Black Life Book.

2 A Leap for Freedom
The Anti-Slavery Movement

I didn't know I was a slave until I found out I couldn't do the things I wanted to do.
(Ex-slave in Virginia, in Marsh, ed., 27)

There was no such thing as being good to slaves. Many white people were better than others, but a slave belonged to his master, and there was no way to get out of it.
(Thomas Lewis, in Mellon, ed., 453)

Though conditions on plantations varied widely from place to place, the myth of the "happy darky" perpetuated in the minstrel show is just that, a myth. Most people were never content with their condition of enforced servitude. Their bodies trapped, but their spirits yearning to be free, the people who could not fly talked, wrote, and organized to gain their freedom. They traded information about those who had escaped, about means of escape, about a completely different world reached by following the North Star. Secrets flew from mouth to ear. Via the underground railroad, they walked and ran a thousand miles toward freedom.

This chapter is about abolitionists who worked in the North as well as the South in a variety of ways to bring an end to slavery. Two more mythic figures emerged during the anti-slavery movement: the Underground Railroad Conductor who "rode a railroad that had no track" and the Emancipated Interlocutor who escaped from bondage and then told powerful stories to sympathetic audiences about life under slavery. These mythic two, with the help of countless unknown others, ferried enslaved Africans to freedom.

The Angry Abolitionist

Denmark Vesey, Gabriel Prosser, and Nat Turner, revolutionary heroes who led slave rebellions, were all "slave preachers," but they can be distinguished from brush arbor preachers by their anger and from other abolitionists such as the Quakers by their bloodshed (as pacifists, Quakers belong to the Religious Society of Friends, which was founded in England by George Fox in the 17th century).

In August 1800, Gabriel Prosser planned a slave uprising in Henrico County, Virginia. An estimated 1,000 slaves gathered 6 miles outside Richmond, Virginia, in readiness for an assault. Gabriel, an uneducated field worker and coachman, planned to lead this slave army, equipped with makeshift weapons, on a raid against the armory in Richmond. Once armed with real muskets, the rebels would defend themselves against all attackers. Betrayed by another slave and hampered by a freak storm, the rebels were crushed. Some 35 slaves, including Gabriel Prosser, were hanged for participating in the plot.

This is how the writer Arna Bontemps, in his novel *Black Thunder: Gabriel's Revolt* (1936), imagines the trial. The scene is between Gabriel Prosser and the prosecutor at his trial. It can be performed as a scene for two male actors, one white, the other black.

"Here, now, you mean to say you were the one that thought up the whole idea?"

"I was the one. Me."

"Yes, but not all alone, surely –"

"Maybe not all alone."

"Well, then, who were your accomplices? Who helped you think it up?"

Gabriel shrugged. "You got Ditcher and Mingo and Gen'l John. You done hanged a plenty mo'. I talked to some of them. I told them to come on."

"It's plain that you do not intend to implicate anyone not already in custody. You're not telling all you know."

Gabriel looked at the man long and directly. "I ain't got cause to talk a heap, suh."

"You know, Gabriel, it is not impossible to alter the complexion of things even yet. I mean, you have a fine chance to let the court know if you have been made the tool of foreign agitators. If there were white men who talked to you, encouraged –"

That sounded foolish to Gabriel. "White mens?"

"Yes, men talking about equality, setting the poor against the rich, the blacks against their masters, things like that."

Gabriel was now convinced that the man was resorting to some sort of guile. He fixed his eyes earnestly. "I tell you. I been studying about freedom a heap, me. I heard a plenty folks talk and I listened a heap. And everything I heard made me feel like I wanted to be free. It was on my mind hard, and it's right there the same way yet. On'erstand? That's all. Something keep telling me that anything what's equal to a gray squirrel wants to be free. That's how it all come about."

"Well, was it necessary to plot such a savage butchery? Couldn't you have contrived an easier way?"

Gabriel shook his head slowly. After a long pause he spoke. "I ain't got no head for flying away. A man is got a right to have his freedom in the place where he's born. He is got cause to want all his kinfolks free like hisself."

"Oh, why don't you come clean? Don't you realize you're on the verge of hanging? The court wants to know who planted the damnable seeds, what Jacobins worked on you. Were you not treated well by your master?"

Gabriel ignored most of what he said. "Might just as well to hang."

"That's bravado. You want to live. And the best way for you —"

"A lion what's tasted man's blood is a caution to keep around after that."

"Don't strut, nigger."

"No, suh, no strutting. But I been free this last four–five weeks. On'erstand? I been a gen'l, and I been ready to die since first time I hooked on a sword. The others too — they been ready. We all knowed it was one thing or the other. The stars was against us, though; that's all."

(Bontemps, 209–11)

On the second Sunday in July 1822, Denmark Vesey, a former slave in Charleston, South Carolina, who had purchased his freedom in 1800 with earnings from a lottery, organized the largest slave conspiracy in American history. Vesey, a Methodist minister, used his church in the city as a meeting place for the conspirators, who also included four white men. He planned an attack on Charleston and sought assistance from the newly independent black nation of Haiti. Among Vesey's closest lieutenants were the Africans Monday Gell, an Ibo, Gullah Jack, Angolan, and Mingo Harth, Mandingo. Vesey conspired to seize weapons, kill any whites who resisted, and set the city ablaze as a signal for slaves from the surrounding areas to enter Charleston. An estimated 9,000 slaves were involved in the plot, which was revealed to white authorities by two black men. Thirty-five African Americans, including Vesey, were killed for their participation in the conspiracy, and 37 were banished from the state. The Vesey House, his residence during the time of the planned rebellion, is at 56 Bull Street in Charleston, South Carolina. It was declared a National Historic Landmark in 1976.

In the cases of Gabriel Prosser and Denmark Vesey, someone in their ranks betrayed them. Why do you think this happened?

A strong improvisation with an acting partner could be built from an imagined dialogue between two conspirators, one of whom is driven to tell about the plan. What are their motives? What are their obstacles? Is the betrayer driven by fear or a more base human emotion such as envy?

The bloodiest slave rebellion in the United States took place on August 21, 1831, in Southampton County, Virginia. Nat Turner, a mystic and talented man who could read and write, believed that God had ordained him to end slavery. Together with six other slaves, Turner killed his own slave master and marched toward the county seat of Jerusalem (now Courtland), attacking plantations and murdering their white residents. Turner's band of rebels had grown to about 60 by the time they were met by the militia. About 57 whites were killed in the uprising, and more than 100 slaves lost their lives during the rebellion and afterward as whites sought revenge. Turner escaped for two months before he was captured and executed.

The Amistad revolt of 1838 is perhaps the most celebrated case of slave resistance. The *Amistad* was sailing from Havana to Port Principe, Cuba, with a cargo of 54 slaves. During the voyage, the slaves, under the leadership of Joseph Cinque, rose up, killed the captain and his crew, and demanded that the ship sail to Africa. Steven Spielberg's film *Amistad* (1997), starring Djimon Hounsou, chronicles the revolt and the subsequent trial that reached the United States Supreme Court, with former president John Quincy Adams representing the captives.

John Brown, a white man, was another angry abolitionist. He has been described as having all the intensity of an Old Testament prophet. Unlike most abolitionists, he believed that slavery would come to an end only after blood was shed. Relentless in his passion to defeat slavery, he declared that he personally would use whatever methods he felt were necessary to make that happen. In 1859 he raided a US Army depot in Harper's Ferry, Virginia, trying to acquire weapons to defend what he hoped would become an independent homeland in the mountains, where slaves could find shelter. The raid was doomed to failure, with several men killed on both sides. Brown himself was captured and hanged for treason and murder. He remained unrepentant to the end, writing that he was "now quite certain that the crimes of this guilty land will never be purged away, but with blood." His death made him a martyr in the cause of abolition.

These slave uprisings, especially the Nat Turner revolt, sent shock waves throughout the South. As Fannie Berry recalled:

> Back before the sixties, I can remember my mistress, Miss Sara Ann, coming to the window and hollering, "The niggers is a-rising! The niggers is a-rising! The niggers is killing all the white folks, killing all the babies in the cradle!" It must

Angry abolitionist

have been Nat Turner's insurrection, which was sometime before the breaking of the Civil War.

(in Hurmence, 1994, 70)

The Underground Railroad Conductor

As the South became an armed camp against slave uprisings, flight from bondage became the most viable route to freedom. Like Sam Joyner, who ran so fast from the patty rollers "that he nearly flew" (in Yetman, ed., repr. 2000, 34), the people who had lost their wings flew for freedom.

This brief excerpt from Lorraine Hansberry's *The Drinking Gourd*, an original drama for television, commissioned by NBC in 1959 and published in her *Collected Last Plays* (1972), offers insight into what it might be like for an enslaved person to contemplate running away. It can be rehearsed as a scene for a man and a woman, both African American.

> EXTERIOR. MOONLIT WOODS.
> HANNIBAL (*Drawing her close*) Lookit that big, old, fat star shinin' away up yonder there!
> SARAH Shhh. Hannibal!
> HANNIBAL (*With his hand, as though he is personally touching the stars*) One, two three, four – they makes up the dipper. That's the Big Dipper, Sarah. The old Drinkin' Gourd pointin' straight to the North Star!
> SARAH (*Knowingly*) Everybody knows that's the Big Dipper and you better hush your mouth for sure now, boy. Trees on this plantation got more ears than leaves!
> HANNIBAL (*Ignoring the caution*) That's the old Drinkin' Gourd herself!
> *Releasing the girl's arms and settling down, a little wistfully now.*
> HANNIBAL Sure is bright tonight. Sure would make good travelin' light tonight . . .
> SARAH (*With terror, clapping her hand over his mouth*) Stop it!
> HANNIBAL (*Moving her hand*) Up there jes pointin' away . . . due North!
> *He sings softly to himself:*
> HANNIBAL "For the old man is a-waitin' For to carry you to freedom If you follow the Drinking Gourd. Follow–follow–follow . . . If you follow the Drinking Gourd. . ."
> SARAH You aim to go, don't you, Hannibal?
> *He does not answer and it is clear because of it that he intends to run off.*
> H'you know it's so much better to run off? (*A little desperately, near tears, thinking of the terrors involved*) Even if you make it h'you know what's up there, what it be like to go wanderin' 'round by yourself in this world?
> HANNIBAL I don't know. Jes know what it is to be a slave!
>
> (Hansberry, 172–5)

If you can find a spot from which you can see the Big Dipper, you could rehearse the scene from Lorraine Hansberry's *The*

The Big Dipper

Drinking Gourd under the stars to help you imagine what it would have been like for Hannibal that night.

Like Hannibal, most slaves had never set foot off their plantations and knew little about the North or how to reach it. Because of this, signs, symbols, and codes were used to transmit important information to fugitives planning to escape on the Underground Railroad. Common quilt patterns made up one of these codes. The quilts could be hung out to air without being noticed by the plantation owner, yet for people who knew the code, the quilt patterns told them how to plan and carry out their escape. The most important quilt patterns in the Underground Railroad carried the following codes:

- The monkey wrench pattern alerted slaves to gather the tools and supplies they would need when they escaped.
- The wagon wheel pattern told slaves to pack their belongings and provisions to help them survive their journey.
- The tumbling blocks pattern announced that it was time to escape.
- The bear's paw pattern instructed runaways to follow the bear tracks through the mountains, staying away from roads.
- The crossroads pattern directed escaping slaves to travel to Cleveland, Ohio, the major crossroads to Canada.

Detail of a quilt, reminiscent of the wagon wheel pattern

- The log cabin pattern indicated stations where runaways were hidden along the way.
- The shoofly pattern referred to the conductors who guided slaves north on the Underground Railroad.
- The bow tie pattern told slaves to dress in better clothing and disguises so they would not stand out.
- The flying geese pattern instructed runaways to follow the migrating geese north in spring.
- The drunkard's path pattern told escaping slaves to move in a crooked or zigzag path, avoiding major roads.
- The star pattern advised runaways to use the stars and constellations as a map to locating the North Star, a guiding light to freedom.

(Vaughan, Author's note, n.p.)

Escape from bondage for Hannibal would have been terribly difficult. The people didn't know the land, they weren't allowed to see maps or discuss routes, and any dark-skinned person traveling without an owner was suspected of being a runaway. The woods were full of rattlesnakes, wolves, and deer. Hannibal might have to hide for days, weeks, or even months before he found people to help him get to the North. His owner would be searching for him, and so he would have to find secret hiding places. Many fugitives hid in forests and swamps. Some stayed in caves. Others hid in big trees. Hannibal would have had no map or compass to guide him. He would have to travel

Detail of a quilt with people

Searching for the Big Dipper

mostly at night, under cover of darkness. On clear nights he could rely on the stars to lead him north; the constellations of the Big Dipper and Little Dipper are easy to spot, and point to the beacon of the North Star. On cloudy nights it was all too easy to get turned around and to travel the wrong way. But if

Hannibal could just get to the first "station" on the Underground Railroad, there were people waiting to help him.

The great majority of fugitives ran away between 1830 and 1860. They traveled on the most famous "road" of the day. This network was called the Underground Railroad because of the story of a runaway slave named Tice Davids. He is said to have escaped from his owner's home in Kentucky and swam across the river to the town of Ripley, Ohio. The owner could see Davids in front of him crossing the river. But when Davids landed on the shore, he vanished from sight. The owner searched all through the town, but Davids was nowhere to be found. Finally the owner gave up and went home to Kentucky. He could not figure out what had happened to Tice Davids. Bewildered, he shook his head and said, "He must have gone on an underground road!" Soon many people knew about Tice Davids' escape. Steam-engine trains had just been introduced, and people began to say that Davids had escaped on an "underground railroad." The name stuck. And from then on, whenever slaves escaped, people said they had traveled on the Underground Railroad. It was a perfect name – "underground" because it was secret, indeed invisible, and "railroad" because it seemed to run regularly and swiftly. The "railroad" became a term for the series of stopping points that ran northward along many paths. Thousands of brave men and women defied the federal fugitive slave laws to operate the Underground Railroad.

If Hannibal were successful in his leap for freedom, he would have been hidden in houses along the way called "stations." People waiting to help him were called "railroad workers," some of whom were "conductors." They would lead him to the next station. "Station masters" would feed Hannibal and give him a place to sleep. More than 100,000 enslaved people may have escaped north via the Underground Railroad. Homes in dozens of cities, especially along the Mason-Dixon line, served as stations on the Underground Railroad, sheltering fugitives until it was safe for them to travel farther north or to Canada.

Hannibal would have discovered that there were many kinds of hiding places. There were secret attic rooms and fake closets. There were trapdoors and hidden tunnels that led to tiny rooms. In some houses, pushing a button would make a whole wall turn and the fugitive could hide behind it. There were sliding panels covered by pictures. Move the picture, push the panel, and there would be a hiding place. In one farmhouse, a secret room in the cellar was particularly elusive as a hiding place – the only way to get to it was through a trapdoor from the room above. So many fugitives had hidden there that the house was called "Liberty Farm." Others hid in secret compartments contained within the wagons in which they traveled. One man built a false bottom on his cart. He put straw in the hidden bottom for fugitives to lie on. Then he filled the top part of the wagon with vegetables and drove off to the market.

Incidents in the Life of a Slave Girl by Harriet Jacobs (published in January 1861 under the pseudonym Linda Brent) is a rare first-hand account of a secret hiding place. Harriet Jacobs lived for seven years in self-imposed exile, hiding in a coffin-like "garret" attached to her grandmother's porch until she could escape from her cruel owner to the north.

The following scene is a touching one in which Harriet says goodbye to her little daughter whom she hasn't seen for five years. Written in the style of women's novels popular at the time, the prose may now seem a little old-fashioned and/or melodramatic. However, if you think of it as a period piece and approach it as you would an Elizabethan text, it will be easier to make real and honest. You can use a combination of dialogue, improvisation and inner monologue to make the scene resonate in the parts where there is no dialogue. This scene could be dramatized with two female actors, both African Americans.

> *Inner monologue:* I thought to myself that I might perhaps never see my daughter again, and I had a great desire that she should look upon me, before she went, that she might take my image with her in her memory. It seemed to me cruel to have her brought to my dungeon. It was sorrow enough for her young heart to know that her mother was a victim of slavery, without seeing the wretched hiding-place to which it had driven her. I begged permission to pass the last night in one of the open chambers, with my little girl. I slipped through the trap-door into the storeroom, and my uncle kept watch at the gate, while I passed into the piazza and went up stairs, to the room I used to occupy. It was more than five years since I had seen it; and how the memories crowded on me!
>
> *Begin scene here (in silence):* In the midst of these meditations, I heard footsteps on the stairs. The door opened, and my uncle Phillip came, leading Ellen by the hand. I put my arms round her, and said,
>
> "Ellen, my dear child, I am your mother."
>
> She drew back a little, and looked at me; then, with sweet confidence, she laid her cheek against mine, and I folded her to the heart that had been so long desolated. She was the first to speak.
>
> Raising her head, she said, inquiringly, "You really are my mother?"

Improvise this into dialogue: I told her I really was; that during all the long time she had not seen me, I had loved her most tenderly; and that now she was going away, I wanted to see her and talk with her, that she might remember me.

With a sob in her voice, she said, "I'm glad you've come to see me; but why didn't you ever come before?

"I couldn't come before, dear. But now that I am with you, tell me whether you would like to go away."

"I don't know," she said, crying. Can't you go with me? O, do go, dear mother!"

Improvise: I told her I couldn't go now; but sometime I would come to her, and I asked if she would like to have me stay all night and sleep with her.

"O, yes," she replied.

Improvise: I took her in my arms and told her I was a slave, and that was the reason she must never say she had seen me. I told her to say her prayers, and remember always to pray for her poor mother, and that God would permit us to meet again. All night she nestled in my arms, and I had no inclination to slumber. The moments were too precious to lose any of them. Once, when I thought she was asleep, I kissed her forehead softly, and she said,

"I am not asleep, dear mother."

Before dawn they came to take me back to my den. I drew aside the window curtain, to take a last look of my child. The moonlight shone on her face. She gave her last kiss, and whispered in my ear,

"Mother, I will never tell."

And she never did.

(Jacobs, repr. 2001, 595–7)

The Underground Railroad workers also made use of clever secret signals which could speed Hannibal on his way. For example, in one city, fugitives were told to go to the boat dock late at night. If they saw a man come off a certain boat and sprinkle ashes on the ground, it was safe to go on board. Or, because Illinois was a free state and Missouri had slaves, students from an Illinois school would cross the Mississippi River on Sunday nights and go into Missouri. They walked along the shore and softly tapped stones together. If Hannibal were hiding in the woods, he would listen for the tapping. When he heard it, he knew it was safe to come out. The students would lead him back across the river and take him to a red barn that was an Underground Railroad station.

Some of the "conductors" aided great numbers to escape. Robert Purvis and William Still, blacks from Philadelphia, were said to have helped 9,000 fugitives. Levi Coffin and Thomas Garret, white Quakers, each speeded almost 3,000 runaways. However, Harriet Tubman was the most prominent conductor on the Underground Railroad. Born a slave in Maryland, she escaped to Canada at the age of 28. As a fearless activist, she carried a gun and prevented frightened runaways from fleeing or telling her secret. She became known as "Moses," after the Old Testament prophet (Sarah Bradford's biography of Tubman, published in 1886, is subtitled *The Moses of her People*). She went down deep into "Egypt-land" 19 times to rescue over 300 slaves. As her exploits became known, the reward for her capture reached $12,000 – an incredible sum at that time. "I think slavery is the next thing to hell," she declared. Among the many she led out of Egypt-land were her brother Henry and their aged parents.

Theodore Brown's play *Go Down Moses* (1938) is based on the life and exploits of Harriet Tubman. In addition to her work on the Underground Railroad, she scouted for the Union army during the Civil War. Brown's play portrays Harriet as an architect of black freedom. It reveals her inner life and celebrates the Iwa which animates the mythic figure. In the last scene, as she leads her band of fugitives to the promised land, she falls to cradle the head of a dying black soldier who sees Canaan in the glowing sunset. Brown's Harriet is a natural leader – chosen, like Moses, by God (Craig, 51).

Playwright May Miller, who devoted much time to anthologizing historical dramas, gives depth and breadth to several major African American heroines in her plays. *Harriet Tubman* (1935), set in Maryland, juxtaposes the activist's heroism toward slaves with the disloyalty of the mulatto house servant, a theme that continues to dominate black literature. Tubman's indomitable will is expressed in such terms as "Trouble or no trouble, thar's two things Ah got de right to, an' they is death an' liberty. One or de other, Ah mean to have. No one will take me back into slavery alive" (Miller in Brown-Guillory, 277). Miller comments on slavery as a corrupt institution in the way that it engenders mistrust and deception among an enslaved people, and on the existence of strong black male and female relationships that have endured in spite of that reality. Miller's Harriet knows how it feels to be a "stranger in a strange land" (Prince, 84) and this knowledge compels her to reach out to free those in bondage.

If Hannibal did decide to take off from his plantation that night long ago, guided by the North Star, his journey would have been long and arduous. Success was by no means guaranteed. But had he been lucky enough to get aboard Harriet's train, he would have made it all the way to Canada, because Harriet "never lost a passenger" (Prince, 85). Further tributes to Harriet Tubman are found in the work of Faith Ringgold, a versatile artist and writer who designs and creates museum-quality story quilts. Her vibrant children's book *Aunt Harriet's Underground Railroad in the Sky* (1992) includes illustrations of the ex-slave flying.

Harriet Tubman (left) and six unidentified persons

The Emancipated Interlocutor

When Sarah H. Bradford was planning to publish *Scenes in the Life of Harriet Tubman* (1869), Harriet asked Frederick Douglass for a letter of support to appear at the beginning of the book:

> ROCHESTER, August 29, 1868.
>
> DEAR HARRIET: . . . You ask for what you do not need when you call upon me for a word of commendation. I need such words from you far more than you can need them from me, especially where your superior labors and devotion to the cause of the lately enslaved of our land are known as I know them. The difference between us is very marked. Most that I have done and suffered in the service of our cause has been in public, and I have received much encouragement at every step of the way. You on the other hand have labored in a private way. I have wrought in the day – you in the night. I have had the applause of the crowd and the satisfaction that comes of being approved by the multitude, while the most that you have done has been witnessed by a few trembling, scarred, and foot-sore bondsmen and women, whom you have led out of the house of bondage, and whose heartfelt "God bless you" has been your only reward. . . .
>
> Your friend, FREDERICK DOUGLASS.
>
> (in Prince, 86)

By the 1830s, former bondspeople were beginning to tell their stories in print. Many of these tales were very widely read, spreading a powerful anti-slavery message. However, these narratives are different from the ones discussed in chapter 1, which were gathered in the 1930s and are retrospective accounts of what it had been like to live as a slave. Eleanor Traylor calls the stories explored here "emancipatory narratives;" they were delivered during slavery in an attempt to bring about its end (Traylor, 45–70).

Such narratives were spoken by free people who had recently escaped slavery. They wanted people in the North to know about slavery and to help abolish it. I call those who delivered emancipatory narratives the Emancipated Interlocutor. This free man or woman had in many cases wrestled his or her own freedom from the slave states without waiting for Abraham Lincoln's emancipation proclamation. This Interlocutor, unlike the center man in minstrelsy who only pretended to be smart and dignified, resisted the caricature of "slave." He humanized himself by telling his own story for the first time on American soil. The Emancipated Interlocutor arrived on the stage having come over the Underground Railroad and then later functioned as a conductor. One such, Solomon Northrup, was born free but was later kidnapped in Washington and enslaved for twelve years in Louisiana. His story, taken down by a northerner in the year of his rescue, 1853, sold 27,000 copies in two years.

With the arrival of this formerly enslaved narrator, a new literary voice announces itself. He (and much more rarely, she) often first told their tales from the pulpits of welcoming abolitionist churches. Their rhythms had a new cadence. It was an emancipatory cadence, decrying slavery and demanding freedom. The lyrics of their songs changed from "Nobody Knows the Trouble I Seen" to "Go down, Moses." When the enslaved person spoke such words as "My name is," "I was born in," "I lived as a beast of burden and escaped to become free," it was the first step to publicly unmasking the Iwa underneath the mask and revealing the spirit of freedom. This bold and self-affirming act figuratively killed the slave and gave birth to a free person. Many of the playwrights and other cultural figures examined in this book dedicated their lives and work to writing against the concept of a person of African descent being less than human. From the Emancipated Interlocutor, who humanized himself by telling his own story, emanates the emancipatory spirit which led to the Civil Rights and Black Power Movements.

Frederick Douglass is perhaps the best-known Emancipated Interlocutor. His autobiography, the *Narrative of Frederick Douglass*, which he delivered to sympathetic audiences in person before it was published in 1845, sets the patterns that most other narratives in this genre followed. They generally begin with the facts of birth, as his does:

> I was born in Tuckahoe, near Hillsborough, and about twelve miles from Easton, in Talbot County, Maryland. I have no accurate knowledge of my age, never having seen any authentic record containing it. By far the larger part of

Frederick Douglass

the slaves know as little of their ages as horses know of theirs, and it is the wish
of most masters within my knowledge to keep their slaves thus ignorant.

(Douglass, in Gates, ed., 1987, 339)

The narratives then proceed to catalogue the evils of slavery. The
following grueling description of his aunt's beating will make a powerful monologue. He paints an indelible portrait of the reality of
slavery. It is here, as well, that he recognizes that he is "both within

and without the circle," both "a witness and participant" (read the whole narrative for a better understanding of these concepts):

> I have often been awakened at the dawn of day by the most heart-rending shrieks of an own aunt of mine, whom he [the overseer] used to tie up to a joist, and whip upon her naked back till she was literally covered with blood. No words, no tears, no prayers, from his gory victim, seemed to move his iron heart from its bloody purpose. The louder she screamed, the harder he whipped; and where the blood ran fastest, there he whipped longest. He would whip her to make her scream, and whip her to make her hush; and not until overcome by fatigue, would he cease to swing the blood-clotted cowskin. I remember the first time I ever witnessed this horrible exhibition. I was quite a child, but I well remember it. I never shall forget it whilst I remember anything. It was the first of a long series of such outrages, of which I was doomed to be a witness and a participant. It struck me with awful force. It was the blood-stained gate, the entrance to the hell of slavery, through which I was about to pass. It was a most terrible spectacle. I wish I could commit to paper the feelings with which I beheld it.
>
> (343)

The emancipatory narratives then go on to describe the means of escape and the joy with which the newly free person met Freedom:

> I have been frequently asked how I felt when I found myself in a free State. I have never been able to answer the question with any satisfaction to myself. It was a moment of the highest excitement I ever experienced. I suppose I felt as one may imagine the unarmed mariner to feel when he is rescued by a friendly man-of-war from the pursuit of a pirate.
>
> (421)

Born a slave in Maryland, Douglass escaped in 1838. He settled first in New Bedford, Massachusetts, where he joined the abolitionist movement and became the foremost North American black leader of the 19th century. The most important and longest running black newspaper before the Civil War was the *North Star*, which Douglass edited in Rochester, New York. His autobiography mentions that because of his location in Rochester, as well as his notoriety, he was very naturally the conductor and station-master at that city. In 1889 he became the US minister to the island of Haiti.

Georgia Douglas Johnson's play *Frederick Douglass* (1935), set in Baltimore, centers on Frederick's love for his girlfriend, Ann. This focus on Douglass' personal life, as opposed to his political life, is not captured in history books. Johnson shows the couple expressing love and tenderness. Again, a playwright looks behind the iconic figure and/or stereotype to reveal the whole person, pulsing with Iwa. When Ann chides Frederick about not wanting her once he is free, Douglass tenderly answers, "Oh my little honey, I'm goin' to love you all my life. We goin' to work together, you an' me, in that great big free coun-try up North" (Brown-Guillory, 14). Throughout the play, Johnson empha-sizes the need for blacks to educate themselves and to give back to their community. When Douglass escapes dressed as a sailor, Johnson shows the spirit of High John still flowing through the people who could not fly.

In their plays, May Miller and Georgia Douglas Johnson created folk heroes and heroines of the race who possess great strength, wisdom, and courage. They defied the stereotypes of black people still lingering in the American imagination. Their voices were unwelcome in the commercial theater of the period. These historical dramas, written to teach the race about their heroes and heroines, offer many opportunities for monologues and scenes for the stu-dent actor. According to Ted Shine, black playwrights write historical dramas

> to liberate the black audience from an oppressive past, to present a history that provides continuity, hope, and glory. Such feelings and knowledge have posi-tive survival value for the race. This emphasis on the black folk hero represents a new pride in the black person's past, particularly the militant past.
>
> (Hatch and Shine, 1974, 371)

Miller and Johnson were early black women playwrights who were part of a group that Elizabeth Brown-Guillory calls "Mother Playwrights." These women were an overlooked but integral part of the Harlem Renaissance and the New Negro Movement (see chapter 4). They wrote mainly one-act plays about middle-class and common folk. Lynching, poverty, disenfranchised war heroes, race pride, and women's rights are subjects they frequently explored. "With feeling hearts, they present a slice of United States history from the unique perspective of women who have been both midwives and pallbearers of African American dreamers" (Brown-Guillory, 20). Writing between 1910 and 1940, these women were instrumental in paving the way for black playwrights between the 1950s and 1980s. Because of the strides made in content, form, characterization, and dialogue by the mother play-wrights, there could be Broadway and off-Broadway productions for Alice Childress, Lorraine Hansberry, and Ntozake Shange.

Many of these women were acquaintances of W. E. B. DuBois who in 1926 strongly advocated community theater by writing in an essay: "If it is a Negro play that will interest us and depict our life, experience, and humor, it cannot be sold to the ordinary [commercial] theatrical producer, but can be produced by our churches, lodges, and halls" (in Brown-Guillory, 4). With this admonition in mind, these early dramatists conscientiously wrote for the black community where their plays were produced in black-owned and black-operated community theaters, churches, schools, social club halls, and homes. Brown-Guillory speaks eloquently of the unnaturally suppressed inner life rousing and coming to the fore in the works of these women who well understood Iwa: "They are, indeed, the missing pieces to a multifaceted puzzle of black life during those decades when blacks were becoming aware, and awakening to their own self-worth, and struggling for an identity robbed from them as a result of mutilated African roots" (5). Georgia Douglas Johnson and other members of this group, including Angelina Weld Grimke, Alice Dunbar Nelson, Mary Burrill, and Marita Bonner, are discussed further in later chapters.

Another Emancipated Interlocutor, William Wells Brown, a lecturer, writer, and conductor, was one of the best-known abolitionists. Born into slavery in Lexington, Kentucky, around 1814, he was the son of a white man but his mother was a slave, and thus so was he. When he was approaching the age of 20, he decided to make his break for freedom. His public addresses on behalf of the Anti-Slavery Society were legendary. Built from these public addresses, Brown's published autobiography describes his escape as well as the fascinating details of those early years in bondage. Entitled *Narrative of William W. Brown, A Fugitive Slave, Written by Himself* (1847), it was wildly successful in both North America and Britain. Later, in 1856, he wrote a play based on his emancipatory narrative. *The Escape or A Leap for Freedom* is the earliest extant play written by a descendant of African slaves. For that reason, histories of African American theater usually use Wells Brown's play as a starting point. Though the author did not expect his play to be staged, James Spruill took on the task twice, first at Emerson College in December 1971 and then at Boston University in February 1977.

Elizabeth Keckley, also an Emancipated Interlocutor, worked in the White House as a seamstress for Mrs. Abraham Lincoln. She was there for Lincoln's second inauguration and also on the night he was assassinated. Her emancipatory narrative, *Behind the Scenes or Thirty Years a Slave and Four Years in the White House* (1868), follows the pattern set out by Frederick Douglass and William Wells Brown.

The following scene takes place after she has escaped slavery and is making a living for herself as a seamstress. It can be dramatized as a scene for two women, one black, one white.

> Mrs. Lincoln came to my apartments one day towards the close of the summer of 1864, to consult me in relation to a dress. And, as usual, she had much to say about the Presidential election. After some conversation, she asked:

"Lizzie, where do you think I will be this time next summer?"

"Why, in the White House, of course."

"I cannot believe so. I have no hope of the re-election of Mr. Lincoln. The canvass is a heated one, the people begin to murmur at the war, and every vile charge is brought against my husband."

"No matter," I replied, "Mr. Lincoln will be re-elected. I am so confident of it, that I am tempted to ask a favor of you."

"A favor! Well, if we remain in the White House I shall be able to do you many favors. What is the special favor?"

"Simply this, Mrs. Lincoln – I should like for you to make me a present of the right-hand glove that the President wears at the first public reception after his second inaugural."

"You shall have it in welcome. It will be so filthy when he pulls it off, I shall be tempted to take the tongs and put it in the fire. I cannot imagine, Lizabeth, what you want with such a glove."

"I shall cherish it as a precious memento of the second inauguration of the man who has done so much for my race. He has been a Jehovah to my people – has lifted them out of bondage, and directed their footsteps from darkness into light. I shall keep the glove, and hand it down to posterity."

"You have some strange ideas, Lizabeth. Never mind, you shall have the glove; that is, if Mr. Lincoln continues President after the 4th of March next."

[After Lincoln is re-elected]

I finished dressing Mrs. Lincoln [for the second inaugural ball], and she took the President's arm and went below. It was one of the largest receptions ever held in Washington. Thousands crowded the halls and rooms of the White House, eager to shake Mr. Lincoln by his hand, and receive a gracious smile from his wife. The jam was terrible, and the enthusiasm great. I held Mrs. Lincoln to her promise. The President's hand was well shaken, and the next day, on visiting Mrs. Lincoln, I received the soiled glove that Mr. Lincoln had worn on his right hand that night.

That glove is now in my possession, bearing the marks of the thousands of hands that grasped the honest hand of Mr. Lincoln on that eventful night. Alas, it has become a prouder, sadder memento than I ever dreamed – prior to making the request – it would be.

(Keckley, repr. 1988, 153–5).

Frederick Douglass was among those to shake hands with President Lincoln that evening, but as Mrs. Keckley recounts he almost didn't get in:

Many colored people were in Washington, and large numbers had desired to attend the levee, but orders were issued not to admit them. A gentleman, a member of Congress, on his way to the White House, recognized Mr. Frederick Douglass, the eloquent colored orator, on the outskirts of the crowd.

"How do you do, Mr. Douglass? A fearful jam to-night. You are going in, of course?"

"No – that is, no to your last question."

"Not going in to shake the President by the hand! Why, pray?"

"The best reason in the world. Strict orders have been issued not to admit people of color."

"It is a shame, Mr. Douglass, that you should thus be placed under ban. Never mind; wait here, and I will see what can be done."

The gentleman entered the White House, and working his way to the President, asked permission to introduce Mr. Douglass to him.

"Certainly," said Mr. Lincoln. "Bring Mr. Douglass in, by all means. I shall be glad to meet him."

The gentleman returned, and soon Mr. Douglass stood face to face with the President.

Mr. Lincoln pressed his hand warmly, saying:

"Mr. Douglass, I am glad to meet you. I have long admired your course, and I value your opinions highly." Mr. Douglass was very proud of the manner in which Mr. Lincoln received him. On leaving the White House he came to a friend's house where a reception was being held, and he related the incident with great pleasure to myself and others.

(Keckley, repr. 1988, 158–60)

Lynn Nottage's play *Intimate Apparel* was inspired by the life of her great-grandmother, Ethel Boyce, a gifted seamstress who earned her living from that work around 1905 – a woman much like Mrs. Keckley. It had its premiere at the Center Stage in Baltimore in February 2003 and received five national awards for best play. In 2007 Lynn Nottage was the recipient of the McArthur Genius Award.

Abraham Lincoln is called the great emancipator because he wrote and issued the Emancipation Proclamation that eventually freed the enslaved laborers of the South. He was considered a "secular saint" by the people who could not fly. Emancipation was at first a dream come true; the "truth 'vealed to the old time preachers." Liberation was described in ecstatic terms, for example: "Freedom came and was like having been to the Devil and come back." (Sabe Rutledge, in Rhyne, 47); "I never forget de day we was set free. You is your own bosses now and you don't have to have no passes to go and come" (Katie Rowe, in Mellon, ed., 30); "We had everything to eat you could call for. No, didn't have no common eats. We could sing in there, and dance old square dance all us choosed. Lord, Lord! I can see them gals now on that floor, just skipping and a-trotting. And honey, there was no white folks to set down and eat before you" (Fannie Berry, in Hurmence, 1994, 74). As *The Liberator* of July 21, 1865, proclaimed:

Slavery is dead
and will be buried so deep
that the Judgment will not find it!

Some accounts burst into song:

> Glory! Glory! Yes, child, the Negroes are free, and when they know that they
> were free, oh, baby, began to sing:

> Mammy, don't you cook no more,
> You are free, you are free.
> Rooster, don't you crow no more,
> You are free, you are free.
> Old hen, don't you lay no more eggs,
> You free, you free.

(in Mellon, ed., 345)

The American Civil War began in April 1861 and ended five Aprils later, in
1865, when General Robert E. Lee, leader of the Southern troops, surren-
dered to General Ulysses S. Grant, commander of the Northern army. With
the Confederate attack on Fort Sumter in Charleston harbor on April 12,
Frederick Douglass immediately recognized that slavery lay at the heart of the
conflict. Although President Abraham Lincoln justified the war as a means of
preserving the Union, Douglass championed the battle as a way to free
the slaves. At Douglass's urging, on January 1, 1863, Lincoln's Emancipation
Proclamation took effect, freeing the slaves in the seceded states only, making
them eligible to fight in the Union army. Approximately 180,000 black men
fought in the Union army and 30,000 in the navy during the war. About one
in five black males over the age of 15 joined the Union forces. They served in
all-black units under the command of white officers. (For more on black
soldiers who fought in the Civil War, see chapter 6.) Two years after the
Emancipation Proclamation, "The end of the War came like that – like you
snap your fingers" (in Mellon, ed., 344). As another voice put it: "I was still
little when the war came, but I can remember when the horn blew, telling us
that the war was done over and we were free. I thought Judgment Day had
come!" (Eison Lyles, in Rhyne, 100).

The Civil War turned out to be only the beginning of African Americans'
fight for freedom. Initially, the Union government gave hope to its black
citizens. It abolished legal slavery in 1865 through the 13th Amendment to
the Constitution. In 1868 it guaranteed African Americans equal rights
and equal protection under the law with the 14th Amendment. The 15th
Amendment (1870) gave black men the right to vote. The federal government tried to remake the South into a real democracy during the Radical
Reconstruction era (1867–77). US soldiers were posted throughout the
former Confederacy to back up the rights of freedmen. Black men functioned
as citizens and were elected to office, including two to the Senate and 14 to
the House of Representatives.

But blacks remained economically enslaved to the large landholders who had once owned them. Now "sharecroppers," the freedmen farmed the fields for a share of the cotton crop, which never produced enough income to pull them out of debt to their masters. White southern Democrats fought to overthrow the Republican Reconstruction state governments. The federal government deserted the slaves it had freed and left the South to its own devices.

A month after Charleston, South Carolina, was captured by Union forces in February 1865, the city's black men and women organized a parade:

> It was a jubilee of freedom, a hosanna to their deliverers. First came the marshals and their aids, followed by a band of music; then the Twenty-first Regiment, then the clergymen of the different churches, carrying open Bibles, then an open car drawn by four white horses. In this car there were 15 colored ladies dressed in white – to represent the 15 recent Slave States. A long procession of women followed the car. Then the children – 1,800 in line, at least. After the children came the various trades. The fishermen, with a banner bearing an emblematical device and the words, "The Fishermen welcome you, General Saxton." Carpenters, masons, teamsters, drovers, coopers, bakers, paper-earners, barbers, blacksmiths, wood-sawyers, painters, wheelwrights and the fire companies. The carpenters carried their planes, the masons their trowels, the teamsters their whips; the coopers their adzes. The bakers' crackers hung around their necks; the paper-carriers [had] a banner, and each a copy of the *Charleston Courier*; the wheelwrights a large wheel; and the fire companies, ten in number, their foremen with their trumpets. A large cart, drawn by two dilapidated horses, followed the trades. On this cart was an auctioneer's block and a black man with a bell represented a Negro trader. This man had himself been sold several times and two women and a child who sat on the block had also been knocked down at auction in Charleston. As the cart moved along, the mock-auctioneer rang his bell and cried out: "How much am I offered for this good cook? She is an excellent cook, gentlemen. She can make four kinds of mock turtle soup – from beef, fish or fowl. Who bids?"
>
> "Two hundred's bid! Two fifty! Three hundred."
>
> "Who bids? Who bids?"
>
> Women burst into tears as they saw this tableau and forgetting that it was a mimic scene, shouted wildly:
>
> "Give me back my children! Give me back my children!"
>
> (*New York Daily Tribune*, April 4, 1865)

Golliwhopshus Names

Like Kunte Kinte in *Roots*, the people who could not fly were never able to even choose their own names:

> Marse Henry ladled out some golliwhopshus names that day, such as, Caesar Harrison, Edward Cades, and Louis Brevard. He said, "Louis, I give you the name of a judge. Dan, I give you a Roman name, Pompey. He gave Uncle Sam the name of Shadrack. When he reached Uncle Aleck, he 'lowed as how he would add two fine names to Aleck: names of a preacher and a scholar, Porter Ramsey.
>
> (Ned Walker, in Rhyne, 93)

Things had not changed much since the days of slavery:

> All the enslaved Africans had to go to Winnsboro and register and get a name. One of Marse's boys was a dwarf, and he said, "Marse, I don't want no little name, I want a big-sounding name." Marse wrote on the paper, then he read, "Your name is Mendozah J. Fernandez, and I hope that's big enough for you." The little dwarf seemed powerful pleased and registered his new name. The rest of us spoke to Marse and he said there was no better name than Woodward, so we took that name.
>
> (Alex Woodward, in Rhyne, 63)

Of course some people chose the name "Freedman" or "Freeman."

The Year of Jubilee

Following emancipation, there was an immediate sense of elation and rush. As Felix Haywood recalled: "[R]ight off, colored folks started on the move. They seemed to want to get closer to freedom, so they'd know what it wuz – like it wuz a place or city. Me and my father stuck close as a lean tick to a sick kitten" (in Mellon, ed., 345). In another account:

> As word of freedom trickled into the remote places, isolated from newspapers and other human contact, the newly Emancipated began their long journeys to petition for their newly gained rights. They came from the plantations and the towns. A few had the benefit of formal training; others were almost wholly self-educated. Many were preachers, some teachers, a few lawyers, the others farmers or artisans. Soon, freedmen all over the South were meeting, informally and in convention, to ask for their rights. For a people only months from slavery these meetings were remarkable affairs. Black soldiers who had learned to read in the army, runaway slaves who had lived in the North and were returning home, free-born blacks from the cities and freedmen fresh from the plantations debated, drew up petitions, chose officers, appointed committees as if they had been following parliamentary procedure all their lives.
>
> (Sterling, ed., 60)

The Freedman's Bureau – originally intended to be a one-year bridge from slavery to freedom – distributed rations to the needy, helped organize

Memorial Marker Of
Madison (Matt) Kilpatrick

Sunday, April 29, 1973   Hempstead, Texas

Matt Kilpatrick, if he knew his parents
or any other forbear he never spoke of them.
It is presumed they lived in Alabama, where
he eventually admitted he came from (he was a
runaway slave).

In the period shortly after the close
of the Civil, War, he was chosen by the
Reconstructionists as Waller County's first
treasurer.

Madison "Matt" Kilpatrick, my great-grandfather. Born into slavery, he became treasurer of Waller County, Texas, during Reconstruction

schools, churches, and medical facilities, and was the only court of appeal for black people. During the Year of Jubilee, the churches and schools became the most important institutions to the newly emancipated. The black church, known as the "invisible institution" during slavery, became highly visible in the South after emancipation. The Baptist, the African Methodist Episcopal, and the African Methodist Episcopal Zion churches organized congregations throughout the South. Together with the Freedman's Bureau, black churches were instrumental in establishing what have come to be known as HBCUs (Historically Black Colleges and Universities). Hampton Institute in Virginia had its beginnings under an oak tree, where Mary Peake, a free black woman, held classes for children of fugitive slaves during the war. Abolitionists such as Francis Ellen Harper and other veterans of the anti-slavery crusade, flooded the South to raise funds, recruit teachers, write textbooks, and open the schools in the South. The children knew little or nothing of the world beyond the plantation. Many had never seen a book or newspaper; some did not know right from left, and had no concept of time. Yet they learned to read, well and swiftly, under the guidance of these committed teachers. Within a few years some schools had progressed so rapidly that they were training blacks to go out and teach. The ordinary people who had been called slaves were finally free to express their unnaturally suppressed inner life.

Tuskegee Institute Senior Class, Alabama, 1913

A Louisiana freedman stated:

> I wants my children to be educated because I can believe what they tells me. If I go to another person with a letter in my hand, he can tell me what he pleases is in that letter and I don't know any better. But if I have got children who read and write, they will tell me the contents of that letter and I will know it's all right.
>
> (in Sterling, ed., 291)

Paul Laurence Dunbar, a master of Iwa, stands out for his ability to uncover the unnaturally suppressed inner lives of enslaved Africans and to put his discovery into poetic form. He was the first published poet to rise to a height from which he could take a perspective view of his own race. He was the first to see objectively its humor, its superstitions, its shortcomings; the first to feel sympathetically its heart-wounds, its yearnings, its aspirations, and to voice them all in a purely literary form. Dunbar's fame rests chiefly on his poems in Negro dialect. Of course, Negro dialect poetry was written before Dunbar wrote, most of it by white writers; but the fact stands out that Dunbar was the first to use it as a medium for the true interpretation of Iwa. The title of Maya Angelou's first volume of autobiography is taken from Dunbar's poem "Sympathy" (written in 1896, not in dialect):

> I know why the caged bird sings, ah me
> When his wing is bruised and his bosom sore
> When he beats his bars and he would be free;

It is not a carol of joy or glee,
But a prayer that he sends from his heart's deep core,
but a plea that upward to Heaven he flings –
I know why the caged bird sings!

(Dunbar, 102)

As the century drew to a close, the heroic abolitionists turned their attention to building a new world for themselves and for the people who had forgotten how to fly. James Weldon Johnson named the people who could not fly "Aframericans." In the next chapter, this is how I refer to those resilient, resourceful citizens, so recently enslaved, saddled with names they did not choose. Most were born in the American place. They did not come through the Middle Passage on slave ships, accompanied by High John the Conqueror. They embraced him instead as their trickster hero. They fought so hard, ran so fast on their thousand miles to freedom that gradually, gradually they seemed to lose the memory of their ancestral homes. Were it not for the tales of High John, who never deserted them, they would not even know that once there were people who could fly. Aframericans. A brand new name for a brand new century.

Food for Further Thought

For a better understanding of the oral tradition in African American life and language, read Henry Louis Gates's *The Signifying Monkey* (1988). Eleanor Traylor's seminal essay, "Two Afro-American Contributions to Dramatic Form" (1980), furthers the dialogue and sheds light on the emancipatory narrative.

Who do you consider a race hero or heroine today? Try your hand at writing a scene about this person. Perhaps it will grow into a short historical drama like the ones by May Miller and Georgia Douglas Johnson, which were written to "teach the race about their heroes and heroines."

Can you take a pivotal event in your life and write it as an emancipatory narrative for your Black Life Book? The emancipatory narrative begins with the circumstances of birth, describes life before the moment of emancipation, and underscores the journey that leads to the cataclysmic moment of liberation. Think of a moment of particular enlightenment in your life, comparable to going from an enslaved mind to an emancipated one. It can be a moment of new-found knowledge or a realization of a truth not previously understood. Draw inspiration from Frederick Douglass's words, "You have seen a man become a slave, now you will see a slave become a man." To help with this exercise, you may also find it useful to read one of the emancipatory narratives I describe in this chapter in its entirety.

3 We are Climbing Jacob's Ladder
Progressing and Migrating

We have spent the greater part of the first fifty years of FREEDOM thinking of the past.
Let us spend the next fifty years thinking of the future.

(Joseph R. Gay, Publisher's Preface, n.p.)

The problem of the twentieth century is the problem of the color line.

(W. E. B. DuBois, 1903, vii)

A Snake called Freedom

In the year 1899 the United States was little more than a century old. In the final 50 years of the 19th century, the people who could not fly witnessed the end of slavery and the rise of Reconstruction. However, by 1900 a new myth of white supremacy had gripped the national mind. Anna Julia Cooper called the *fin de siècle* a "transitional and unsettled time." As Aframerican people stepped into the 20th century, their living conditions were constricted by a US Supreme Court decision known as *Plessy vs. Ferguson*, which established the doctrine of separate but equal. Issued in 1896, this decision made segregation of the races the law of the land and Jim Crow was wheeling and jumping across the South again. The exuberance that at first followed emancipation soon sobered:

> When Freedom come,
> folks left home,
> out in the streets,
> crying,
> praying,
> singing,
> shouting,
> yelling,
>
> Some shot off big guns. Then come the calm.
> It was sad then.
> So many folks done dead,
> things tore up,
> and nowheres to go

and nothing to eat,
nothing to do.
Some folks starved nearly to death.

(in Meltzer, 1984, 87)

Some used stories to describe their dire straits:

> Slaves prayed for freedom. Then they got it and didn't know what to do with it. They was turned out with nowhere to go and nothing to live on. They had no experience in looking out for themselves, and nothing to work with, and no land. They make me think of the crowd one time who prayed for rain, when it was dry in crop time. The rain fell in torrents and kept falling till it was about a flood. The fields was so wet and miry you could not go in them, and water was standing in the fields middle of every row, while the ditches in the fields looked like little rivers, they was so full of water. Then one of the brothers said to the other brothers, kinder easy and shameful like, "Brothers, don't you think we overdone this thing?" That's what many a slave thought about praying for freedom. Slavery was a bad thing, and freedom, of the kind we got, with nothing to live on, was bad. Two snakes full of poison. One lying with his head pointing north, the other with his head pointing south. Their names was slavery and freedom. The snake called slavery lay with his head pointed south, and the snake called freedom lay with his head pointed north. Both bit the nigger, and they was both bad.

(Hurmence, 1984, 79–80)

The first years of the new century, called the Progressive Era, were marked by an urgency to uplift the race. These admonitions, which now sound rather quaint, appeared in a book published in 1913 (since out of print) called *Progress and Achievements of the 20th Century Negro*:

> Character; Education; Industry; Wealth. These are the successive stages on the road to success, and they follow in their regular order. Character belongs to every man individually, and can not be copied from another. It lies in the man; that is all anybody can tell about it. The power to succeed in business is character. Progressive Colored Americans must seek opportunity which does not come of itself, and which has been denied them in the past.
>
> Start Right In Life By Avoiding Foolish and Unnecessary Extravagances. Economy tells us we must learn to do without many things we would like, and forego all unnecessary luxuries, recreations and pleasures which call for money. We can be happy without these things and enjoy the forgotten pleasures of home. Cut down on rent, table, clothes, etc.
>
> Educate Your Children. It can not be doubted that education is the father and mother of opportunity and success in life. We are progressing far beyond the dreams of your youth, and your children are tied to the car of progress. Think this over and let it sink into your mind.

(Gay, 126–8)

Drafting class at Hampton Institute, Virginia

The Fourth Annual Conference of the National Association for the Advancement of Colored People in Chicago, attended by W. E. B. DuBois, 1912

Black Person of the Blacks

From the ranks of those bestowed with their "golliwhopshus" names rose a new folk hero, the Race Man. Race Men took it as their duty to lead the race "up from slavery." Those who had received education and other opportunities

59

before and after the Civil War felt they had a solemn obligation to help lift others up Jacob's ladder of success. I follow John Langston Gwaltney in calling these new race heroes "Black Persons of the Blacks," a phrase he uses to describe "members of the core black culture" (Gwaltney, xv).

The Race Men began to establish professional organizations during the early 20th century. After Frederick Douglass's death in 1895, his mighty mantle was picked up by two very different Black Persons of the Blacks: Booker T. Washington and W. E. B. DuBois. Booker T. Washington founded Tuskegee Institute in Alabama in 1881 on the theory that the newly emancipated needed labor skills. Dubois felt that a "talented tenth," educated and middle-class, must arise to lead the race. Popularized by W. E. B. DuBois in *The Souls of Black Folk* (1903), the "Talented Tenth" referred to the stratum of well-educated and skilled African Americans. Historian Evelyn Brooks Higginbotham adapted the term to "Female Talented Truth" to call attention to the leadership role assumed by black women in the late 19th and early 20th centuries.

Perhaps a mythic way to understand these two titans is to think of Booker T. Washington as descended from the Old-Time Negro Preacher and DuBois as descended from the Angry Abolitionist. In his Atlanta Cotton States Exposition Address (1895), Washington first uttered his now famous words, "In all things that are purely social we can be as separate as the fingers, yet one as the hand in all things essential to mutual progress." He counseled Aframericans to "cast down your bucket where you are," or to make the most of their situation in the South. Washington advocated economic development as the means to achieve racial equality. He was willing to forgo political participation and protest against racial oppression. Once Aframericans acquired important skills and provided essential services, Washington maintained that the southern states, indeed the nation, would accord them the rights and privileges of first-class citizenship. This story from Washington's autobiography may offer us some insight into his philosophy:

> In order to defend and protect the women and children who were left on the plantations when the white males went to war, the slaves would have laid down their lives. The slave who was selected to sleep in the "big house" during the absence of the males was considered to have the place of honour. Anyone attempting to harm "young Mistress" or "old Mistress" during the night would have had to cross the dead body of the slave to do so.
>
> (Washington, 35)

The dichotomy in the philosophies of the two men is captured in Dudley Randall's poem "Booker T. and W. E. B.":

> "It seems to me," said Booker T.,
> "It shows a mighty lot of cheek

To study chemistry and Greek
When Mister Charlie needs a hand
To hoe the cotton on his land,
And when Miss Ann looks for a cook,
Why stick your nose inside a book?"

"I don't agree," said W. E. B.,
"If I should have the drive to seek
Knowledge of chemistry or Greek,
I'll do it. Charles and Miss can look
Another place for hand or cook.
Some men rejoice in skill of hand,
And some in cultivating land,
But there are others who maintain
The right to cultivate the brain."

"It seems to me," said Booker T.,
"That all you folks have missed the boat
Who shout about the right to vote,
And spend vain days and sleepless nights
In uproar over civil rights.
Just keep your mouths shut, do not grouse,
But work, and save, and buy a house."

"I don't agree," said W. E. B.,
"For what can property avail
If dignity and justice fail.
Unless you help to make the laws,
They'll steal your house with trumped-up clause.
A rope's as tight, a fire as hot,
No matter how much cash you've got.
Speak soft, and try your little plan,
But as for me, I'll be a man."

"It seems to me," said Booker T. –

"I don't agree,"
Said W. E. B.

(Randall, 131–2)

Like many other black intellectuals, W. E. B. DuBois was disturbed by the implications of Washington's so-called Atlanta Compromise. To DuBois, the policy seemed like surrender, a permanent acceptance of inferior status. His answer was *The Souls of Black Folk* in which he stated "the problem of the twentieth century is the problem of the color line." With Washington accepted by the overwhelming majority of white Americans as the leading

Aframerican spokesman, DuBois consigned himself to the role of dissenter. The split was also sharp within the black community.

William Edward Burghardt DuBois was born on February 23, 1868, three years after the end of the Civil War, in Great Barrington, Massachusetts. DuBois became a seminal figure in the intellectual history of the 20th century, an architect of black protest. A sociologist, writer, historian, lecturer, teacher, and activist, he was near the center of every significant movement involving Aframericans. He was the first black man to earn a Ph.D. from Harvard. A harbinger of black nationalism and Pan-Africanism, DuBois, together with William Monroe Trotter and other Aframericans, formed the Niagara Movement in 1905 to protest racial oppression, to gain the ballot, and to improve educational opportunity. The Niagara Movement led the way to the National Association for the Advancement of Colored People (NAACP) in 1909. DuBois went to Africa, at the age of 93, to help edit an African encyclopedia in Ghana. On August 27, 1963, on the eve of the March on Washington, DuBois died in Accra, Ghana. The W. E. B. DuBois Memorial in Great Barrington, Massachusetts, is on the site of the DuBois family home.

The Race Woman: Lifting as she Climbs

Anna Julia Cooper, the quintessential Race Woman, lived for 105 years. Her life is framed by especially momentous years in US history: the final years of slavery and the climactic years of the Civil Rights Movement. She was largely based in Washington, DC, a shining example of the ways in which progressive era Race Women worked toward the uplift and betterment of the race. As she put it in her essay "A Voice from the South" (1892):

> Only the Black woman can say
> "when and where I enter,
> in the quiet, undisputed dignity of my womanhood,
> without violence and without suing or special patronage,
> then and there
> the whole race enters with me."
>
> (in Lemert and Bhan, eds., 63)

It will be well to remember that during this time Aframerican women could not inherit property. They could not speak in public. Once married they could not work outside the home. Speaking from the pulpit or holding original spiritual ideas was unheard of. There were no hair products that "tamed" their unruly hair. Nonetheless, though the most visible race heroes during the Progressive Era were male, the Black Person of the Blacks was also a woman.

Race Women worked as teachers, lecturers, social workers, and journalists. They were more committed to the idea of uplift of the race than to their own personal advancement, partly because they did not choose to isolate themselves from the problems of poor black women. These Race Women built strong social organizations, such as the National Association of Colored Women formed in 1896 to counter the stereotypical images of Aframerican women as ignorant, lewd, and licentious Jezebels.

Besides Anna Julia Cooper, well-known Race Women include Mary Macleod Bethune and Mary Church Terrell. Mary McLeod Bethune (1875–1955) was the founder of the National Council of Negro Women and Vice-President of the NAACP. She was awarded the Haitian Medal of Honor and Merit, the highest award in the island republic. In Liberia she received the honor of Commander of the Order of the Star of Africa. She founded the Daytona Normal and Industrial Institute for Negro Girls (now Bethune-Cookman College) in 1904, serving as president from 1904 to 1942 and in 1946–7. Mary Church Terrell (1863–1954) founded the National Association of Colored Women in 1896 and was its first president. She was one of two women who were charter members of the NAACP and assisted in the founding of the Delta Sigma Theta sorority at Howard University.

Anna Julia Cooper was born into slavery to Hannah Stanley and the man who owned them both, George Washington Haywood. In 1880 she won a scholarship to Oberlin College, Ohio, where she earned both a Bachelor's and a Master's degree in mathematics. She went on to teach at M Street High School, the only black high school in Washington, DC, where she became principal in 1901. Having begun coursework for a Ph.D. at Columbia University, New York, in 1914, she gained that degree from the University of Paris-Sorbonne in 1925. She spoke at the 1893 World's Congress of Representative Women as well as at the 1900 Pan-African Congress Conference in London. In 1905 she helped found the Colored Women's YWCA. This was part of a national trend toward the establishment of clubs and organizations in which Aframerican women took leadership roles. Despite her vibrant activism, Cooper has been described as a solitary woman in the history of her time, as in the following poem by Georgia Douglas Johnson:

> The heart of a woman goes forth with the dawn
> As a lone bird, soft winging, so carefully on
> Afar o'er life's turrets and vales does it roam
> In the wake of those echoes the heart calls home.
>
> The heart of a woman fall back with the night,
> And enters some alien cage in its plight,

An African sculpture invoking the spiritual "Climbing Jacob's Ladder"

And tries to forget it has dreamed of the stars,
While it breaks, breaks, breaks on the sheltering bars.

(in Hughes and Bontemps, eds., 57)

The Great Migration

Beginning in 1910 and continuing through to the 1940s, the children of the people who could not fly were slowly transformed from a rural to an urban people. A restlessness grew among the people of the south. Booker T. Washington could not hold them. Events outside their control pushed the people north, this time on an overground railroad. Though the federal government had tried to remake the South into a real democracy during the Radical Reconstruction era (1867–77), Aframericans remained economically enslaved to the large landholders who had once owned them. Now called "sharecroppers," the newly emancipated farmed the fields for a share of the cotton crop. Their labors, however, never produced enough income to pull them out of debt.

This first-hand account can be performed as a monologue for a black male actor. Use your powers of inner image to understand the conflict the speaker faces when he can't speak out in deference to his mother. What would his inner monologue be?

> There was nine of us kids in the family and we all had to work a lot. I flunked two grades in school because of the unjust system we had to live under. I stayed out of school a lot of days because I couldn't let my mother go to the cotton field and try to support all of us. I had to decide which was more important, getting an education or letting my mother suffer alone. When my father stopped working I had to stay out of school more than ever before. I picked cotton and pecans for two cents a pound. I went to the fields in the morning and worked until seven in the afternoon. When it came time to weigh up, so to speak, my heart, body and bones would be aching, burning and trembling. I stood there and stared the white men right in their eyes while they cheated me, other members of my family, and the rest of the Negroes that were working. They had their weighing scales loaded with lead and the rod would always be pointing toward the sky. There were times when I wanted to speak but my fearful mother would always tell me to keep silent. The sun was awful hot and the days were long. It was like being baked in an oven. When I went to bed at night, I could see bolls of cotton staring me right in the face.
>
> (Charlie H. Wingfield, Jr., in Marsh, ed., 35)

This excerpt from Sterling Brown's poem "Old Lem" is based on WPA oral histories discussed in chapter 1. To make a longer scene for two male actors, you could find the whole poem and combine it with the monologue. The person speaking the monologue could be "Old Lem." The second actor, the "interviewer", can intertwine the poem as Lem is speaking the monologue, in a point-counterpoint or call-and-response style.

> I talked to old Lem
> And old Lem said:
> "They weigh the cotton
> They store the corn
> We only good enough
> To work the rows;
> They run the commissary
> They keep the books
> We gotta be grateful
> For being cheated;
> Whippersnapper clerks
> Call us out of our name
> We gotta say mister
> To spindling boys
> They make our figgers
> Turn somersets
> We buck in the middle
> Say, 'Thank yuh, sah.' "

(in Hughes and Bontemps, eds., 87)

By 1877, the Democrats were back in charge of the southern states. The federal government deserted the slaves it had freed and left the South to its own devices. As Boston Blackwell recalled: "That old story about forty acres and a mule, it make me laugh. They sure did tell us that, but I never knowed any person which got it. Nothing ever hatched out of that, neither" (in Yetman, ed., repr. 2000, 28). By the 1890s, the door to opportunity that had opened for Aframericans during Reconstruction closed shut. In the South the return to the old Jim Crow ways was called "Redemption." The most aggressive Redeemers were a secret organization of "true blue" southerners called the Ku Klux Klan. Klan members hid their identities under hoods and sheets. They mutilated, killed, or otherwise bullied freedmen:

After us colored folks was 'sidered free and turned loose, the Ku Klux broke out. Some colored people started to farming, like I told you, and gathered the old stock. If they got so they made good money and had a good farm, the Ku Klux would come and murder 'em. The government built schoolhouses, and the Ku Klux went to work and burned 'em down. They'd go to the jails and take the colored men out and knock their brains out and break their necks and throw 'em in the river. There was a colored man they taken, his name was Jim Freeman. They taken him and destroyed his stuff and him 'cause he was making some money. Hung him on a tree in his front yard, right in front of his cabin.

(Pierce Harper, in Botkin, 267)

Other recollections of the Ku Klux Klan are equally vivid: "Captain, them mens look like they ten feet high, an' they hosses big as elephants" (Henry Garry, in Mellon, ed., 394); "Baby, them Ku Klux was a pain. The paddyrollers was bad enough, but them Ku Klux done lots of devilment." (Talitha Lewis, in Mellon, ed., 394). This warning to a sharecropper was written in red ink, to simulate blood:

K.K.K.
Beware! Beware! Beware!
Your doom is sealed in blood
Take heed, stay not.
Here the climate is too hot for you.
We warn you to flee.

(*New National Era*, May 25, 1871)

Ida B. Wells (also referred to as Wells-Barnett after her marriage to the attorney F. L. Barnett in 1895) was a fiery teacher-turned-journalist who had been born to Mississippi slaves in 1862. She is best known for having launched an anti-lynching crusade that some historians consider the beginning of the Civil Rights Movement. In 1892 she was writing a column for a black newspaper in Memphis, Tennessee, when three local black men were lynched. In her editorial, she claimed that the crime of black men raping white women was usually unsubstantiated and often a myth. Fearless as Harriet Tubman, Wells was such a fierce anti-lynching campaigner that she became a target of white anger. Friends advised her to ease up on her editorials, warning her that her life was at risk. A gunman had been spotted at the station whenever one of the trains from the North on which she often traveled was due. Instead, like Harriet, Wells decided to carry a pistol. "[I had] already determined to sell my life as dearly as possible if attacked," she later recalled (Pearson Education, online). American newspapers referred to her as the "slanderous and nasty-minded mulattress" (Mindich, 113).

In 1906 Wells-Barnett joined with DuBois and others to further the Niagara Movement, and she was one of two Aframerican women to sign

THE DEPARTMENT OF THEATRE AND DRAMA
in association with
THE RACKHAM SCHOOL OF GRADUATE STUDIES
presents

a rehearsed reading of

THE BRIDGE PARTY

a lynching drama
by
Sandra Seaton

featuring

MS. RUBY DEE
and
a distinguished ensemble of actors

Directed by
Glenda Dickerson

April 30, 1998
7:30 p.m.

Rackham Auditorium
915 East Washington
Ann Arbor, MI

THE BRIDGE PARTY

Invitation to *The Bridge Party*, a lynching drama I directed in 1998, featuring Ruby Dee

"the call" to form the NAACP. A dynamic, controversial, temperamental, uncompromising Race Woman, she broke bread and crossed swords with some of the movers and shakers of her time: Frederick Douglass, Susan B. Anthony, Marcus Garvey, Booker T. Washington, W. E. B. DuBois, and

President William McKinley. Wells-Barnett died in Chicago on March 25, 1931, at the age of 68. In 1950 the city of Chicago named her one of the 25 most outstanding women in its history.

A number of Race Women, Black Persons of the Blacks, wrote plays to protest against lynching as the practice spiraled out of control. Angelina Grimke's play *Rachel* (1916) is the earliest extant full-length drama written by an Aframerican woman; it is also said to be the first play by an Aframerican, excluding musicals, to be produced and publicly performed by Aframerican actors. Produced originally at the Myrtill Miner School in Washington, DC, with a subsequent production in 1917 at the Neighborhood Playhouse in New York, *Rachel* remains a black classic. It centers around the Lovings, a proud middle-class family that has suffered the lynching of the husband and the eldest son. Mr. Loving was lynched for writing a column in a "colored" newspaper to protest against the lynching of another man. His teenage son was lynched for trying to save his father. Grimke vilifies the lynching of innocent black people by white Christians. Her lyrical, almost sermonizing language can be heard, for example, when Tom, Mrs. Loving's son, comments on the condition of blacks because of what he sees as the moral degeneracy of whites: "Their children shall grow up in hope; ours in despair. Our hands are clean; theirs are red with blood – red with the blood of a noble man – and a boy. They're nothing but low, cowardly, bestial murderers" (in Perkins and Stephens, eds., 49).

Georgia Douglas Johnson (1886–1966) wrote approximately 20 plays, several of which Kathy Perkins and Judith Stephens call "lynching plays." These include *Blue-Eyed Black Boy, Safe,* and *A Sunday Morning in the South,* all of which level an indictment against lynching. Tom, the protagonist of *Sunday Morning* is accused of raping a white woman, a crime that supposedly took place two hours after he had gone to sleep. Though the young white woman can only vaguely recollect what her assailant looks like, Tom is arrested because he comes close to the stated description, "age around twenty, five feet five or six, brown skin." Johnson's point here is that a white mob cannot be contained or pacified until black blood is spilled.

Johnson was the most prolific of the black women dramatists writing during what would come to be called the New Negro Movement or the Harlem Renaissance. She spent the bulk of her life in Washington, DC, where her home was christened "Halfway House." For four decades this was a mecca for such intellectual and artistic giants as Langston Hughes, May Miller, Owen Dodson, Sterling Brown, Alain Locke, Angelina Grimke, Zora Neale Hurston, James Weldon Johnson, Claude McKay, and others who were the architects of the New Negro Movement.

The Redeemers often used the excuse of imagined misbehavior of the brutal black buck (explored in chapter 1) to deprive sharecroppers of their

KRIGWA PLAYERS
LITTLE NEGRO THEATRE

AN attempt to establish in High Harlem, New York City, a Little Theatre which shall be primarily a center where Negro actors before Negro audiences interpret Negro life as depicted by Negro artists; but which shall also always have a welcome for all artists of all races and for all sympathetic comers and for all beautiful ideas.

A. DOUGLAS

At their Playhouse
Basement of the 135th Street Branch, New York Public Library

Reproduction of a poster designed by Aaron Douglas for DuBois' Krigwa Players

economic growth. Thomas Dixon's book and play *The Clansman* (1905), which inspired D. W. Griffith's film *Birth of a Nation* (1915), solidified brutal stereotypes in the national imagination. In reaction to such racist misrepresentations, DuBois wrote his pageant *The Star of Ethiopia* (1913). DuBois had three goals: to "get people interested in the development of Negro drama;" to teach "the colored people themselves the meaning of their history and their rich emotional life through a new theatre;" and "to reveal the Negro to the white world as a human, feeling thing." The play opened at the 12th Regiment Armory in New York on October 22, 1913. *The Star of Ethiopia* covers a period of 10,000 years and has a cast of over 1,000 actors. Beside two excerpts from Verdi's *Aida*, all facets of the production – music, costume, lighting, set design, and stage direction – were conceived and produced by Aframericans. The production joined dance, music, and re-enactments of African history, the Middle Passage, slavery, emancipation, and Reconstruction in order to celebrate black heritage. In 1924 DuBois and Regina M. Anderson founded the Krigwa Players, which he described as "an attempt to establish [. . .] a Little Theatre which shall be primarily a center where Negro actors before Negro audiences interpret Negro life as depicted by Negro artists."

The Promised Land

> Boll weevil got the cotton
> Cut worm in the corn
> Debil in the white man
> We's going on.
> (Traditional)

In 1898 the tiny boll weevil ate its way east across the South. Crops were devastated and thousands of sharecroppers were thrown off the land. The onset of war in Europe in 1914 brought a halt to European immigrant workers. An alternative supply of labor was needed to meet the increased demand for war supplies. The South, with its surplus of workers, became very attractive to northern manufacturers. The tightening of Jim Crow laws and nearly daily lynchings led many to leave the South. For many, the Great Migration was like a religious revival. Letters from the North were often read in churches, where "fresh news on the exodus was given out." Churches formed migration clubs to exchange information and facilitate passage north. Rumors were said to be powerful in the exodus, and the devout saw the migration as a sign from heaven. Why else, they argued, would so many become obsessed with the same impulse? Some believed a great calamity would finally befall the South. "Floods and destructive twisters were seen as a sign of God's anger. Judgement Day was coming." The Progressive Era people seemed to be seized by a northern fever and headed north toward "the promised land" where a better life and a different opportunity was promised. By 1917, the term "exodus" was widely used to describe the migration, and the migrating people were called "exodusters." As George Haynes put it:

> The movement among the colored people is striking in many ways. [It] is without organization or opportunities. The Negroes just quietly move away

71

Turn of the century Pullman Porters in their uniforms

without taking their recognized leaders into their confidence any more than they do the white people about them. A Negro minister may have all his deacons with him at the mid week meeting but by Sunday every church officer is likely to be in the North. They write the minister that they forgot to tell him they were going away.

(in Marks, 2)

On May 15, 1917, publisher Robert Abbott launched what he called "The Great Northern Drive" in the *Chicago Defender,* a weekly newspaper he had founded in 1905. The object of the drive was to exhort southern blacks to come to Chicago, in order to make money and live under the legal benefits of citizenship. Abbott artfully combined the roles of race crusader and businessman. He invented slogans ("The Flight out of Egypt") and promoted songs ("Bound for the Promised Land," "Going into Canaan") that pounded home a comparison with the events described in the Book of Exodus. The *Defender* emphasized southern racial injustice and provided Aframericans in the region with information about jobs and social opportunities that they could read nowhere else. Southern landowners were desperate to retain their exploited labor. Police in several cities confiscated copies of the *Defender,* but vendors responded by smuggling them in from rural areas. Copies were mailed in packages that disguised their contents. Black porters acted like conductors on the Underground Railroad by secretly delivering bales of the paper on their trips from Chicago (Dodson and Diouf, eds., 122).

These rail servants, known as Pullman Porters, were a fixture on long-distance trains that crisscrossed the nation. As they traveled between Chicago and southern towns they spread the word (and passed out the *Defender*) on their stops. A common evening pastime was visiting the depot to ask the Chicago porters numerous questions about the city.

In the Aframerican community, employment as a railroad porter was considered honorable, an occupation usually taken by sophisticated men with college degrees who were unable to find better jobs in their chosen professions. This prosperous, respected elite derived their name from the Chicago company that manufactured sleeping cars. Later they organized into a union called the Brotherhood of Sleeping Car Porters.

To learn more about the Pullman Porters, the impressive cadre of uniformed, clean-shaven men who appeared shortly after the Civil War, see the television film by Robert Townsend starring Andre Brauger and Charles Dutton, *10,000 Black Men Named George* (2000), which is about Union activist Asa Philip Randolph and his efforts to organize the black porters of the Pullman Rail Company in 1920s America. The documentary *Rising from the Rails: The Story of the Pullman Porter* (2006), directed and produced by Brad Osborne, features extended interviews with porters and their families. It is based on Larry Tye's book *Rising from the Rails: Pullman Porters and the Making of the Black Middle Class* (2004). If there are stories in the documentary that appeal to you, you might want to read Tye's book to find possibilities for monologues and/or scenes.

A series of paintings by Jacob Lawrence (1917–2000) illustrates the mass exodus of African Americans who moved to the North in search of a better life. The paintings, dated 1940–43, are now part of the Phillips Collection, housed in the Museum of Modern Art, New York. The whole series is available on the museum's website. You may be inspired to create silent improvisations from some of the powerful images of scenes ranging from riots to church services.

The reasons for leaving the South varied: "freedom and independence," better wages, educational opportunities for children. Some people intended to stay only long enough to save a bit of money and return. One migrant, asked why she left the South, replied:

> "I left Georgia because I wanted better privileges." Did that mean mixed schools and association with white people generally? "No," she responded, "I don't care nothing about that, but I just want to be somewhere where I won't be scared all the time that something is going to break loose."
>
> (in Dodson and Diouf, eds., 119)

The *Chicago Defender* was remarkably successful in encouraging Aframericans to migrate from the South to Chicago, often listing names of churches and other organizations to whom they could write for help. As a result, thousands of prospective migrants wrote letters like the three quoted below to black churches, such as the Bethlehem Baptist Association in Chicago.

> While reading the *Defender* I saw where you needed laborers in Chicago. I have children and I lost my wife a few years ago. I would like to properly educate them. I am a barber by trade, and have been barbering for twenty years. I have saved enough money for our fare.

> Dear Sir: I saw your add [sic] in the *Chicago Defender* for laborers. I am a young man and want to finish school. I want you to look out for me a job on the place working morning and evening. I would like to get a job in some private family so I could continue taking my piano lesson. I can do anything around the house but drive and can even learn that. Send me the name of the best High School in Chicago. How is the Wendell Phillips College. I have finish the grammar school.

> BIRMINGHAM, ALA., MAY 1917 SIR: I am in the darkness of the south and I am trying my best to get out. Do you no where about I can get a job in New York. I wood be so glad if could get a good job. O please help me to get out of this low down county. I am counted no more than a dog. Help me please help me. O how glad I wood be if some company would send me a ticket to come and work for them. No joking, I mean business. I [will] work if I can get a good job.

In a matter of months over 400,000 men, women, and children were mobilized and transported from all across the South. The exodusters headed to the large industrial centers – Detroit, Pittsburgh, New York, and most of all Chicago. In Chicago alone the black population grew from 44,000 in 1910 to 109,000 in 1920, and then to 234,000 in 1930. A local commission on race relations reported that 50,000 black people had moved to Chicago from the South in 18 months during the war.

"Farewell – We're Good and Gone," the title of the familiar migration poem, was neatly chalked on one of the special trains heading north, symbolic of a collective hunger for deliverance.

It true we love de South all right,
But, yes we love God, too.
An' when he comes ter help us out,
What's left for us ter do?

Den comes de North and wages high,
Saying, come on up de horn,
An' den you think we'll stay down here?
"Not us" – Good bye, we're gone.

An' let one race have all de South,
Where color lines are drawn,
For "Hagar's Child" done [stem] de tide
Farewell – we're good and gone.

(Traditional)

Claude Brown's autobiography *Manchild in the Promised Land* (1965) encapsulates another migration story: "Going to New York was goodbye to the cotton fields, good-bye to 'Massa Charlie', good-bye to the chain gang, and, most of all, good-bye to those sunup-to-sundown working hours. One no longer had to wait to get to heaven to lay his burden down; burdens could be laid down in New York" (in Dodson and Diouf, eds., 141).

The people traveled to the North over an imaginary overground bridge from the near and deep South, led by the siren song of the bright lights in the big cities. They themselves were a bridge between the dark days of slavery and sharecropping in the South and the new days promised by industrial opportunities in the North. The exodusters, following in the tradition of Ida B. Wells and other Black Persons of the Blacks, placed their very bodies at risk to bridge the gap between their pasts and their children's futures. They worked hard to join the Pullman Porters and others in the new black middle class. Doctors, lawyers, and teachers followed their patients, clients, and students to the cities of the North. The newcomers who came north created a voluminous demand for different kinds of services, giving rise to a large group of professional and business men and women who constituted a new leadership class in the community.

Madam C. J. Walker was part of this new leadership class. Born Sarah Breedlove on December 23, 1867, to former slaves on a plantation in Delta, Louisiana, she transformed herself from an uneducated farm laborer and laundress into one of the 20th century's most successful women. Friendships with other Aframerican women who were members of St. Paul AME Church and the National Association of Colored Women exposed her to a new way of viewing the world. In 1905, the same year Abbott founded the *Chicago Defender* with 25 cents and a handful of pencils, Sarah changed her name to "Madam" C. J. Walker. She founded her own business and began selling Madam Walker's Wonderful Hair Grower, a scalp-conditioning and healing formula, which she claimed had been revealed to her in a dream. (Incidentally, she did not invent the straightening comb, though many people believe that to be true.) To promote her products, she traveled for a year and a half throughout the heavily black South and Southeast, not only door to door, but demonstrating her scalp treatments in churches and lodges, and devising sales and marketing strategies. In 1908 she temporarily moved her base to Pittsburgh, where she opened Lelia College to train Walker "hair culturists." As her business continued to grow, Walker organized her agents into local and state clubs. Her Madam C. J. Walker Hair Culturists Union of America Convention in Philadelphia in 1917 must have been one of the first national meetings of businesswomen in the country. In 2007 Kathleen Shaw's short play *The Making of a Legend: Madame C. J. Walker* premiered as part of the Martin Luther King Day celebration at the University of Louisville, under the direction of Dr. Lundeana Thomas.

On September 9, 1915, Carter G. Woodson and four other black men started the Association for the Study of Negro (now Afro-American) Life and History in Chicago. (He later incorporated the group in Washington, DC, where he managed it from his home.) A year later Woodson, who became known as the "Father of Negro History," began publishing the *Journal of Negro History* (still published as a quarterly, under the title *Journal of African American History*). He created Associated Publishers in 1921, initiated the observance of Negro History Week in 1926, and founded the *Negro History Bulletin* in 1936.

The people did not journey to Chicago and points north alone. With them traveled a mysterious creative spirit, born in the brush arbors. Just as High John had accompanied them on the slave ship to guard their wings, and played tricks during slavery, he seemed to imbue them with the power to create a new collective song on the journey north. This mysterious spirit was manifest in the music, equal parts hope and despair, created by the next generation of the children who could not fly.

Blues and jazz lie at the heart of American popular music and have affected musical styles throughout the world. Radio had a tremendous impact in terms of making people dream of going north one day. Gathered around the radio at night, the soon-to-be exodusters heard music coming from soon-to-be legends, for example Earl "Fatha" Hines, Duke Ellington, Cab Calloway, and the young Count Basie. Legendary blues singer Koko Taylor grew up

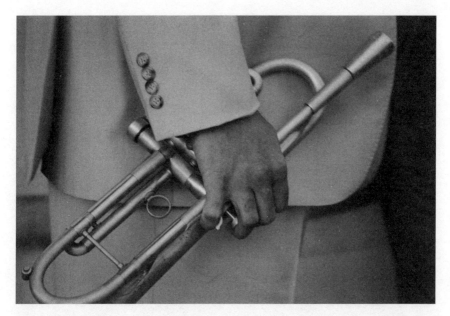

Man traveling with his trumpet

chopping cotton in the Mississippi Delta. She was one of the many thousands who didn't stay:

> When I was 18 years old, I left Memphis, my husband and I. And we got the Greyhound bus up Highway 61 and headed north to Chicago. He didn't have no money and I didn't have no money. We had one box of Ritz crackers that we split between us. With no money, nowhere to live, no nothing; we was just taking a chance. And I figured, if he got enough nerve to take a chance with nothin', I have too. So that's what we did.
>
> (in Dodson and Diouf, 139)

Zora Neale Hurston (1891–1960) was a folklorist, author, and anthropologist, associated with her celebration of the ordinary or common folk. She said of High John, "the sign of this man was a laugh, and his singing-symbol was a drumbeat. [. . .] It was an inside thing to live by. [. . .] Thousands upon thousands of humble people still believe in John de Conquer. John will never forsake the weak and the helpless, nor fail to bring hope to the hopeless" (A. Davis, 156–7).

Zora was herself a migrant, having been raised in the all-black community of Eatonville, Florida, and then journeying north to matriculate at Howard University, one of the HBCUs established during Reconstruction. It was while she was at Howard that she wrote her play *Color Struck* (1925), which makes the point that migration, while affording some positive opportunities,

Woman left behind during the Great Migration

had its drawbacks. She saw the results of the Great Migration as often devastating to those left behind. The play can be summarized as follows: Emmaline (called Emma throughout) is a dark-skinned Aframerican woman from Jacksonville, Florida. Her lover, John, pursues light-skinned women, thus keeping Emma in a constant state of jealousy. The setting is a railway car where John, Emma, and others from various parts of Florida – Jacksonville, Augustine, and Eatonville – are en route to a cakewalking dance contest. Scene 2 takes place right before the contest, scene 3 during the contest itself. The final scene, 20 years later, depicts John's return from the North and his attempt to reconcile his differences with Emma. Emma, however, rejects John's overtures as too little, too late. Emma embodies the circumstances of rural, southern black women of the time.

Color Struck was completed just before Hurston's entrance into Barnard College, New York, to study anthropology with Franz Boaz. She would eventually become the New Negro Movement's problem child – not only did she refuse to adopt the movement's exclusionary code of silence when it came to literature and drama about simple folks, she often criticized it. But for now, let's just follow Zora as she heads north on her journey to Harlem. In the first week of January 1925, Zora Hurston arrived in New York with $1.50 in her purse, no job, no friends, but like all the other exodusters, filled with hope.

Food for Further Thought

Anna Julia Cooper was the quintessential Race Woman. Read her essay "A Voice from the South" (1892) to find out why. W. E. B. DuBois was a brilliant and sometimes underappreciated groundbreaking scholar and Race Man. His pageant *Star of Ethiopia* (1913) is included in *Black Theatre USA* (1996), edited by James V. Hatch and Ted Shine. To learn more about the Great Migration read *In Motion* (2004), a volume edited by Howard Dodson and Sylviane Diouf, which has many illustrations and maps.

Is there a Black Person of the Blacks in your family, living or dead? If so, and if he or she is still living, would you like to record an oral history? If not still living, would you like to interview another family member? From your research, can you write a biography?

Leaving home was a wrenching experience for the exodusters, though mitigated by exhilaration. Do you remember a trip that took you a long way from home? Were you beset by conflicting feelings? How would you describe the trip for your Black Life Book?

In your Black Life Book, what "admonitions" would you offer to your peers for success in life. How would they differ from those of the turn of the century listed above? Would any of your admonitions be the same or similar to those from *Progress and Achievements of the 20th Century Negro*? One of those I quoted was: "Educate Your Children. It cannot be doubted that education is the father and mother of opportunity and success in life."

4 The Harlem Renaissance
A Sunburst Something like Spiritual Emancipation

"Everybody loves Saturday Night."

(West African high life lyric)

A railroad ticket and a suitcase, like a Baghdad carpet,
transport the Negro peasant from the cotton-field and farm
to the heart of the most complex urban civilization.

(Alain Locke, in Maxwell, 47)

The Harlem that greeted Zora Neale Hurston was a magical place. The urban streets were as different from rural Florida as Booker T. was from W. E. B. The most famous black community in the world, Harlem has been the home of some of the greatest American artists, politicians, entertainers, clergymen, and writers of the 20th century. Subject of poems, novels, songs, plays, and dreams, Harlem is like a mythic place, set high on a hill, a proper launching pad for people who dreamed of flying. The streets were alive with beauty parlors, markets, apartments, and hospital waiting rooms. Doctors, lawyers, real estate brokers, undertakers, and dentists followed the exodusters north and became the "best" people of Harlem.

Zora stepped into a world whirling with images of Eubie Blake and Noble Sissle; of Josephine Baker and Florence Mills; of Claude McKay and Countée Cullen; Duke Ellington and Lena Horne; Langston Hughes and James Weldon Johnson; Marcus Garvey and W. E. B. DuBois. This kaleidoscopic group represented what were in effect two Harlems: one where the regular people danced in the smoky exuberance of nightclubs and rent parties and the other where the elite observed them from the privileged vantage point of Alain Locke's New Negro. Together they made up the Harlem Renaissance. Zora was ideally suited to bridge these two worlds. Just because of who she was, she could lead anyone on a tour of the two Harlems. In your imagination, follow Zora, with her big smile and curious eyes, uptown to 125th Street, where black businesses flourished in buildings owned by white landlords, and listen to the street criers:

Ah got string beans!
Ah got cabbage!
Ah got collard greens!

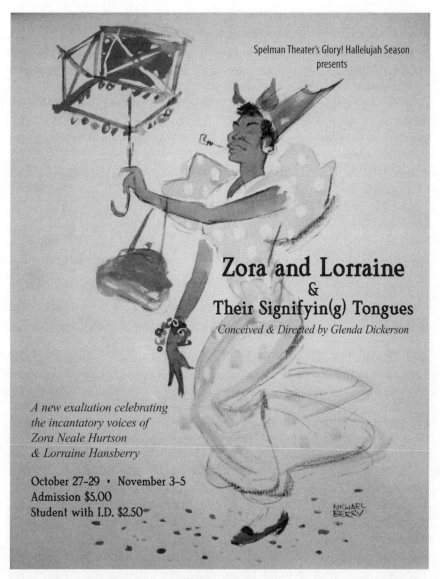

Spelman Theater's Glory! Hallelujah Season
presents

Zora and Lorraine
&
Their Signifyin(g) Tongues

Conceived & Directed by Glenda Dickerson

A new exaltation celebrating
the incantatory voices of
Zora Neale Hurtson
& Lorraine Hansberry

October 27-29 • November 3-5
Admission $5.00
Student with I.D. $2.50

MICHAEL
BERRY

Flyer for *Zora and Lorraine & Their Signifyin(g) Tongues*, a play I conceived and directed in 1995, about an imaginary meeting between Zora Neale Hurston and Lorraine Hansberry

> Ah got um! Ah got um!
> Ah got anythin' you need,
> Ah'm de Ah-got-um man!

At the intersection with 7th Avenue, imagine listening to prophets such as Marcus Garvey, whose Universal Negro Improvement Association (UNIA)

A Harlem Renaissance crowd collects outside the Lafayette Theatre before a performance of *Hallelujah*!

became the largest black organization in the US, with branches throughout the world. He might be advancing his program of racial pride, black economic development, and the return of Negroes to Africa. Garvey was a real-estate magnate who owned large tracts of Harlem property. Having founded the Black Star Shipping Line, he sold thousands of shares of stock to Negroes uptown, where he was worshiped as a black emancipator and visionary.

Wandering up 7th Avenue, known as the Boulevard of Dreams, pause between 130th and 131st Street, where Zora might introduce you to Bill "Bojangles" Robinson. The legendary tap dancer and other Renaissancers would be standing outside the famous Lafayette Theatre, looking for work. The most popular place to see Negro talent, the Lafayette was the scene for aspiring actors, dancers, and performers to mix, gather, and exchange information and gossip. Outside the theater stood the Tree of Hope, a tall chestnut tree believed to bring good luck to all who touched it. The tree came to symbolize the promise that Harlem held for millions of aspiring Negroes. Harlem show-people believed that if you touched the bark of the tree, your wishes would come true. It became a natural place where agents and people in show-business gathered. Many entertainment jobs were handed out under the shade of the tree.

These were the days of prohibition. Selling or consuming liquor was illegal. So Zora, who did not drink, would have rushed you past rowdy speakeasies where bootleggers sold homemade "cawn" liquor and racketeers plied their trade. She might have pointed out a big sign over a vacant lot: "WATCH THE CLOUDS THIS SUNDAY – JULIAN IS ARRIVING FROM THE SKY HERE." The aviator "Lieutenant" Hubert Fauntleroy Julian, MD (for Mechanical Designer), born in Trinidad, learned to fly in the Canadian Air Corps during World War I and made Harlem his home. His Transatlantic flight of 1929, two years after that of Charles Lindbergh, inspired the Calypso musician Sam Manning to record the song *Lieutenant Julian*. Between international flights (and surviving several plane crashes), he toured with his own circus troupe, the Five Blackbirds.

If it was Sunday morning, Zora could take you to the Abyssinian Baptist Church to hear a charismatic sermon preached by the Reverend Adam Clayton Powell, Sr., one of the most famous Negro churchmen of his time. Services at Abyssinian Baptist Church were joyful events which would have reminded her of the Old-Time Negro Preacher still preaching in Eatonville. Spontaneous cries and shouts of "Amen!," "Hallelujah!," and "Praise the Lord!" punctuated the services and resounded throughout the church. During the Depression, Reverend Powell campaigned to feed the poor and for better jobs and city services. Actively involved in the struggle against racism, he was a co-founder of the National Urban League, and an early leader in the National Association for the Advancement of Colored People. Powell so electrified his congregation and much of Harlem that it was only in 1937, on his third attempt, that the church agreed to let him retire. Powell turned over the pulpit to his son, Adam Clayton Powell, Jr., who in 1945 became New York's first black congressman.

Harlem became a beacon for the young, beautiful and talented. Railroad porters, domestic house cleaners, former tenant farmers, and immigrants from the Carribean brought their music, their literature, and their stories with them to Harlem. These seekers from far-flung corners of the world began filling the plentiful housing Harlem had to offer. As soon as one or two black families moved into a block, the whites began moving out. Then the rents were doubled and sometimes tripled. Meeting such exorbitant rents was not easy, so Harlemites began to find new ways of greeting the landlord without empty pockets. The Harlem rent party was born. Tenants opened their doors to party-goers for an admission price of 25 cents. Guests could enjoy fried chicken, pork chops, pig's feet, potato salad, and homemade liquor. Rent parties became an overnight rage and before the evening was over the party-throwers had enough to pay their rent:

> Gimmee a pigfoot and a bottle of beer
> Send me, gate, I don't care

I feel just like I wanna clown
Give the piano player a drink because he's bringin me down.

(in A. Davis, 282)

Because Zora loved the "folk" and made a career of celebrating their tales, she would have been right at home at a rent party. Parties began anytime after midnight and continued sometimes well into dawn with the smells of good food and the pulsing sounds of hot music. Saturday night became the night for rent parties. Family after family opened wide their doors. As quoted at the start of this chapter, "Everybody loves Saturday night."

Zora and a number of other playwrights during this time wrote plays about the people who attended the rent parties. And as the Harlem Renaissance gathered momentum, black playwrights began to look seriously at ordinary black people. Arna Bontemps, Jean Toomer, and Sterling Brown all invested the characters in their plays, which were then called "folk dramas," with dignity and courage.

Eulalie Spence (1894–1981), another playwright who reached her zenith during the Harlem Renaissance, was born in the British West Indies. Her *Undertow* (1929) is a gripping and realistic folk drama about life in Harlem. The central characters are Hattie and Dan, a couple who live through a loveless marriage for 20 years. After Hattie discovers that her husband has been having an affair, she is reduced to nagging and degrading him because of her pain over his betrayal. When Clem, the other woman, returns to rekindle the fire, Hattie and Dan enter a violent physical struggle, leaving Hattie dead. Among her last words to Dan are, "You ain't gonna tro no dust in mah eyes no second time – not ef Ah know it" (in Hatch and Shine, eds., 1974, 195).

In the "other" Harlem, where no one except Langston Hughes admitted ever attending a rent party, a flowering of black art, dance, drama, music, and literature was taking place. It was a period marked by what Arthur Davis calls "a sunburst of writing by and about blacks." Claude McKay's *Harlem Shadows*, the first published book of verse since Paul Laurence Dunbar's *Poems of Cabin and Fields* (1899), came out in 1922. In 1923, Charles Johnson wrote of Jean Toomer's *Cane* that it expressed "triumphantly the Negro artist, detached from propaganda, sensitive only to beauty." In this "other" Harlem, A'Lelia Walker was the great party giver. Her mother was Madame C. J. Walker, of hair-culturalist fame (see chapter 3). Madame Walker had made a great fortune from her products. The daughter used much of that money for fun. A'Lelia made no pretense at being intellectual or exclusive. At her "at homes," numbers bankers mingled with the sunburst writers. Although Zora could probably get you and me into one of A'Lelia's famous parties, we might not be able to meet the hostess herself. These affairs were always overcrowded and most people never got to see A'lelia. But Zora could introduce us to her friend, Countée Cullen.

Countée Cullen was at the center of one of the major social occasions of the Harlem Renaissance. On April 9, 1928, he married Yolande DuBois, only child of W. E. B. DuBois. One of the most lavish weddings in the history of black New York, this event symbolized the union of the grand black intellectual patriarch and the New Negroes. (The marriage lasted only two months, however.) Poet, anthologist, novelist, translator, children's writer, and playwright, Countée Cullen (1903–1946) was secretive about his early life. Though he later claimed to have been born and bred in New York, his birthplace remains uncertain. He graduated from New York University in 1925 and went on to study at Harvard. His poems were published in several prestigious journals, and in 1926 he won the *Crisis* magazine poetry award. Alain Locke wrote in 1926: "Ladies and Gentlemen! A genius! Posterity will laugh at us if we do not proclaim him now." Cullen's poem "From the Dark Tower" inspired A'Leila Walker to name her salon "The Dark Tower":

> We shall not always plant while others reap
> The golden increment of bursting fruit,
> Not always countenance, abject and mute,
> That lesser men should hold their brothers cheap;
> Not everlastingly while others sleep
> Shall we beguile their limbs with mellow flute,
> Not always bend to some more subtle brute;
> We were not made eternally to weep.
>
> (in Hughes and Bontemps, eds., 132)

In mid-March 1924 Charles S. Johnson, editor of the Urban League's *Opportunity* magazine, invited about a dozen young and mostly unknown poets and writers to dine with Dr. DuBois and James Weldon Johnson at the Civic Club. This distinguished group included Jean Toomer, Gwendolyn Bennett, Countée Cullen, Langston Hughes, and Alain Locke. This party is notable for two reasons. First it marked passing the baton on from the "older school" of black letters, represented by DuBois and Johnson, to the younger generation. And second was the birth of an idea that led to the New Negro Movement. Charles Johnson praised DuBois and Johnson as forefathers who had given "invaluable encouragement to the work of this younger group." The floor was then yielded to Alain Locke. A professor of philosophy at Howard University, Locke would later be known as the "father of the Harlem Renaissance," the voice of the "New Negro."

Ironically, Locke himself was not from Harlem and never took up permanent residence there. He had been Zora's teacher at Howard, where he told his students "culture is all there is." The public relations campaign to promote the New Negro Movement was conducted by a small band of men and a few women, but it was Charles Johnson's voice that proved most influential. Zora usually gave what she called the "Niggerati" short shrift, but no praise was ever too much for her Dr. Johnson. The Renaissance "was his work, and only his hush mouth nature has caused it to be attributed to many others," she wrote (Urban League, online).

Johnson's overarching desire and objective was to kill the pernicious stereotypes born in slavery, disseminated by the minstrel show and solidified in the dark days following Reconstruction. This meant, among other things, that folk drama was not the expression of choice and dialect was definitely not approved. Johnson and Locke and the others believed that the "folk" had to be spoken for and interpreted by the literary elite. Like Zora, most of the New Negro writers and artists did not originate in Harlem.

Langston Hughes (1902–67) became the unofficial poet laureate of the Harlem Renaissance and one of America's leading writers. Born in 1902, in Joplin, Missouri, he was raised until the age of 12 by his grandmother, who was the widow of Sheridan Leary, one of the black men killed in John Brown's raid on Harper's Ferry. When Hughes got to Harlem he said: "I stood there, dropped my bags, took a deep breath, and felt happy again." He wrote poems, plays, short stories, novels, essays, history, biography, newspaper columns, and even lyrics for opera composers. *The Crisis* published one of his most enduringly popular poems, "The Negro Speaks of Rivers":

> I've known rivers:
> Ancient, dusky rivers.
> My soul has grown deep like the rivers.
> I bathed in the Euphrates when dawns were young.
> I built my hut near the Congo and it lulled me to sleep.
> I looked upon the Nile and raised the pyramids above it.
> I heard the singing of the Mississippi when Abe Lincoln went down to
>   New Orleans, and
> I've seen its muddy bosom turn all golden in the sunset.
>
> I've known rivers:
> Ancient, dusky rivers.
>
> My soul has grown deep like the rivers.
>
> (in Hughes and Bontemps, eds., 105)

In August 1924, when an issue of *The Crisis* arrived containing his first published poem, Arna Bontemps (1902–73) immediately resigned his job in the Los Angeles post office and bought a ticket for New York. He settled in Harlem, where his career soon intersected with that of Langston Hughes. The two became close friends and went on to collaborate on several works, including the play *St. Louis Woman* (1946), which inspired Vernon Duke's Broadway musical about the Fisk Jubilee Singers. In Harlem, Bontemps also mixed with other artists of the New Negro Movement.

Bibliophile, historian, writer, collector, and curator, Arturo (Arthur) Alfonso Schomburg (1874–1938) was born in Puerto Rico. He began his education in a primary school in San Juan, where his fifth-grade teacher is said to have told him that black people have no history, no heroes, no great moments. Because of this, Schomburg developed a thirst for knowledge about people of African descent and began his lifelong quest studying the history and collecting the books and artifacts that made up the core of his extensive library. He frequently loaned objects from his personal library to the 135th Street Branch of the New York Public Library, which was a center of intellectual and cultural activity in Harlem. In 1926 his collection of 10,000 books and prints was purchased by the New York Public Library, with the assistance of the Carnegie Corporation. This became the cornerstone of the library's Division of Negro Literature, History, and Prints, of which he was invited to be curator in 1932.

Aaron Douglas (1898–1979), whom Charles Johnson had been told was one of the race's finest potential artists, had to be persuaded to come to Harlem: "Better to be a dishwasher in New York than to be head of a high school in Kansas City," Johnson's secretary challenged. He went on to play a vital role in the Harlem Renaissance. He wrote to Langston Hughes and set forth the following strategy for creating an authentic "Negro" art: "Let's bare our arms and plunge them deep through laughter, through pain, through sorrow, through hope, through disappointment, into the very depths of the souls of our people and drag forth material crude, rough, neglected. Then let's sing it, dance it, write it, paint it" (in O'Meally, 192).

Charles Johnson decided that the artists and writers arriving in Harlem needed an established forum with its own standards, rules, and rewards. In September 1925 his editorial in *Opportunity* announced new awards for outstanding creative achievement. His statement of purpose referred to artistic creation as a means of fostering a type of writing by Negroes which "shakes itself free of deliberate propaganda and protest." Zora's *Color Struck* won the literary prize.

The year 1925 ended with publication of Alain Locke's book *The New Negro*, a presentation of poetry and prose spun off from the *Opportunity* contest. There was still a divide between the two Harlems: the high literature promoted by Alain Locke's New Negro Movement and the low appeal of rent parties and speakeasies celebrated in the folk dramas. These lyrics from a Bessie Smith song capture the atmosphere:

Up in Harlem every Saturday night
When the highbrows get together it's just too tight
They all congregate at an all night strut
And what they do is tut, tut, tut

(in A. Davis, 281)

Straining to counteract the "distinctly inferior" perception, some young writers of the early years of the Harlem Renaissance were preoccupied with proving to white America that they were just like them (except for the superfluous matter of color). Two types of "genteel" literature were produced by early black playwrights, the so-called "raceless" and "best-foot-forward" types. These were by writers who felt that literature by and about blacks and using black dialect might be perceived as not only limiting, but as bad literature.

"Raceless" literature de-emphasizes recognizable aspects of black culture. Some of the early works of Countée Cullen, James Weldon Johnson, and Claude McKay may be considered within that category. The "best-foot-forward" approach includes only the best and the positive about blacks, generally middle-class blacks. Grassroots blacks and their sometimes seamy sides are ignored as subjects. These writers aimed to demonstrate that blacks were no different from whites. Thus, when whites read about characters who are only painted black, they would be receptive to the work in question (Brown-Guillory, 11).

As far as the performing arts were concerned, Charles Johnson's *Opportunity* muses were unhappy about the fact that blacks were relegated to musical comedies rather than to the serious dramatic stage. Nonetheless, *Shuffle Along*, the first American musical revue written and performed by African Americans, was the shining jewel in the crown of the Harlem Renaissance. The music was composed in 1921 by Noble Sissle and Eubie Blake, who teamed with George Miller as librettist and Aubrey Lyles as lyricist. By this time, Blake had already won fame as one of the principal composers of ragtime. Noble Sissle's grandfather came from the Cecil plantation and so resented the origin of his name that he changed it to Sissle. Miller and Lyles were blackface comedians who wrote all of their own material, and it was of such quality that they appeared at what became known as "high class" theaters. Similarly, Blake and Sissle had played society music, unlike many Negro musicians who had been confined to the blues circuit and to burlesque theaters. After seeing their act, Miller suggested that they work together to produce a "clean" comedy and a song that people could whistle after the show.

Shuffle Along was written for Broadway, although it was tried out elsewhere to see whether it would appeal to white audiences. It opened at the Cort Theatre on 63rd Street and ran for nearly a year and a half, going on

Sheet-music cover for a song from *Shuffle Along*, by Noble Sissle and Eubie Blake.
Courtesy Kimball and Bolcom

to influence countless subsequent musical comedies. The cast included
Josephine Baker, Florence Mills, and Paul Robeson. The orchestra was conducted by James Rosamond Johnson with William Grant Still in the string
section. The most famous number in the show was "I'm Just Wild about

Noble Sissle and Eubie Blake. Courtesy Kimball and Bolcom

Harry," which Harry Truman used as his presidential campaign song. Langston Hughes, who claimed that he chose to attend Columbia University so that he could see *Shuffle Along*, credited the show with giving a "scintillating send-off to that Negro vogue in Manhattan known as the Harlem Renaissance. For nearly two years it was always packed. It gave the proper push – a pre-Charleston kick – to the vogue that spread to books, African sculpture, music and dancing" (in Woll, 60).

Lilly Lindo, one of the Apollo Theatre dancing girls, wanted to emulate the singing of Florence Mills, of whom she said:

> Florence Mills knocked em' dead ev'vy time she came on the stage. The Duke a Win'sor saw her strut her stuff thirteen times. They even call her the black ambassador to the world, but things like that never went to her head. Her spirit was typical of the black, and did she have pride in her own people! Whenever she was playin' in a show on Broadway she always seed to it that it came to Harlem even for a week so that her own people who didn't have money enough to go down on Broadway would not be denied the privilege of seein' her. People like Florence Mills make this world a better place t'live in. She did a hel-luva lot t'wipe out race prejudice. If all they say about the Hereafter is true, then the Heavenly Gates must a swung ajar for Florence Mills t'enter an' shine in Heaven, cause she sure did shine down here.
>
> (in Bascom, ed., 178)

Among those in the chorus line in *Shuffle Along* on tour in 1921 was Josephine Baker (1906–75), born Freda Josephine McDonald, who became known as "The Black Venus." On October 2, 1925, she opened in Paris at the Théâtre des Champs-Élysées, where she became an instant success for her erotic dancing and for appearing practically nude on stage. She performed wearing only high heels and a skirt made of bananas; she was often accompanied by her pet leopard, Chiquita, who was adorned with a diamond collar.

Though based in France, Baker supported the American Civil Rights Movement during the 1950s, and protested racism in her own way. On tours of the United States, she refused to perform in segregated nightclubs, and her insistence on mixed audiences helped to integrate shows in Las Vegas, Nevada. For the centenary of her birth, Jerome Savary wrote and directed *Looking for Josephine*, a splashy revue that opened at the Opéra-Comique in Paris. The show wove in the history of black American music and paid tribute to New Orleans, both before and after the tragedy of Hurricane Katrina. The production starred Nicolle Rochelle as Josephine Baker and played to sold-out audiences in the 1,000-seat venue.

An equally celebrated black American – indeed the epitome of the 20th-century Renaissance man as exceptional athlete, actor, singer, cultural scholar, author, and political activist was Paul Robeson (1898–1976). In his own words: "To be free – to walk the good American earth as equal citizens, to live without fear, to enjoy the fruits of our toil to give our children every opportunity in life – that dream which we have held so long in our hearts is today the destiny that we hold in our hands" (Electronic New Jersey Project, online). His talents made him a revered man of his time, but his political beliefs all but erased him from popular history.

Josephine Baker and her pet leopard, Chiquita

As an actor, Robeson was one of the first black men to play serious roles in the primarily white American theater. In the mid-1920s he created the leading part in Eugene O'Neill's *All God's Chillun Got Wings* (1924), a drama about a mixed marriage. He went on to star in another play by O'Neill, *The Emperor Jones* (1925) and was also featured in the filmed version (1933). He appeared in the title role of *Othello* in New York nearly 300 times, making Margaret Webster's production the longest-running Shakespeare in Broadway history. Robeson's first professional appearance in this role was in London (1930); he had also starred in a school performance. Perhaps he is most widely known for his singing of "Old Man River" from the musical *Showboat*. His concert career took him well beyond New York, to Vienna, Prague, Budapest, Paris, London, Moscow, Nairobi, and elsewhere. He was usually welcomed with open arms and standing ovations. His travels taught him that racism was less prevalent in Europe than in the United States, where he couldn't enter theaters through the front door or sing without intimidation and protest. Robeson believed in the universality of music and that by performing Negro spirituals and other traditional folk songs, he could promote intercultural understanding. As a result, he became a citizen of the world, singing for peace and equality in at least 25 languages.

Marita Bonner (1905–71) was a pioneering experimenter with form during the Harlem Renaissance. Her play *The Purple Flower*, which first appeared in *The Crisis* in 1928, is a fantasy populated by characters who serve as a vehicle for her to make serious comments on reality in America. Devoid of humor, it is biting and militant, every bit as powerful as the radical plays of the 1960s. In her essay entitled "On Being Young – a Woman – and Colored" (1925), she wrote: "You long to explode and hurt everything white; friendly, unfriendly. But you know that you cannot live with a chip on your shoulder . . . For chips make you bend your body to balance them. And once you bend, you lose your poise, your balance, and the chips get into you. The real you. You get hard." The play is set on a hill called "Somewhere inhabited by White Devils" (whites) and in the valley called "Nowhere peopled by the Us's" (blacks). Bonner describes the White Devils as "artful little things with soft wide eyes such as you would expect to find in an angel. Soft hair that flops around their horns. Their horns glow red all the time – now with blood – now with eternal fire – now with unholy desire" (in Hatch and Shine, eds., 1974, 202). On the other hand, Bonner says of the Us's, "They can be as white as the White Devils, as brown as the earth, as black as the center of a poppy. They may look as if they were something or nothing" (202). In this fantasyland, the White Devils scheme to keep the Us's off the hill and away from the Purple Flower, which represents the good and the best in life. Several Us's offer suggestions about how to get up the hill. *The Purple Flower* was a powerful example for such later writers as Amiri Baraka, Sonia Sanchez, and Ed Bullins.

With the death of A'Lelia Walker in August 1931, the morning after she had hosted one of her lavish parties, Harlem began to feel something of its own mortality. The Reverend Adam Clayton Powell, Sr., gave a stirring eulogy at her funeral, which Langston Hughes described as "grand" and

> very much like a party. Mrs. Mary McLeod Bethune spoke in that great deep voice of hers, as only she can speak. She recalled the poor mother of A'Lelia Walker in old clothes, who had labored to bring the gift of beauty to Negro womanhood, and had taught them the care of their skin and their hair, and had built up a great business and a great fortune to the pride and glory of the Negro race – and then had given it all to her daughter, A'Lelia. After that the girls from the various Walker beauty shops throughout America brought their flowers and laid them on the bier. That was really the end of the gay times of the New Negro era in Harlem, the period that had begun to reach its end when the crash [of the Stock Exchange of October 29, 1929] and the white people had much less money to spend on themselves, and practically none to spend on Negroes, for the depression brought everybody down a peg or two. And the Negroes had but few pegs to fall.
>
> (in Huggins, 1976, 96–7)

Nevertheless, during the 1930s, Langston Hughes directed his plays at the 135th Street branch of the Public Library, calling his company the Suitcase Theatre. His *Don't You Want to be Free?*, which lasts only an hour, endeavored to capture the entire scope of Negro history from Africa to America. It was to be presented in a "modern manner," with no curtains or stage effects other than a lynch rope which hangs at the back center of the stage throughout the performance, to serve as a symbol of Negro oppression. The play opened in February 1937 and ran for 135 performances, the longest-running play in Harlem during his life. His last play was titled *Jericho – Jim Crow* (1964). He died in 1967 at the age of 65. An edition of his collected works was published in 2001.

Zora Neale Hurston, having received her anthropology degree from Barnard College in 1927, soon left New York to collect folk stories from the South. Many of these are published in her book *Mules and Men* (1935). She wrote seven novels (of which *Their Eyes were Watching God*, 1937, is the most famous), numerous short stories, plays, and magazine articles. During her few return visits to New York she collaborated briefly with Langston Hughes, for example in the play with music, *Mule Bone: A Comedy of Negro Life*; while not performed in its day, it was produced at the Lincoln Center, New York, in 1989. For all her wide-eyed wonder, political manipulation, mentors and admirers, and her supreme talent, Zora died penniless in Florida in 1961. Perhaps she was too far ahead of her time. She lay in an unmarked grave until Alice Walker placed a marker on it in 1972. After this, Zora was rediscovered and is now hailed as one of the great American novelists of the 20th century, able to span the two Harlems and the two worlds of A'Lelia Walker and Alain

Locke. As you read any of her diverse writings, you will see that Zora remains a splendid guide as you search for the many ways Iwa has been expressed by the children of the people who could not fly.

Food for Further Thought

For a sampling of many different writers from the Harlem Renaissance, consult Nathan Irvin Huggins' *Voices from the Harlem Renaissance* (1976) and *Harlem on my Mind* (1968), edited by Allon Schoener.

Listen to an album by Bessie Smith. Also, look at the photographs in *Van der Zee: Photographer, 1886–1983* (1993) by Deborah Willis-Braithwaite and Rodger C. Birt. Charles Van der Zee documented both the rent party-goers and the "New Negroes."

If you are in New York, visit Harlem to explore the Schomburg Collection.

Have you ever had a group experience like that of the New Negroes, perhaps in a fraternity or sorority? How would you like to see that experience expressed artistically?

For your Black Life Book, how would you describe the main street in your hometown? Is it as vibrant as Harlem in the 1920s? However you find it, write about how it strikes you now.

5 War Stories
Buffalo Soldiers, Black Bird Men, and the Bloods

Black Crispus Attucks
Taught us how to die
Before white Patrick Henry
Uttered the battle cry:
"Yay, give me liberty or give me death."

(Melvin B. Tolson, in Chapman, ed., 1968, 388)

By the God of Heaven, we are cowards and jackasses if now that the war is over, we do not marshal every ounce of our brain and brawn to fight the forces of hell in our own land.

(W. E. B. DuBois, 1919, 13)

"The Bloods is us."

(Gene Woodley, former combat paratrooper, Vietnam)

Between the Harlem Renaissance and the advent of the militant theater of the 1960s, the New Negroes continued to gain experience on Broadway, off-Broadway, in community theaters, and in drama groups in HBCUS. The Federal Theatre Project grew out of the Depression, providing work for unemployed theater people during the 1930s, particularly in its Negro Unit.

The American Negro Theatre (ANT) was a pioneering African American company and school in which several hundred black actors, writers, and technicians began their careers. It was founded in Harlem in 1940 by the black writer Abram Hill and the black actor Frederick O'Neal, who aimed to create opportunities for African American artists and entertainment for African American audiences on Broadway. Such actors as Ruby Dee, Ossie Davis, Sidney Poitier, Harry Belafonte, and Alice Childress were all affiliated with the American Negro Theatre.

Two dramas reached Broadway in the 1940s: *Native Son* (1941) by white playwright Paul Green and Richard Wright; and Theodore Ward's *Our Lan'* (1947). The former is a dramatization of Wright's novel about the "brute Negro" Bigger Thomas and the corrosive effects that American society had on him. *Our Lan'* concerns a group of newly freed people who search for economic independence and security toward the end of the Civil War and during the early Reconstruction period. In the 1950s off-Broadway teemed with plays by Negroes. To name just a few, these included William Branch's *Medal for Willie* (1951) and *In Splendid Error* (1955); Alice Childress's *Trouble in Mind* (1955), and Loften Mitchell's *Land beyond the River* (1957).

Among the playwrights to have captured the contradiction of black men sent off to war, fighting with great courage and sometimes dying for a country in which they still had less than full rights, are Alice Dunbar-Nelson, Mary Burrill, William Branch, and Charles Fuller. They are all examined in this chapter. Melvin Tolson's poem quoted above refers to Crispus Attucks (1723–70), known as a martyr for the cause of American independence. He was the first soldier to be killed during the American Revolution, in which 5,000 Africans fought. The 1st Rhode Island Regiment was the only all-black unit to fight; the other units were integrated. After this war, the military instituted a policy of segregation which lasted until the Korean War (1950–3).

Black soldiers have distinguished themselves in war ever since Crispus Attucks was killed. In a letter written from Fort Pickens, Florida, on December 19, 1864, one soldier wrote:

> Dear Friend: I have not as yet been in any regular battle, but have been on scouting parties a number of times. The last scout we were on we met the rebs, who had six companies of colored soldiers with them, all armed with guns. As soon as the colored soldiers among the rebs saw our colored troops they threw down their arms and ran over to us, crying out "we are free, we are free!"
>
> (in Redkey, ed., 153)

Approximately 180,000 black men fought in the Union army and 30,000 in the navy during the Civil War. About one in five black males over the age of 15 joined the Union forces. They served in all-black units under the command of white officers. Among the 16 men to be awarded the Congressional Medal of Honor was Sgt. William H. Carney, who received it for his valiant stand at Charleston Harbor. Carney belonged to the 54th Massachusetts Colored Infantry, which was led by Col. Robert Gould Shaw (a white). On July 18, 1863, Confederate guns were entrenched in Fort Wagner, which guarded the approach to Charleston Harbor. In attempting to dislodge the enemy, the 54th lost more than 1,500 men, many of them mangled by artillery shells shot at close range. When Shaw was killed, Sgt. Carney, who was twice wounded in the engagement, led the final charge after picking up the colors from the fallen standard bearer. The battle was dramatized in the film *Glory* (1988), in which Denzel Washington plays the fugitive slave Trip, a role that won him an Academy Award for best supporting actor.

Soldiers from the 9th and 10th Cavalry and the 24th and 25th Infantry were stationed in the West after the Civil War. Twelve soldiers from those units won Congressional Medals of Honor during the Indian Wars. The

Sgt. W. H. Carney, 54th Massachusetts Colored infantry. Mark E. Mitchell Collection of African American History

"Buffalo Soldiers," as the Indians called these troops, saw action in Arizona, Colorado, Montana, New Mexico, South Dakota, and Texas. Henry O. Flipper was a buffalo soldier who had been born into slavery in 1856. The first black graduate of the US Military Academy at West Point, he ranked fifth in a class of 76. His initial years in Company A, Tenth US cavalry, one of four all-black regiments, allowed him to display his engineering skills and leadership in battle. His troop joined the chase of Victorio, a brilliant Apache leader, over 1,200 miles. When the Apaches crossed the Rio Grande River into southwest Texas, Flipper rode 98 miles in 24 hours to alert headquarters to the danger. Once he delivered his message he collapsed to the ground. His four-year tour came to a halt with dubious charges of embezzlement, of which he was later exonerated. Flipper was awarded a posthumous honorable discharge from the army in 1976 and pardoned by President Bill Clinton in 1999.

Charge of the 54th Infantry on Fort Wagner, South Carolina, July 1863. Mark E. Mitchell Collection of African American History

The Buffalo Soldiers were race heroes. Black newspapers and magazines tracked their movements and reported their activities. Poetry, dramas, and songs all celebrated their service and valor. As Rayford Logan said:

> Negroes had little, at the turn of the century, to help sustain our faith in ourselves except the pride that we took in the 9th and 10th Cavalry, the 24th and 25th Infantry. Many Negro homes had prints of the famous charge of the colored troops up San Juan Hill [with Teddy Roosevelt and his "Rough Riders" in Cuba in 1898]. They were our Ralph Bunche, Marian Anderson, Joe Louis and Jackie Robinson.
>
> (in Morehouse, 17)

Hell Fighters: World War I

When the United States entered World War I in 1917, the flow of exodusters moving from south to north was temporarily slowed. Thousands of black men volunteered to fight. Two figures from the heyday of the Harlem Renaissance, Noble Sissle and James Reese Europe, saw action in the war as part of the all-black 369th US Army Regiment, known as the Harlem Hell Fighters. Sissle describes an incident that nearly precipitated a race riot just before they were sent to France. *One Sunday night after church Jim told him to*

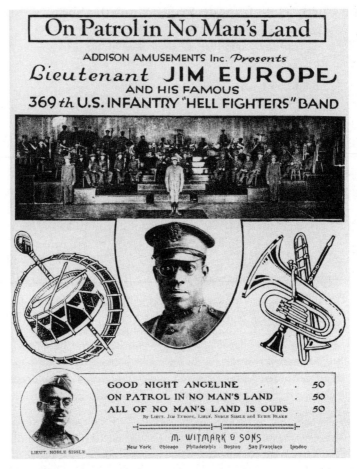

Flyer advertising a concert by Jim Europe and his infantry band, known as the "Hell Fighters." Courtesy Kimball and Bolcom

"go over to the hotel and get every paper that has the words New York on it." He later recalled:

> When I went to the stand, I was roughly grabbed in the collar from behind, and before I realized what had happened my service hat was knocked from my head.
>
> A gruff voice roared, "Say, nigger, don't you know enough to take your hat off?"
>
> Well, the first thing that came to me was maybe I was guilty of a breach of etiquette, but a quick glance around showed it was because of my color – every citizen and officer had on his hat. I reached for my hat and as I did so received a kick accompanied by an oath. Lost for words, I stammered out:
>
> "Do you realize you are abusing a United States soldier and that is a government hat you knocked to the floor?"

"Damn you and the government too," the man replied. "No nigger can come into my place without taking off his hat."

I left as soon as I could, but not before I received three other kicks. The regiment found out about it quickly enough, as there were several witnesses, and it took the military police and Jim's cool head to prevent a brawl from breaking out.

The next day they rushed the regiment north to Hoboken and after several delays we sailed for the front, arriving at the coast of France on New Year's Day 1918 – the first American Negro combat unit to set foot upon French soil.

(in Bolcom and Kimball, 65)

Similar stories are told in Stephen L. Harris's book *Harlem's Hell Fighters: The African-American 369th Infantry in World War I* (2003). The award-winning documentary film maker Ken Burns commented in his review:

The story of James Reese Europe and the Hell Fighters is one of the best I know, and here it is told superbly. It is a story of bravery and courage, creativity and controversy, tragedy and transcendence. It reminds us, in nearly every line, of the extraordinary contributions African Americans have made – not just to American life, but to the very essence of what it means to be an American.

(Burns, online)

Before, during, and after the Harlem Renaissance, some women ("Mother Playwrights") were writing plays to bring about social change while their male counterparts were concerning themselves with matters of behavior. Alice Dunbar-Nelson and Mary Burrill both wrote plays which addressed the reality of black soldiers during World War I.

Alice Dunbar-Nelson (1875–1935), born in New Orleans, Louisiana, was a graduate of Straight University (now Dillard University) and went on to teach in West Medford, Massachusetts. When she married Paul Laurence Dunbar she moved to Washington, DC, where she became a member of the Women's Committee on the Council of Defense, helping to organize southern black women in nine states for the war effort. In her protest play *Mine Eyes Have Seen* (1918), the central character is a young man called Chris, who has been drafted to fight in World War I but who debates whether he should honor the draft. Dunbar-Nelson suggests that black men who gladly fight for their country should not have to return to find that the freedom they fought for is for white Americans only. She has Chris comment bitterly: *"Haven't you had your soul shriveled with fear since we were driven like dogs from our home? And for what? Because we were living like Christians. Must I go and fight for a nation that let my father's murder go unpunished?"* (in Hatch and Shine, eds., 1974, 175). Chris's father had been shot while trying to save his home, which a mob had set on fire. Dunbar-Nelson is clearly indignant about soldiers who are drafted to defend their country overseas, but are still faced with violence and injustice at home.

Mary Burrill's *Aftermath* (1919) similarly levels an indictment against an American society that encourages blacks to fight in foreign wars but does not protect them from terrorists at home who lynch and burn. Set in South Carolina, the play centers on the homecoming of John, a black soldier who earned the French War Cross for single-handedly fighting off 20 Germans, thereby saving the lives of his entire company. John's glory is short-lived, however. On his return he discovers that his father, who had argued with a white man over the price of cotton, has been burned to death. Perhaps responding to DuBois's statement quoted at the beginning of this chapter (which refers to the black soldiers who had fought in World War I), Burrill calls for violent retaliation as John goes out in search of retribution. Gun in hand, John says:"You mean to tell me I mus' let them w'ite devuls send me miles erway to suffer an' be shot up fu' the freedom of people I ain't nevah seen, while they're burnin' an' killin' my folks here at home!" (in Hatch and Shine, eds., 1974, 61).

World War II: Black Bird Men and Buffalo Soldiers

The combat achievement of the black pilots of the 332nd Fighter Group is a shining example of men overcoming prejudice and discrimination in the 1940s to make their mark in history. The black fighter pilots who fought during World War II are known as Tuskegee Airmen. About 1,000 Americans of African ancestry completed their flight training at Tuskegee Army Air Field. Despite initial obstacles, as many as 445 served as combat pilots in Europe, North Africa, and the Mediterranean. Flying bomber escort and ground attack on 15,533 sorties between May 1943 and June 9, 1945, the Tuskegee Airmen are renowned for never having lost a passenger. A simple outdoor monument at Walterboro Army Airfield in Walterboro, SC, commemorates these men as follows:

> In reverence white American bombers called them "Red Tail Angels", because they never lost an aircraft. Because of their unwavering bravery during the war in Germany, they were called Schwartze Vogelmenschen – Black Bird Men – by the Germans who feared and respected them. The legacy of the Tuskegee Airmen was the eventual desegregation of the USAF, the recognition that black pilots were equal to white pilots and the respect and admiration earned by former Tuskegee pilots like General Benjamin Davis, Jr. and General Daniel "Chappie" James.

In 2006 the Black Bird Men were awarded the Congressional Gold Medal.

During World War II another generation of "Buffalo Soldiers" was born. In 1942 the army activated two all-black infantry divisions, the 93rd Blue Helmets and the 92nd Buffalo Soldiers. In August 1944 the first combat team of Buffalo Soldiers arrived in Italy. They were cheered on by hundreds of black service-unit soldiers who were in the area waiting to greet them. Ulysses Lee of the army's Historical Division related the story of their arrival:

> As the thousands of black fighting men, in single file, debarked from the crowded troopships, they presented an impressive and awe-inspiring spectacle. Armed with basic weapons and full field battle dress, proudly wearing the circular shoulder patch with the black buffalo, they moved smartly and efficiently into their unit formations. As they marched away, every man in step, every weapon in place, chins up and eyes forward, a low rumbling babble of sound came from the troops on the dock, then swelled to a crescendo of thunderous cheering which continued until the last Buffalo unit had disappeared from sight.
>
> (in Morehouse, 161)

World War II ended in 1945 with the surrender of German forces. Americans had fought throughout Europe and continued to do so in Southeast Asia. Once they returned to American shores, the veterans began changing the social structure of the US. The coming together of one million black men during the war was a significant community-building event, one that would be the precursor to the Civil Rights and Black Power Movements. Not content to live within the constraints of segregated society, the black veterans of World War II became foot soldiers in the fight for equality.

A Medal for Willie, a one-act play by William Branch, falls in the tradition of the black veteran who fought abroad for freedoms he did not have at home. The central character, Willie Jackson, has been killed fighting abroad. His mother is to receive a posthumous medal for her son, but she bravely disrupts the public ceremony. This excerpt from scene 7 can be performed as a monologue for a man or woman. The ceremony is in progress. The mayor has just announced the posthumous award to Willie Jackson and invited Mrs. Jackson to come to the podium to read a speech he has written for her. Mrs. Jackson, in simple, direct language, refuses the medal:

> You-all 'spect me to 'cept this medal and read that speech you had all ready for me, say, "Thank you kindly, suhs," and then go home an' be happy about the whole thing. But I can't! I can't go through with this – this big LIE. (The others are shocked.) Yes, I said lie. What has all your fine talk ever meant to Willie?

Sailor during the 1940s

He walked around this town nearly all his young life and nobody cared. You jim-crowed him and shunned him and you shoved him off in a corner. You gave him a third-rate schoolin' and when he wasn't quiet like a mouse, you put him out in the street. You looked down on him and you kept him down 'cause he was black and poor and didn't know no better than to believe that was the way things is supposed to be! Yes, my Willie was dumb in a lotta ways. He didn't know nothin' 'bout no i-de-lol-logies or whatever you calls it. He wasn't fightin' 'cause he hated anybody. He joined the Army 'cause he couldn't get a decent job here. Willie thought if he did what they told him in the Army and didn't get in no trouble, maybe someday he could come back home and walk down the street and be somebody. Willie tried so hard, he got himself killed. But he didn't know. 'Cause even while you-all's here supposed to be honorin' Willie, you keep talkin' 'bout keepin' things the way they is. Willie didn't want things to stay the way they is. 'Cause it always meant he come out holdin' the short end of the stick – the Jim Crow end, the poor folks end. That's why this is all such a big lie.

(in King and Milner, eds., 470)

Branch turned down an offer from a white producer to option the play when it involved rewrites the playwright could not accept. Instead he gave it to the Committee for the Negro in the Arts (CNA), a cadre of former American Negro Theatre members. *A Medal for Willie* first opened at Club Baron at 132nd Street and Lenox Avenue in Harlem on October 15, 1951. The very next day Branch was inducted into the army to fight in the Korean War.

Charles Fuller, a veteran who served in Korea and Japan, wrote a full-length drama, *A Soldier's Play*, which won the Pulitzer Prize in 1982. It is more complex in theme and characterization than the earlier one-act plays discussed above. In focusing on a different kind of conflict for black soldiers – how to confront self-loathing within their own ranks – it is another step forward in the search for Iwa. Departing from the trajectory begun with the Emancipated Interlocutors writing themselves into humanity, Fuller's play marks a different kind of maturity in the race's expression of Iwa. Charles Fuller first received critical acclaim in 1969 for his play, *The Perfect Party*. He won an Obie award for *Zooman and the Sign* in 1980.

The first scene of *A Soldier's Play* has a middle-aged black army officer, Tech. Sgt. Vernon Waters, stumbling about in the shadows. The setting is Fort Neal, Louisiana, in 1944. Drunk and raving, Waters screams "They still hate you! They still hate you!" Then two shots ring out, and he falls to his death. Another black officer, Capt. Richard Davenport, is sent to the scene of the crime to investigate the murder. In the process, another, larger drama is played out. The soldiers, who have not seen any wartime action, wait in desperate hope that they may get orders for overseas, so that they can prove that "colored boys can fight" Hitler as well as white boys. But in the playwright's view, this aspiration is just another version of Waters's misplaced ambition to deny his blackness by emulating whites – and just as likely to end in tragic self-annihilation. The play was directed by Douglas Turner Ward and presented by the Negro Ensemble Company at Theater Four, 424 West 55th Street, New York, in November 1981. A film version was released in 1984.

Denzel Washington in the film *A Soldier's Story* (1984), based on the play by Charles Fuller

You may find it interesting to see the names of the actors who were in the Negro Ensemble Company's original cast. How many names do you recognize?

Tech. Sgt. Vernon C. Waters ....Adolph Caesar
Capt. Charles Taylor...................................Peter Friedman
Cpl. Bernard Cobb.....................................Eugene Lee
Pfc. Melvin Peterson..................................Denzel Washington
Corporal Ellis...James Pickens, Jr.
Pvt. Louis Henson......................................Samuel L. Jackson
Pvt. James Wilkie ....Steven Jones
Pvt. Tony Smalls...Brents Jennings
Capt. Richard Davenport ....Charles Brown
Pvt. C. J. Memphis.....................................Larry Riley
Lieutenant Byrd...Cotter Smith

In February 2007 the History Channel featured a program about black soldiers who served in World War II. Entitled *A Distant Shore: African Americans of D-Day*, it includes interviews with seven octagenarians who recount their experiences as overlooked and underserved veterans.

Vietnam: The Bloods

Between the Korean War and the Vietnam War, the army became fully integrated. Blacks now not only took part in combat, but were appointed to positions of leadership. After Korea, the army provided fuller and fairer employment opportunities than could be found in civilian society. But Vietnam was a different kind of war and eventually used a different kind of soldier. Wallace Terry's *Bloods: An Oral History of the Vietnam War by Black Veterans* (1984) features 20 soldiers who describe how their experiences differed from those of the Buffalo Soldiers, the Black Bird Men or even the ordinary characters depicted in the plays by Durbar-Nelson, Burrill and Branch. The countryside itself presented an overwhelming challenge to navigate. The nights were darker than on the Underground Railroad. The soldiers had to endure drenching rain, swamp, monsoon, "rednecks flying rebel flags," wait-a-minute vines that grabbed and tangled, and fierce little bamboo snakes that bit and killed. They listened to recordings by John Coltrane, Eric Dolphy, Pharaoh Sanders, Miles Davis, and the Beatles to

My father, Harvey Dickerson, retired from the US Army as a colonel after 30 years. He
served in both Korea and Vietnam

remind them of home. In the "Nam," they were caught up in a war they
seemed unable to win:

> HAROLD "LIGHT BULB" BRYANT: I thought we had got into the beginning of a
> war. But I found out that we were just in another phase of their civil wars. And
> we weren't gaining any ground. We would fight for a hill all day, spend two days
> or two nights there, and then abandon the hill. Then maybe two, three months
> later, we would have to come back and retake the same piece of territory [. . .].
> We lost 20 men the first time saving it, 30 or 40 men the next time retaking it.
>
> (in Terry, 21)

These men were turned into what they themselves called "animals":

> ARTHUR GENE: I went to Vietnam as a basic naive young man of eighteen.
> Before I reached my nineteenth birthday, I was a animal. When I went home
> three months later, even my mother was scared of me. The only thing they
> told us about the Viet Cong was they were gooks. They were to be killed.
> Nobody sits around and gives you their historical and cultural back ground.
> They're the enemy. Kill, kill, kill. That's what we got in practice. Kill, kill, kill.
>
> (in Terry, 236)

They became socially aware:

> ROBERT MOUNTAIN: Well, I was getting more of a revolutionary, militant atti-
> tude. It had begun when I started talking with friends before leaving Nam

about being a part of the struggle of black people. About contributing in the world, since Vietnam was doing nothing for black people. They killed Dr. King just before I came home. I felt used. [I noticed] that in my city, which is 95 percent black, that there were a lot of black combat veterans coming back not able to find any employment because of bad discharges, or killing their-selves or dopin' up. We started the Wasted Men Project, and I have been counseling at veterans centers ever since.

(in Terry, 36)

They hate war and will never forget what they went through. As Stephen A. Howard declared: "I think we were the last generation to believe, you know, in the honor of war. There is no honor in war" (in Terry, 129).

George C. Wolfe's *The Colored Museum* (1986), a satirical play consisting of 11 vignettes, is discussed in chapter 9. However, turning to one of its darker monologues, "Soldier with a Secret," can be useful here to compare the Vietnam soldier with the soldier now serving in Iraq. Think about the landscape that soldiers went through in Vietnam. Can you create from news sources an accurate picture of the landscape in Iraq? What about the weight that soldiers carry in Iraq? Use your thoughts on these questions as inner images and obstacles as you rehearse "Soldier with a Secret." How would the landscape and the weight keep the soldier from achieving his objective: to free his comrades from coming pain?

The final story in this chapter, an account by Private First Class Reginald Edwards about his connection to the Black Panthers, leads naturally to the next chapter, which concerns the turbulent times of the Civil Rights and Black Power Movements. It can be performed as a monologue for a black man:

When I went to Quantico, my being black, they gave me the black squad, the squad with most of the blacks, especially the militant blacks. And they started

An incendiary message from the Black Panthers, Oakland, California, *c.* 1966

hippin' me. I mean I was against racism. I didn't even call it racism. I called it prejudice. They hipped me to terms like "exploitation" and "oppression." [After I was kicked out of the Corps] I went to the Panther office in D.C. and joined. I felt the party was the only organization that was fighting the system.

I liked their independence. The fact that they had no fear of the police. Talking about self-determination. Trying to make Malcolm's message reality. This was the first time black people had stood up to the state since Nat Turner. I mean armed. It was obvious they wasn't gonna give us nothing unless we stood up and were willing to die. They obviously didn't care anything about us, 'cause they had killed King. For me the thought of being killed in the Black Panther Party by the police and the thought of being killed by Vietnamese was just a qualitative difference. I had left one war and came back and got into another one. Most of the Panthers then were veterans. We figured if we had been over in Vietnam fighting for our country, which at that point wasn't serving us properly, it was only proper that we had to go out and fight for our own cause. We had already fought for the white man in Vietnam. It was clearly his war. If it wasn't, you wouldn't have seen as many Confederate flags as you saw. And the Confederate flags was an insult to any person that's of color on this planet. I rose up into the ranks. I was an artist immediately for the newspaper. Because of my background in the military, obviously I was able to deal with a lot of things of a security nature. And eventually I took over the D. C. chapter.

(Edwards, in Terry, 11–12)

Sparked in part by the assassinations of Malcolm X and Martin King, northern inner cities exploded into riots in the mid-1960s, with the most serious rebellions in the loss of lives and property taking place in Harlem (1964), Watts (1965), Newark (1967), and Detroit (1967). Between 1964 and 1968, there were about 329 riots in 257 cities across the US. By 1969 a new black soldier had appeared. The war had used up the professionals. Replacing the careerists were black draftees, many just steps removed from marching in the Civil Rights Movement or rioting in the rebellions that swept the urban ghettos from Harlem to Watts. This person was filled with a new sense of black pride and purpose. He became radicalized in Vietnam and returned to make a different kind of impact on American society as the Black Freedom Movement swept the country with sit-ins, boycotts, and marches.

Food for Further Thought

To find out more about the Federal Theatre Project and its Negro unit, read E. Quita Craig's *Black Drama of the Federal Theatre Era* (1980) and *Free, Adult, Uncensored: The Living History of the Federal Theatre Project* (1978), edited by John O'Connor and Lorraine Brown. For a succinct overview of the American Negro Theatre, see Loften Mitchell's *Black Drama* (1967). See also the *History of African American Theatre* (2003) by Errol G. Hill and James V. Hatch.

Black soldiers are portrayed in the film *Stormy Weather* (1943), directed by William LeBaron. Bill "Bojangles" Robinson plays a soldier just returning from World War I. Lena Horne makes an unforgettable rendition of the title song, Fats Waller of "Ain't Misbehavin'," and the Nicolas Brothers offer a dance number that will leave you breathless. Try writing a movie review.

If you know a person who served in any of the wars, record an oral history of his or her experiences. Whether the person is living or dead, write some details for posterity, together with photos for your Black Life Book.

6 Sitting Down, Sitting In, and Standing Up
The Black Freedom Movement

Wheel about and turn about and do just so
Every time I wheel about I jump Jim Crow.

I and my children are craving light–
the entire colored race is craving light.

(Silas Hardrick Fleming, a parent suing the
Topeka Board of Education, 1951)

We who believe in freedom cannot rest.

("Ella's Song," recorded by the women's vocal group
Sweet Honey in the Rock)

It is important to remember that for much of the 20th century America was a segregated country. In 1954 Thurgood Marshall was the Chief Counsel for the National Association for the Advancement of Colored People (NAACP). Known as the "warrior lawyer," Marshall spearheaded the landmark decision in *Brown vs. Board of Education of Topeka, Kansas*, which held that separate (primarily in schools) was not equal. That decision was one of the first major victories in the battle against Jim Crow.

Brown vs. Board of Education has a broad and bright visibility; but there were other movements not fought in the courts, other warriors less well-known who were involved in striving for racial equality in the US. These foot soldiers were responsible for the sit-ins, the freedom rides, the bus boycotts and the historic marches. The ordinary people who, as they struggled, symbolized their transformation by changing their nominal identity from Colored to Negro to Afro-American and finally Black. These are therefore the adjectives I use in the next two chapters. These ordinary people tell extraordinary stories. They were as important to the struggle as were the iconic figures.

A year after the Supreme Court decision in *Brown vs. Board of Education*, a young man was murdered in what came to be called the hate crime that changed America. Mamie Till was an exoduster who left Money, Mississippi, in the Great Migration for Chicago. On August 20, 1955 her son Emmett boarded the City of New Orleans train to spend the summer in his mother's former home town. The landmark court case had little impact on the Mississippi that Emmett visited during the last summer of his short life. The state was filled with fear and hatred. Black housekeepers had separate drinking cups. When rest-rooms for Negroes were available at all in department stores and restaurants, they were marked "colored." White people received preferential treatment in stores. Colored shoppers were forbidden to try on clothes before buying them. Knowing your place, not being "uppity" was sometimes the only way to keep yourself safe from violence. Fathers walking with their children were forced to tip their hats to any passing white person; to say "yes, sir" and "yes, ma'am" to whites who condescendingly addressed them as "boy" or "uncle."

The details of Emmett's death are still shrouded in confusion and misun-derstanding. What is clear is that Emmett went into a local store owned by Roy Bryant and whistled. Was this intended as a joke, or in response to getting "stuck on a word"? (His mother believes this to be the case because he had a stuttering problem.) Whatever the reason for his whistling, the owner's wife Carolyn Bryant felt that she had been offended by Emmett and communi-cated that to her husband. Her story was embellished each time it was retold. Roy Bryant and several others abducted Emmett from his uncle's home and within days his dead and mutilated body was recovered from the Tallihatchie River. A gin fan was tied around his neck with barbed wire. This real story sounds very much like the one in Georgia Douglas Johnson's *A Sunday Morning in the South* (see chapter 3).

The Mississippi coroner's office warned Mamie Till not to open her son's coffin; but she insisted on looking. She later said: "I looked at the bridge of his nose. It looked like someone had beat it with a meat cleaver. . . . I looked at his teeth. I was so proud of his teeth. There were only two." Mamie Till then made the decision to show Emmett's ruined face to the whole country. "Let the people see what I've seen," she said. The photograph published in *Jet* magazine (1955) horrified Americans who had never been near a lynching. Suddenly the mortal consequences of living under Jim Crow became clear to even the most detached.

James Baldwin's play *Blues for Mr. Charley* (1964) offers a fictionalized version of the Emmett Till story. Dedicated "to the dead children of Birmingham," it has a militancy that challenged the conventional stereotypes of southern blacks. According to the author's introduction: "The play takes place in Plaguetown, U.S.A., now. The plague is race, the plague is our concept of Christianity, and this raging plague has the power to destroy every human relationship" (in Oliver and Sills, eds., 243). The play opened at the ANTA (American National Theatre and Academy) Playhouse in New York on April 23, 1964, with a distinguished cast that included Diana Sands, Al Freeman, Jr., and Rosetta Lenoire. Although it closed after only 146 Broadway performances, the drama became a standard for black colleges over the next 30 years; some people consider it to be as power-ful as Baldwin's earlier play *Amen Corner* (1954).

Sitting Down

Rosa Parks (1913–2005) is enshrined in the national memory as the mother of the Civil Rights Movement. On December 1, 1955, with quiet dignity, she refused to yield her seat to a white man on a bus in Montgomery, Alabama. Her courageous action led to the coinage of the phrase "sitting down to stand up," and to the Montgomery Bus Boycott of 1955–6. The boycott propelled both Rosa Parks and Martin Luther King to international prominence, though it was Jo Ann Gibson Robinson, head of the Women's Political Council (WPC), who – with the backing of thousands of Colored women in Montgomery – became the decisive force in winning it. The WPC had been preparing for this historic moment for years.

The following reminiscence by Mrs. Robinson can be performed as a monologue for a black woman. She provides you with all the actions necessary to block the scene. Perform each action with close attention to detail: really drop the coins into the box and carefully observe the other (imaginary) passengers. Imagine how it would feel to be a northerner sitting on the bus, ignorant of Montgomery's bus seating practices which always reserved the front ten seat for white riders. Would you feel fear or anger when accosted by the bus driver? Or perhaps a combination of both? How would you dramatize her statement, "I felt like a dog"?

> I boarded an almost empty city bus, dropped my coins into the proper place, and observed the passengers aboard, only two – a white woman who sat in the third row from the front, and a black man in a seat near the back. I took the fifth row seat from the front and sat down, immediately closing my eyes and envisioning, in my mind's eye, the wonderful two weeks' vacation I would have with my family and friends. From the far distance of my reverie I thought I heard a voice, an unpleasant voice. Immediately I sat up in that seat. The bus driver had stopped the bus and was speaking to me! Suddenly the driver left his seat and stood over me. His hand was drawn back as if he were going to strike me. "Get up from there!" he yelled. He repeated it, for, dazed, I had not moved. "Get up from there!" I leaped to my feet, afraid he would hit me, and ran to the front door to get off the bus. It suddenly occurred to me that I was supposed to go to the back door to get off, not the front! However, I was too upset, frightened, and tearful to move. I never

could have walked to the rear door. Then the driver opened the front door, and I stumbled off the bus and started walking back to the college. [. . .] I felt like a dog.

(in Garrow, ed., 16)

That experience, which took place in 1949, convinced Jo Ann Gibson that the WPC ought to target Montgomery's segregated bus seating for immediate attention. "It was then that I made up [. . .] my mind to stage a bus boycott when the time was ripe and the people were ready" (17). The right time came six years later, in December 1955, when Rosa Parks – already active in the NAACP – was treated with equal lack of respect by a bus driver from Equality, Alabama. Because she refused to move to the back of the bus, she was arrested and charged with a violation of Montgomery segregation laws. At her trial four days later, she was found guilty of disorderly conduct and fined $10 plus $4 in court costs. On December 4, 1955, plans for the boycott were announced throughout the city. The next day, the Montgomery Bus Boycott began. The people walked for 381 days, organizing group rides in cars and suffering abuse. Across the nation, black churches collected new and slightly used shoes to replace the tattered footwear of boycotters like Mother Pollard, who said "My feets is tired, but my soul is rested" (Pitts, online). A lawsuit brought by the NAACP made its way to the Supreme Court, which handed down a decision in favor of the association on November 13, 1956. Fearing financial ruin, the bus company finally capitulated to the demands of the WPC and the boycott ended on December 20, 1956.

Although Douglas Turner Ward's play *Day of Absence* was not written until 1965, it is relevant here for being set in a small southern town whose residents wake up one day to discover that all the "Nigras" have vanished and chaos has descended. The play, which calls for 15 black actors performing the roles of about 19 whites, is "conceived for performance by a Black cast, a reverse minstrel show done in white face." The owners of the Montgomery bus company probably felt similar to the characters in Ward's play when the buses rode empty of working-class Colored women and men for over a year. *Day of Absence* had its off-Broadway premiere at the St. Marks Playhouse on November 15, 1965, part of a double bill with Ward's *Happy Ending*.

Integrating

On Labor Day 1957, nine young Colored students were enjoying the last day of their summer vacation – Carlotta Walls, Jefferson Thomas, Elizabeth Eckford, Thelma Mothershed, Melba Pattillo, Ernest Green, Terrance

NOTICE

COLORED

Riding the bus after the successful Montgomery Bus Boycott

Roberts, Gloria Ray, and Minnijean Brown. Daisy Bates, then president of the local NAACP, had made plans for them to continue their education at the segregated Central High School in Little Rock, Arkansas. Everywhere in Little Rock, there were rumors that segregationist forces from hard-core states, the "solid south," were organizing for a fight to the finish against integration in public schools. Little Rock was to be the battleground. Arkansas governor, Orville Faubus, promised that "blood will run in the streets."

On the first day of school Elizabeth Eckford was unfortunately separated from the other eight students. Because her parents did not have a phone, she did not receive word that the nine were to meet at a designated location before approaching the building. Her dignity and control in the face of the jeering mobsters and the indifferent guards was filmed by television cameras and recorded in pictures flashed to newspapers around the world. Her story was told in many languages. Elizabeth became a national heroine, but the incident took an unseen toll on the little girl. Elizabeth went into a shell and the only time she showed real excitement over the next year was when Thurgood Marshall came to town to meet with the young warriors. Melba Pattillo Beals, another of the Little Rock Nine (who finished school in Santa Rosa, California, with financial assistance from the NAACP), later recalled: *"I marvel at the fact that in the midst of this historic confrontation, we nine teenagers weren't maimed or killed"* (Beals, 309).

117

Elizabeth Eckford trying to enter Central High School in Little Rock, Arkansas

Elizabeth Eckford's story is paraphrased in *In White America: A Documentary Play* (1963) by Martin Duberman. The following extract gives a flavor of the apprehension and then terror that she experienced:

> Before I left home, Mother called us into the living room. She said we should have a word of prayer. Then I caught the bus and got off a block from the school. I saw a large crowd of people standing across the street from the soldiers guarding Central. As I walked on, the crowd suddenly got very quiet. For a moment all I could hear was the shuffling of their feet. Then someone shouted, "Here she comes, get ready!" The crowd moved in closer and then began to follow me, calling me names. I still wasn't afraid. Just a little bit nervous. Then my knees started to shake all of a sudden and I wondered whether I could make it to the center entrance a block away. It was the longest block I ever walked in my whole life. Even so, I still wasn't too scared because all the time I kept thinking that the guards would protect me. When I got right in front of the

school, I went up to a guard. He just looked straight ahead and didn't move to let me pass him. I stood looking at the school – it looked so big! Just then the guards let some white students go through. The crowd was quiet. I guess they were waiting to see what was going to happen. When I was able to steady my knees, I walked up to the guard who had let the white students in. He too didn't move. When I tried to squeeze past him, he raised his bayonet and then the other guards closed in and they raised their bayonets. They glared at me with a mean look and I was very frightened and didn't know what to do. I turned around and the crowd came toward me.

(Duberman, online)

Ernest Green was the only one of the 13 to graduate that year. The others, who were not seniors, did not attend the ceremony because of their fear of violence. With support from Governor Faubus and the Arkansas State Legislature, the school board cancelled the entire 1958–9 academic year for all three Little Rock high schools rather than integrate them.

Sitting In

Ted Shine's play *Contribution* (1969) takes a darkly humorous look at the Civil Rights Movement and different generational attitudes to it. Eugene, the young protagonist, berates his grandmother for being an "Uncle Tom" and not supporting the struggle. But in the end, Grandmother Love has a surprise for the young warriors. She makes her own "contribution" when she sends the sheriff her "specially seasoned" cornbread, which leads to his painful death at the peak of the showdown with the students. *Contribution* was first produced by the Negro Ensemble Company in 1969 and is published in *Black Theatre USA* (1996), edited by Hatch and Shine.

A turning point for the Civil Rights Movement was instigated by a North Carolina teenager named Ezell Blair, Jr., who on the last day of January 1960 announced to his mother: "Mom, we are going to do something tomorrow that may change history, that might change the world." He was attending an HBCU college in Greensboro, the North Carolina Agricultural and Technical. On Monday afternoon, February 1, 1960, he and three classmates, Franklin McCain, David Richmond, and Joseph McNeil, went downtown to Woolworth's department store, took a seat at the lunch counter, and ordered a doughnut and coffee. "I'm sorry," said the waitress, "we don't serve you here." Though whites-only lunch counters were a fact of southern life, one of the students replied, "We just beg to disagree with you." Before sitting down, they had deliberately bought some school supplies (the store was open to everyone, but the lunch counter was exclusively for whites). Holding up a receipt, they

The four students who initiated the sit-ins at Greensboro, North Carolina, in 1960

pointed out that they had just been served at a nearby cash register. Using such tactics of resistance, the youths initiated a nationwide wave of "sit-ins." Within a week, the Greensboro Four had grown to hundreds. Within two months, protests had taken place in 125 cities in nine states. The Greensboro Woolworth Store is being converted into a museum to commemorate the four young warriors, whose footsteps are cast in bronze on the sidewalk outside.

The sit-ins sparked a freedom flame which marked a new era of activism. At the time, Martin Luther King, Jr. had just turned 31. The main thing he and the movement's other veterans had accomplished since the Montgomery Bus Boycott was to form a preacher-led group of southern activists called the Southern Christian Leadership Conference (SCLC). The co-founder was Fred Shuttlesworth, a hot-headed Baptist minister from Birmingham, Alabama, who was fond of saying, there is a "bomb with my name on it," and "They can't kill hope." When Shuttlesworth visited one of the North Carolina sit-ins that February, he called SCLC headquarters in Atlanta, Georgia. "You must tell Martin that we must get with this," Shuttlesworth said to Ella Baker, the staff director "and really, this can shake up the world."

For a Colored college student hoping to move up in the world, going to jail was especially humiliating. But as the sit-ins spread outside North Carolina, and the police started making arrests, going to jail for the movement became a badge of pride. When sit-in fever reached King's Atlanta, Martin Luther King found himself torn between the newly energized students and the more cautious older leaders. He was the man who could command the spotlight and get the results. But he often needed the young people, like those lunch counter pioneers, to push him to the next frontier.

On October 19, 1960, after much soul-searching, King went with some college students to the Magnolia Room restaurant at Atlanta's finest department store and got himself arrested. This set off a national uproar, but it was only the first of many later arrests. On April 16, 1963, he composed his famous Letter from Birmingham City Jail, the most articulate explanation he had yet given of his belief in nonviolent confrontation and civil disobedience. He wrote: "One day the South will know that when these disinherited children of God sat down at lunch counters, they were in reality standing up for what is best in the American dream" (Hoyt, 29).

Actor/activist Harry Belafonte was an early supporter of the Civil Rights Movement in the 1950s and one of Martin Luther King's confidants. It was he who bailed King out of the Birmingham city jail. He raised thousands of dollars to release other imprisoned Civil Rights protesters. He also financed the Freedom Rides, supported voter-registration drives, and, because of Jim Crow laws, refused to perform in the South from 1954 until 1961. He has since become an outspoken critic of the policies of the Bush administration.

The musical, which had been shunned by most creative artists during the 1950s, was given a new lease on life as an acceptable vehicle for expressing black protest with *Fly Blackbird* (1962), which has music and lyrics by James Hatch and Clarence Jackson. In two acts, the show revolves around a group of HBCU students who, following the example of the lunch-counter rebels, launch a drive for integration. It explores two conflicting philosophical approaches to achieving equality: William Piper and his daughter Josie, a Sarah Lawrence graduate, believe that "Everything Comes to those who Wait;" on the other hand, Josie's boyfriend Carl counters that things have to be changed, "Now." Ultimately, Piper shifts to Carl's sense of urgency, and in a poignant final scene, sings "Who's the Fool?"

Fly Blackbird can be performed simply with piano or small combo and calls for an integrated cast of about 18. It was first produced in Los Angeles, then moved to off-Broadway, and was awarded an Obie Award for best musical, all in 1962. Following is an excerpt of Carl's duet with Josie, "Now," which captures the exuberant determination of the young people:

(Carl enters. He carries a sign which reads "Now!" He walks to the edge of the stage, sings directly to the audience.)

121

Sheet-music cover for *Fly Blackbird*. Courtesy Hatch-Billops Collection

CARL
I do believe . . .
that the sun can shine in the middle of the night.
We're gonna walk.
JOSIE *(has entered, carries a sign saying "Wake up!")*
We're gonna walk!
CARL
We're gonna talk!
JOSIE
We're gonna talk!
CARL AND JOSIE
There is a new day waiting at your door.
JOSIE
The sun's gonna shine this morning.
The night will be no more. . .
I'm gonna open my window wide.

CARL and JOSIE
See the new day waiting at your door.
CARL
We're gonna walk
JOSIE
We're gonna walk
CARL
We're gonna talk
JOSIE
We're gonna talk
CARL AND JOSIE
We're gonna sit at the table with our heads up high!

(in Reardon and Pawley, eds., 228–9)

Freedom Summer

During the 1960s, civil rights activism moved beyond lunch-counter sit-ins. The Student Nonviolent Coordinating Committee (SNCC, pronounced SNICK) decided to open freedom schools throughout the South to teach reading, writing, arithmetic, and black history. These alternative schools and camps were all part of freedom summer. A thousand volunteers, who had been trained in nonviolent techniques in Oxford, Ohio, prepared to leave for the South to teach in these schools. They were warned of violence and even death. Among the volunteers was Andrew Goodman, who left on his 20th birthday, riding with James Chaney and Michael Schwerner. The three were never to return home. Their names have become synonymous with the often anonymous violence associated with the struggle. Their indomitable spirit is captured in such freedom songs as this:

> I'm taking a ride on the Greyhound bus line
> I'm traveling in the front seat to Jackson this time.
> Hallelujah, I'm traveling
> Hallelujah ain't it fine
> Down freedom's main line
> Listen, Jim Crow is dead this time.

In 1961 John Lewis (current Congressman from Georgia) was a 21-year-old student. As a member of SNCC in Nashville, Tennessee, he and his comrades had succeeded in getting the local lunch counters desegregated after leading a huge march to City Hall. Now John Lewis was starting out on a new history-making protest: the Freedom Ride. Based on an earlier model established by CORE (Congress for Racial Equality), the Freedom Ride would send 13 volunteers,

Negro and white, around the South on regular buses to integrate the whites-only waiting rooms. Their first nine days on the road through the upper South were uneventful; but once they crossed the state line into Alabama, a white mob rushed the Greyhound bus, waving chains and clubs. Someone heaved a firebomb through the window. Birmingham's Ku Klux Klan was the most violent in America, and it had friends in high places, not least the city's most powerful elected official, Commissioner Eugene "Bull" Connor. Connor had assured local clansmen that his police department would give them 15 minutes to assault the Freedom Riders before any city officers arrived on the scene. "I don't give a damn if you beat them, bomb them, murder, or kill them," a police detective told his Klan contact. "We don't ever want to see another nigger ride on the bus into Birmingham again" (McWhorter, 2004, 63).

John Lewis was smashed over the head with a wooden Coca-Cola crate. He was lying bleeding on the street when the attorney general of Alabama bent over him and handed him papers ordering an end to the Freedom Rides. There is an excellent account of the Freedom Rides in the 14-hour award-winning documentary, *Eyes on the Prize*. Produced in two parts (1987 and 1990) by Henry Hampton, who founded the film company Blackside in 1968, it takes its title from a Civil Rights song: "I know the one thing we did right/Was when we started to fight/Keep your eyes on the prize, hold on."

Fannie Lou Hamer, known as the lady who was "sick and tired of being sick and tired," was born on October 6,1917, in Ruleville, Mississippi. She was the granddaughter of enslaved people. In 1962, when Hamer was 44 years old, SNCC members arrived to hold a voter registration meeting. She was surprised to learn that Negroes had a constitutional right to vote. When the SNCC members appealed to those assembled to register (despite the risk of a white backlash), Hamer was the first to raise her hand. On their arrival at the courthouse, the volunteers were jailed and beaten by the police. Hamer was then thrown off the plantation where she had been a sharecropper. She also began to receive frequent death threats and was even shot at. As she recalled, "The only thing they could do to me was to kill me, and it seemed like they'd been trying to do that a little bit at a time ever since I could remember" (Hamer, 17). Still, Hamer would not be discouraged. She became a SNCC Field Secretary and traveled around the country speaking and registering people to vote. To call this dangerous work is an understatement. Imagine a lone black woman in some small town in Alabama or Mississippi, asking questions that no one wanted to answer, encouraging people to take action that might result in their losing their jobs, their homes or even their lives.

In 1964 the Mississippi Freedom Democratic Party was formed, with Hamer elected as Vice-Chair. Despite their fears of retaliation, 60,000 people signed up to the party. For many it was reminiscent of Reconstruction. The

Fannie Lou Hamer

MFDP had been organized specifically to challenge the all-white Mississippi delegation to the Democratic National Convention in Atlantic City, New Jersey. Party leaders caused a storm at the convention when they refused to seat the MFDP contingent, favoring the white delegates from the official party. Hamer made national news when she testified before the credentials committee about the beatings that she and others were given and the threats they faced for trying to register to vote. The MFDP kept up its agitation within the convention even after it was denied official recognition.

Hamer was an inspirational figure to many involved in the struggle for civil rights. Like Chaney, Goodman, Schwerner, Medgar Evers, James Meredith, and Jimmy Lee Jackson (whose beating death precipitated the historic march from Selma to Montgomery), she took a chance with her life, believing the prize was worth it. The prize was freedom. Fannie Lou Hamer died on March 14, 1977, at the age of 59. Jayne Cortez honors her in this poem, written in 1982:

> Big fine woman from Ruleville
> great time keeper
> and dangerous worker
> magnificent ancestor
> warrior friend
> most beautiful sister
> I kiss the mud of this moment
>   (in Baraka and Baraka, 94–5)

Playwright Endesha Ida Mae Holland (1944–2006) went to jail 13 times for the Civil Rights Movement. Her play *From the Mississippi Delta*, which covers her life story and her days as an SNCC worker in Mississippi, was described by the *New York Times* in 1987 as "a joyful celebration of survival against what seemed to be impossible odds and of fulfillment in a harsh world of injury and deprivation" (Bruckner, 24).

Martin Luther King led the historic March on Washington for Jobs and Freedom in August 1963. When he delivered his "I Have a Dream" speech on the steps of the Lincoln Memorial, he was standing on the shoulders of thousands who had marched before him. In April 1939 the Negro contralto Marian Anderson also stood on the steps of the Lincoln Memorial, forced to deliver an open-air concert as she had been denied entrance to the segregated Constitution Hall by the Daughters of the American Revolution. It was Eleanor Roosevelt who arranged for her to sing at the Lincoln Memorial instead. Anderson went on to star at the Metropolitan Opera in New York and toured throughout the US and in Europe, both in opera and as a concert artist, often including impeccably performed spirituals.

From the plaintive wails raised in the brush arbors, the spirituals sung by the Fisk Jubilee Singers, the blues guitar of B. B. King, the kinetic energy of Stevie Wonder's harmonica, the improvisational scatting of Ella Fitzgerald and the ecstatic voice of Marian Anderson, music has been a deep and abiding vessel for the people who could not fly to access and express their Iwa.

Marian Anderson performing on the steps of the Lincoln Memorial in Washington, DC, 1939

Ossie Davis, then a student at Howard University, was there when Marian Anderson sang in 1939. As he recalled:

> And I think it was April 16th – Easter – a cold and dreary day. And Marian Anderson was on the front steps in her mink coat, as it were. But standing there, there were 75,000 people, of course, and the student body was included – standing there listening to her. All of a sudden, I had a transformation that was almost of a religious nature. Something in her singing, something in her voice, something in her demeanor entered me and opened me up and made me a free man. And in a sense, I never became – I never lost that.
>
> (O. Davis, 2000, online)

The March on Washington was attended by over 200,000 people. Among them was an "arts contingent," which included Harry Belafonte, Ossie Davis, Ruby Dee, Lena Horne, Diahann Carroll, and Paul Newman. Josephine Baker, dressed in her French army uniform, was the only woman to speak at the rally. After some discussion among the male leaders, it was decided that there would be only a "tribute to women," among them Rosa Parks.

On September 15, barely two weeks after the march, Birmingham's Sixteenth Street Baptist Church was celebrating Youth Day. The church was full of children. A bomb was flung from a speeding car. Three 14-year-old girls perished – Addie Mae Collins, Carol Robertson, and Cynthia Wesley, as did the 11-year-old Denise McNair:

> Maxine McNair searched desperately for her only child until she finally came upon a sobbing old man and screamed, "Daddy, I can't find Denise!" The man helplessly replied, "She's dead, baby. I've got one of her shoes." He held a girl's white dress shoe, and the look on his daughter's face made him scream out, "I'd like to blow the whole town up!"

(Branch, 889)

While Negroes in the South dismantled segregation and appeared to be making remarkable improvements in their lives, Negroes in the North faced deteriorating ghettos, police brutality, inadequate recreational facilities, poor housing, few public services, and rising unemployment. Like the returning Vietnam veterans, more and more ordinary people were becoming militant in attitude and less patient with nonviolent tactics. Ordinary people were taking matters into their own hands. Lynda Bryant Hall was witness to a groundshaking moment in the freedom struggle in 1966, when Martin Luther King visited Chicago, which he once described as more racist than the deep south. In reply to the interviewer's question, "How was the character of the Cicero march different from Dr. King's [. . .] marches in Chicago?," Hall stated:

> Well, Dr. King's marches in Chicago were usually made up of movement people. This march was community people. These people had not attended any workshops on nonviolence; they had not listened to any lectures on love and loving your fellow man and all; they were just people who were angry about what was happening and wanted to do something. And when they all decided to go on this march, and people started to throw bricks and bottles at us, a couple of people caught the bricks and threw them back, threw rocks back; they even would jump in-between a lady sometimes. Women who were on the march were very protected. [. . .] These people were saying, you know, Yeah, we're going to come to Cicero and we're not going to go limp. We're going to march through Cicero, and we're going to march to the point that we said we were going to march to, and we're going to come

back. And that in itself was a triumph, because people just didn't do that in Cicero.

(in Carson et al., eds., 315)

Equally inextricably associated with the Civil Rights Movement is Malcolm X, whose name and face have become cultural icons. In a speech entitled "The Ballot or the Bullet" (1964) he stated:

> We need to expand the civil-rights struggle to a higher level – to the level of human rights. Whenever you are in a civil-rights struggle, whether you know it or not, you are confining yourself to the jurisdiction of Uncle Sam. Human rights are something you were born with. Human rights are your god-given rights. Human rights are the rights that are recognized by all nations of this earth.
>
> (Malcolm X, online)

Such concepts as power, solidarity, rebellion, and the ultimate refusal to assimilate or to be placated remain attached to his memory. He was in the public eye from 1959 to 1965 and eloquently identified the contradiction between America's principles and practices. Malcolm X was assassinated in a rain of bullets on February 21, 1965, in New York's Audobon Ballroom. He left behind a pregnant widow, Betty Shabazz, and three little girls. His collected papers, after almost being lost, are now at the Schomburg Center for Research in Black Culture, the 135th Street branch of the New York Public Library.

N. R. Davidson's sweeping epic drama, *El Hajj Malik: The Dramatic Life and Death of Malcolm X,* was developed out of a group improvisation by the playwright and other students in the MFA program at Stanford University in spring 1967. It is based on Malcolm X's biography and speeches, using poetry, chants, slides, music, dancers, and dramatic narration to move from his roots in Detroit through his days as a hoodlum, a prisoner, a convert to Islam, and a pilgrim to Mecca. The trip transformed his separatist philosophy into a Pan-African vision. The play is an ensemble piece, written for 12 voices, all of which dip in and out of the character of Malcolm X. It was published in *New Plays from the Black Theatre,* edited by Ed Bullins, having been premiered by the Black American Theatre in Washington, DC, in the summer of 1971. In November that year Ernie McClintock's Afro-American Studio produced the play off-Broadway at the Martinique Theatre.

The person who delivered the eulogy at Malcolm's funeral, calling him "our black shining prince," was Ossie Davis. A play that I conceived and directed, *Malcolm Little and the Holy City Mecca,* which I call a "miracle play," was premiered at Atlanta's Spelman College on February 25, 1993. Part of its text is from Ossie Davis's eulogy:

MALCOLM LITTLE
AND THE HOLY CITY MECCA
A Miracle Play, Conceived and Directed by Glenda Dickerson
February 25-28, 1993

For Reservations Call: 404-681-3641 ext. 2227

Performances
Thursday, Friday, Saturday: **8:00** Sunday: **3:00**
Baldwin Burroughs Theater, Rockefeller Fine Arts Building, **Spelman College**

A flyer for *Malcolm Little and the Holy City Mecca*, a play I conceived and directed, 1993

Here – at this final hour, in this quiet place – Harlem has come to bid farewell to one of its brightest hopes – extinguished now, and gone from us forever. For Harlem is where he worked and where he struggled and fought – his home of homes, where his heart was, and where his people are – and it is, therefore, most fitting that we meet once again – in Harlem – to share these last moments with him. For Harlem has ever been gracious to those who have loved her, have fought for her and have defended her honor even to the death. It is not in the memory of man that this beleaguered, unfortunate, but nonetheless proud community has found a braver, more gallant young champion than this Afro-American who lies before us – unconquered still. I say the word again, as he would want me to: Afro-American – Afro-American Malcolm, who was a master, was most meticulous in his use of words. Nobody knew better than he the power words have over minds of men. Malcolm had stopped being a Negro years ago. It had become too small, too puny, too weak a word for him. Malcolm was bigger than that. Malcolm had become an Afro-American, and he wanted – so desperately – that we, that all his people, would become Afro-Americans, too. However we may have differed with him – or with each other about him and his value as a man – let his going from us serve only to bring us together, now. Consigning these mortal remains to earth, the common mother of all, secure in the knowledge that what we place in the ground is no more now a man – but a seed – which, after the winter of our discontent, will come forth again to meet us. And we will know him then for what he was and is – a prince – our own black shining prince! – who didn't hesitate to die, because he loved us so.

(O. Davis, 1965, online)

Standing Up: Black Power Movement

Malcolm's inspiration had a great deal to do with the growing militant attitude among the people who could not fly. In the words of a traditional song that became associated with the Civil Rights Movement:

> We shall not, we shall not be moved,
> We shall not, we shall not be moved.
> Just like the tree standing by the water,
> We shall not be moved.

In 1966 James Meredith set out from Memphis, Tennessee, to serve as an example of individual courage so that others in the state would actively seek to exercise their right to vote. A shotgun blast abruptly ended his planned walk to Jackson, Mississippi. Members of SNCC, the SCLC, and CORE were determined to pick up the march from where Meredith had been ambushed. Stokely Carmichael, chairman of SNCC, and Martin Luther King argued over tactics on how to continue. Their disagreements came to symbolize the increasing friction between the two approaches for achieving equality, as dramatized in *Fly Blackbird*.

Cleveland Sellers remembers the moment during the Meredith March when Stokely Carmichael first proclaimed the slogan "Black Power":

> Later that afternoon, a group drove out on the highway to the spot where Meredith had been ambushed, and we walked for about three hours. We wanted to advertise that the march would be continued. [. . .] Stokely, who'd been released from jail just minutes before the rally began, was the last speaker. He was preceded by [Floyd] McKissick, Dr. King and Willie Ricks. Like the rest of us, they were angry about Stokely's unnecessary arrest. Their speeches were particularly militant. When Stokely moved forward to speak, the crowd greeted him with a huge roar. He acknowledged his reception with a raised arm and clenched fist.
>
> "This is the twenty-seventh time I have been arrested and I ain't going to jail no more!" The crowd exploded into cheers and clapping.
>
> "The only way we gonna stop them white men from whuppin' us is to take over. We been saying freedom for six years and we ain't got nothin'. What we gonna start saying now is Black Power!"
>
> The crowd was right with him. They picked up his thoughts immediately.
>
> "BLACK POWER!" they roared in unison.

Martin King, Floyd McKissick, and Stokely Carmichael

> Willie Ricks, who is as good at orchestrating the emotions of a crowd as anyone I have ever seen, sprang into action. Jumping to the platform with Stokely, he yelled to the crowd,
> "What do you want?" "BLACK POWER!"
> "What do you want?" "BLACK POWER!!"
> "What do you want?" "BLACK POWER!! BLACK POWER!!! BLACK POWER!!!!"
>
> (in Carson et al., eds., 280–1)

Can you imagine the scene that day? How would you stage it?

Women playwrights were equally concerned with black power as a means of taking control of their own lives. Beginning with her work in the American Negro Theatre in the 1930s, Alice Childress blazed a path for other black women playwrights to follow from Lorraine Hansberry to Ntozake Shange. Childress (1916 [or 1920]–94) had a career in the theater as actor, director, and playwright. In 1956 her first play produced outside

Black Power Fist

Harlem, *Trouble in Mind*, won the Obie Award for best original off-Broadway play; she was the first woman to win an Obie and the first black woman to have a play produced professionally off-Broadway. Though her plays were optioned for Broadway itself 11 times, they did not reach the theaters there because she would not compromise her vision. Childress has described her plays as an attempt "to interpret the 'ordinary' because they are not ordinary."

Alice Childress's *Wine in the Wilderness* takes place in Harlem, on a summer night in 1964. There is a riot outside. Bill Jameson, an aspiring artist, opens his doors during the riot to Oldtimer, a Harlem eccentric, and his married friends Sonny-Man and Cynthia. Sonny-Man and Cynthia bring with them another Harlem resident named Tommy, who has lost her apartment to the rioters. The couple believe Tommy will be the perfect model for the "messed up chick" in Bill's planned three-part painting (triptych) of "African womanhood." According to James Hatch:

> Bill, Sonny-Man, and Cynthia are victims of the old Black bourgeois values. They are empty, artificial people, preaching Blackness, brotherhood, and love simply because it is in vogue; they remain self-centered individuals who reflect the values of the old slave masters. Tommy is the source of inspiration that they all so desperately need to find themselves and their Blackness.
>
> (in Hatch and Shine, eds., 1996, 341)

Like Zora Neale Hurston, Alice Childress chose to express Iwa, the inner life of blackness, through extraordinary ordinary people. In Tommy, Childress created a powerful, new black heroine who emerges from the depths of the community. Ella Jo Baker was in many ways much like Alice Childress's Tommy: a simple woman who emerged from the depths of her community. In a career that spanned five decades (1930–80), Ella Jo Baker was a role model and mentor for an entire generation of activists, in which capacity she touched thousands of lives and contributed to over 35 organizations. Born in 1903 in Norfolk, Virginia, Ella Baker was a daughter of the Jim Crow South and a granddaughter of slaves. She played a pivotal role in the three most prominent black freedom organizations of her day – the NAACP, SCLC, and SNCC. She worked alongside such male leaders as W. E. B. DuBois, Thurgood Marshall, George Schuyler, Walter White, A. Philip Randolph, Martin Luther King, Jr., and Stokely Carmichael. Ella Baker's life shows how certain connections and continuities can form a strong chain of links in a long tradition of resistance. Each intergenerational organization she joined, each story she told, each lesson she passed on was a part of the connective tissue that formed the Black Freedom Movement in the United States.

A question often posed by Ella Baker, "Now who are your people?," symbolizes Baker's approach to life-history. This was important to her, not to establish an elite pedigree, but to locate an individual as a part of a family, a community, a region, a culture, and an historical period. On Saturday, December 13, 1986, she died quietly in her sleep in her Harlem apartment. In their diversity, those who gathered to mourn her death represented the breadth and depth of the Black Freedom Movement and of Ella Baker's influence on 20th-century American politics. Her biographer Barbara Ransby gives a vivid account of Baker's funeral:

> It was a cold and rainy day in New York City and a week before Christmas when the overflow crowd piled into Harlem's historic Abyssinian Baptist Church to remember and to celebrate a woman who had touched more lives than she herself could have realized. Those who came to honor Ella Baker wore fur coats, African prints, Islamic kufis, and yarmulkes. They were young with dreadlocks and elderly with graying temples and receding hairlines. They were black and white and a myriad of shades in between, men and women, rich and poor, those formally educated and those self taught. Among those who gathered were politicians, religious leaders, entertainers, and renowned scholars. Crowded in among the celebrities were those whom Ella Baker sometimes referred to as the little people: people without credentials or titles, but people she had valued and respected in her life, and who now honored her in death. The voice that echoed most powerfully through the cavernous church where Ella Baker's funeral was held was that of Bernice Johnson Reagon, founder and lead singer of Sweet Honey in the Rock and one of Ella Baker's political daughters. Her commanding voice drew attention to every line of Ella Baker's favorite movement song, "Guide my feet, while I run this race . . . because I don't want to run this race alone . . . because I don't want to run this race in vain." And Ella Baker did neither. She ran long, she ran hard, and she ran with a diverse assortment of folks over some fifty years.
>
> (Ransby, 10–12)

The "diverse assortment" of folks with whom she ran for over fifty years: these were Ella Baker's people.

Eight-year-old Sheyann Webb was Martin Luther King's "smallest freedom fighter." Whenever he visited Selma, he would hold her on his lap at the pulpit and let her lead her favorite freedom song, "Ain't Gonna Let Nobody Turn Me Around." Little Sheyann asked her reluctant parents to register to vote as a present for her ninth birthday. In 2006 the Voting Rights Act named for Rosa Parks and Fannie Lou Hamer (among others) came up for renewal. Over the strenuous protests of some southern representatives, it was extended for another 25 years. When it again comes up for renewal, remember how the title of one of Spike Lee's films echoes the words of Martin Luther King. The time is always right to do the right thing.

Food for Further Thought

There are many, many books about the Black Freedom Movement. Just a few that I would recommend are *Warriors Don't Cry* (1994) by Melba Patillo

Beals, *The Long Shadow of Little Rock* (1962) by Daisy Bates, *A Dream of Freedom* (2004) by Diane McWhorter and *Ella Baker & the Black Freedom Movement* (2003) by Barbara Ransby. I also highly recommend the companion volume to the *Eyes on the Prize* documentary: *Eyes on the Prize Civil Rights Reader* (1991), edited by Clayborne Carson, D. Garrow, G. Gill, V. Harding, and D. Hines.

Both *In White America* and *Fly Blackbird* call for integrated casts, so they can be performed by all kinds of drama groups.

Do you know or have you read about a person like Ella Baker who rose "from the depths of her community" to make intergenerational change? Can you research and write about that person's intergenerational work for your Black Life Book? Also for your Black Life Book, how would you answer Ella Baker's question, "Now who are your people?"

7 Black is Beautiful
Protest and Performance

What time is it? It's Nation Time!
(Amiri Baraka, in Carson et al., eds., 480)

Black Art is the aesthetic and spiritual sister of the Black Power concept.
(Larry Neal, 29)

I never knew I was Black until I read Malcolm.
(Denise Nicholas, actress with the Free Southern Theater)

In 1966–8, between the Meredith March and the assassination of Martin Luther King, a mysterious spirit of Blackness moved across the movement. As Stokely Carmichael asserted in 1966: "We have to stop being ashamed of being Black. A broad nose, a thick lip and nappy hair is us and we going to call that beautiful whether they like it or not" (in Van Deburg, 201).

This notion resonated broadly among the people who could not fly. A transformation of the mind, a reanimation of Iwa, grabbed hold to the people striving anew for freedom, now called liberation. The reanimation of Iwa transformed American Negroes to Black Americans through a new way of expression that became known as Soul. Soul was perceived as being the essence of Afro-American culture. Soul embraced much of the Brer Rabbit aura of sly confidence and assumed superiority that surrounded the "brothers" and "sisters" who strode the urban streets. It was like James Brown, the "Godfather of Soul," commanding the audience to "Say it loud. I'm Black and I'm proud." As comedian Godfrey Cambridge noted, "You can't learn it, because no one can give you all those black lessons" (in Van Deburg, 195). You just had to be Black. Suddenly Black with a capital B was beautiful. Suddenly the people remembered that once they could fly.

Harlem during the 1960s and into the 1970s was as vibrant a place as during the Harlem Renaissance. There was a market at 125th and Lenox which was alive with vendors selling food, spices, and African fabrics. Harlem was once again the center of intellectual ferment in writings by such powerful voices as Malcolm X, Angela Davis, Nikki Giovanni, and James Baldwin. After Malcolm's death, a new generation of artists/activists, daughters and sons of the black shining prince, combined art and politics in what Larry Neal called "the Black Arts Movement" (BAM).

Woman wearing a dress influenced by West African fashion

High John appears again among the people who could not fly in the lyrics of this blues song by Bessie Smith:

> Got myself some snakeroot,
> John the Conqueror, too
> Chewed them both together,
> I know what they will do.

The most potent root in conjuration, High John the Conqueror is named after the trickster figure of slave folklore who could always outwit the master. High John the Conqueror root incorporates the spirit of hope – the hope of a people still striving to be free – and metaphorically captures the soul of Black American culture. High John was the source of their new soul and their rearoused ancient laughter. Across the nation, there came an explosion of dashikis and djellabas, gold and ivory beads and earrings, cowrie shell belts, bubas, caftans, agbadas and geles, African heritage medallions and elephant hair bracelets.

Like Malcolm X before them, many people took African or Muslim names, used African proverbs in their speeches, and echoed his belief that Blacks in the northern hemisphere needed to involve themselves in a spiritual and cultural back-to-Africa movement. The people described themselves as soul sister and soul brother; living their Blackness, embracing their ancestral past. The souls of Black folk were valuable, worthy, even sacred. As Lance Jeffers put it: "My blackness is the beauty of this land, my blackness, tender and strong, wounded and wise. My blackness is the beauty of this land" (in Major, ed., 72). Others expressed it differently, for example Barbara Ann Teer:

> The way we talk (the rhythms of our speech which naturally fit our impulses), the way we walk, sing, dance, pray, laugh, eat, make love, and finally, most important, the way we look, make up our cultural heritage. There is nothing like it or equal to it, it stands alone in comparison to other cultures. It is uniquely, beautiful and personally ours and no one can emulate it.
>
> (in Joseph, ed., 192)

Or Joseph Walker:

> Hero with an Afro
> Mojo in indigo
> Gonna overthrow
> The status quo.
>
> (in Van Deburg, 276)

A natural hairstyle served as a highly visible imprimatur of Blackness; a tribute to group unity; a statement of self-love. Rejecting white-influenced beauty standards, Black Americans cleared hot irons, chemical straighteners,

Striding with black pride

and permanents from their medicine cabinets. In those days Angela Davis identified herself as "a young soldier for the revolution" (hooks, 10). Her Afro became iconic, a powerful symbol of soul and resistance. Despite her work as a soldier for the revolution, her incarceration, her published books, and sold-out lectures, she is still most readily identified with and by her hair: in

Angela Davis (center) at a press conference, 1976. Star Collection, reprinted by permission of the DC Public Library; © *Washington Post*

"Afro Images: Politics, Fashion, and Nostalgia," she reports, somewhat ruefully, that today people who do not immediately recognize her face or even her name, are prompted into memory when she is described as "the Afro" (in James, ed., 1998: 273–8).

In 1977 she looked back into the past and gazed into the future:

> Today, as we reflect on the process of empowering Afro-American women, our most efficacious strategies remain those that are guided by the principle used by Black women in the club movement. We must strive to "lift as we climb". In other words, we must climb in such a way as to guarantee that all of our sisters, regardless of social class, and indeed all of our brothers, climb with us.
>
> (Busby, 572)

Playwrights, novelists, songwriters, and artists all forged their personalized visions of Black Power. They thought of Afro-American culture as a weapon in the struggle for liberation. What we can call cultural workers sought to define the universe in their own terms in three ways: by emphasizing the distinctiveness of Afro-American symbols, myths, and metaphors; by extolling the virtues of Black life-styles and values; and by promoting race consciousness, pride, and unity. They wanted to turn people on, to wake people up, make them conscious of themselves and their environment, and ultimately to push everybody to the stage where their very lives would be poetry (Joseph, ed., 181). This new breed of freedom fighter was trying to bring about a cultural revolution. An evolving communal consciousness, a new way of

Kwanzaa candles

expressing Iwa/Soul, moved people toward rituals that would celebrate, promote, and preserve Black history and culture. As Iya Afin recorded in the *Eyes on the Prize* project:

> I met some people in my apartment building who invited me to a feast. The feast took place in Los Angeles in 1967. They were celebrating [. . .] Kwanzaa. The music, the food, the clothes, my people, I was entranced and captivated. For the first time in my life I felt at home in my own skin. I was listening to my people's music and dancing to my people's drums. At last I had a culture of my own. I felt a connection to my ancestors so strong that everything I had ever experienced in my whole life came back to me and I was changed forever.
>
> (in Carson et al., eds., 233)

Or as the poet don l. lee expressed it:

> a people without their culture
> are a people without meaning.
> A people without their culture
> are a people without substance.
> A people without their culture
> are a people without identity, purpose and direction.
> A people without their culture
> are a dead people.
>
> (in Van Deburg, 280)

The plays in those days were agitprop (agitation and propaganda) pieces, meant either to move the "masses" to revolution or to find a new language to express Black culture. Playwrights were less concerned with structure than with content. As Askia Muhammad Toure wrote:

> The role of the revolutionary Black artist is that of a liberator, freeing the collective consciousness of his people by countering the reactionary cultural images of the oppressor with strong, positive affirmative cultural images of revolutionary Blackness, inspiring the people with hope for a better day, of victory and total liberation.
>
> (in Bullins, 1969, 16)

Larry Neal and LeRoi Jones are comparable as personalities with Charles Johnson and Langston Hughes during the Harlem Renaissance. Partly because he died of a heart attack in 1981, Neal, aged only 44, is less well known than Jones (now Baraka). However, it was Neal who wrote a searing essay in 1968; it has since appeared in many anthologies as the manifesto of the Black Arts Movement. Both men were articulate voices in bringing the manifesto to reality in their plays, essays, and poetry.

Like Georgia Douglas Johnson and Jesse Fauset, who opened their homes during the 1920s, the Neal residence on Jumel Terrace in the Sugar Hill section of Harlem served as a magnet for the creative individuals of the new era. Neal is credited with coining some of the most memorable phrases of the era: "Black Arts Movement," "Afro-American ethos," and "the presence of ancestry." It was in his manifesto for the Black Arts Movement that he first declared: "Black Art is the aesthetic and spiritual sister of the Black Power concept," a statement that became a mantra for the new generation.

LeRoi Jones, a poet, writer, political activist, and teacher, used black cultural nationalism as a tool for community building and cultural awareness. Hailed as the leader of the revolutionary Black Arts and Black Theater Movements of the 1960s, he founded and directed Spirit House in Newark, where young Afro-American playwrights' works were performed by the African Revolutionary Movers. Among his own plays that he produced at Spirit House was *Slave Ship* (1967), a ritual drama about the middle passage of African people to America. Other important dramatic works include *Dutchman, The Slave, The Toilet,* and *Black Mass.* In addition to writing for the theater, he has published more than two dozen books, including poetry, fiction, and nonfiction.

In 1964 Jones received the Obie Award for his one-act play *Dutchman*, which had received its first professional production at the Cherry Lane Theater in New York on March 24 that year. The title variously refers to the Dutch man-of-war *The Treasurer*, a slave ship that brought the first 20

LeRoi Jones (Amiri Baraka) directing

Africans to Jamestown in 1619, and the legends of the *Flying Dutchman*: "One night I sat up all night and wrote a play I called *Dutchman*. I had gotten the title from The Flying Dutchman but abstracted it because . . . [i]t didn't quite serve my purpose." The protagonist, Clay, at first seems to be a mild-mannered, middle class, young Black man who is entertained by the odd behavior of Lula, the white woman antagonist. The two have a violent encounter on the New York subway ("the flying underbelly of the city," "the subway heaped in modern myth"), dramatically exposing the suppressed hostility of American Blacks toward the dominant white culture. But under Lula's relentless goading, all layers of respectability are peeled away; Clay's anger bursts into a tirade asserting his manhood. Lula listens coldly and then, as he prepares to leave the train, stabs him to death. For Jones, Clay's murder by Lula, "the Anglo-Saxon bitch-goddess," becomes the symbolic lynching of all Afro-Americans. The play is dense with metaphor and self-examination. Jones uses the white myth of Black male sexuality (the brutal black buck stereotype) to highlight what he considers the systematic and deliberate annihilation of Afro-Americans. *Dutchman* was revived at the Cherry Lane Theater for a limited season in January–February 2007, in a production starring Dule Hill and Jennifer Mudge and directed by Bill Duke.

In 1968 LeRoi Jones changed his name to Amiri Baraka, stating that he killed the slave within by dropping his "slave name." Like the Emancipated Interlocutor, Jones gave birth to his newly free self by renouncing his "gallopwashus" name. He expressed something of this in his poem "We Own the Night":

> We are unfair
> And unfair
> We are black magicians
> Black arts we make
> in black labs of the heart
> The fair are fair
> And deathly white
> The day will not save them
> And we own the night

(in Jones and Neal, eds., 527)

The same title was used for Jimmy Garrett's *We Own the Night: A Play of Blackness* (1968), among the most controversial one-act dramas of the time. It was published in *Black Fire: An Anthology of Afro-American Writing* (1971), edited by LeRoi Jones and Larry Neal, and in *New Plays from the Black Theatre* (1969), edited by Ed Bullins. This play features a conversation between generations very different from that dramatized in Ted Shine's *Contribution* (see chapter 6). In Garrett's play, the confrontation between mother and son is meant to represent the conflict not only between generations but between the old assimilationist "negro" and the new breed of radical freedom fighter. This disturbing work culminates in Johnny shooting his mother to death.

What do you think Jones meant by "the day will not save them and we own the night" in the poem quoted above? Could a Freedom Rider in 1961, singing "If my mother don't go, I'll go anyhow, I'm on my way to freedomland," have imagined that Jimmy Garrett would interpret the notion of freedom in such violent terms?

Robert MacBeth founded the New Lafayette Theatre (NLT) in Harlem in 1967 with the assistance of the Ford and Rockefeller Foundations and the New York State Arts Council (sources of funding that later became contentious issues within the Black Arts community). The New Lafayette was the most prominent site for the new agitprop theater. Named for the original Lafayette, famous during the Harlem Renaissance, it was housed in the same building. Perhaps the most effective demonstration of the NLT's commitment to the Harlem community was its early policy of supplying free tickets to Harlem residents. MacBeth and the NLT strove to give both white and black societies a stereotype-free view of black culture that they theorized was generally unavailable elsewhere at the time.

Who's Got his Own by Black Arts playwright Ron Milner (1938–2004) was one of the initial productions at the NLT. In concerning itself with the disintegration of the Black family due to racism, it is similar in spirit to such works as Lonnie Elder III's *Ceremonies in Dark Old Men* (1965), J. E. Franklin's *Black Girl* (1969), Richard Wesley's *The Past is Past* (1973), and Philip Hayes Dean's two plays, *The Owl Killer* (1971) and *The Sty of the Blind Pig* (1971).

Along with Amiri Baraka and Larry Neal, Ed Bullins was one of the most influential voices of the Black Arts Movement. Ed Bullins was playwright-in-residence at the NLT from 1968 to 1973. Bullins and Larry Neal created a laboratory at that theater to work out the intellectual ideas of the movement and experiment with how performance – music, dance, poetry, and plays – could liberate a people.

In the introduction to his anthology *The New Lafayette Presents* (1974), Ed Bullins says:

> The Black masses were sought out in their ghettos and enthusiastically set upon by the new Black revolutionary artists through almost seemingly spontaneous eruptions of Black street plays. Black arts festivals proliferated, with numerous conferences and symposiums created to discuss the criteria for evaluating Black arts, the role of the artists in the movement and the creation of an alternate Black communications and media system throughout the Black communities of America.
>
> (Bullins, ed., 1974, 3)

The only woman playwright included in the anthology is Sonia Sanchez. She spoke with Ed Bullins about her play *The Bronx Is Next*:

> *The Bronx Is Next* is the first play that I did. I'm trying to say that when I did *The Bronx Is Next* I was talking about Harlem and the tenements in Harlem. How people live in Harlem. It was my opinion at the time and it still is that those same tenements need to be burned down. As a consequence in the play I have, I guess, what you'd probably call the militants, in the terminology of America, I have some men who decided to move Black people out of Harlem and burn down the tenements. At the time I knew that a lot of Black people were dying in the cities. I watched us die. (161)

This was a time of extraordinary activity by Black American cultural workers, not only in Harlem, but in the broader New York community and across the nation. After he and Ron Milner had relocated from Detroit, Woodie King, the most prolific of all Afro-American producers, founded the New Federal Theatre in 1970 at the Henry Street Settlement House in lower Manhattan. The company was named after the Federal Theatre Project of the 1930s.

The Negro Ensemble Company (NEC) can trace its origins back to 1966, when Douglas Turner Ward (whose work is discussed in chapter 6), wrote an article for the *New York Times* entitled "American Theatre: For Whites Only?":

> Despite an eminent handful, Negro dramatists remain sparse in number, productions sporadic at most, and scripts too few to indicate discernible trends. (Last year, during a forum on "What Negro Playwrights Are Saying" not even panel members could cite enough plays to make the plural subject matter viable). [Ward went on to suggest the need for] a theatre concentrating primarily on themes of Negro life, but also resilient enough to incorporate and interpret the best of world drama – whatever the source.
>
> (Ward, DI, 03)

The article drew the attention of the Ford Foundation, which invited Ward to develop a proposal for a new black theater group and later provided generous funding. In 1967 Ward, Gerald Krone, and Robert Hooks (who originated the role of Clay in *Dutchman*) spearheaded the founding of the Negro Ensemble Company. Under the leadership of Ward and others, the not-for-profit organization has produced over 200 plays. It served not only as the training ground and professional home of such actors as Samuel L. Jackson, Lynn Whitfield, Denzel Washington, and Phylicia Rashad, but – like its predecessor, the American Negro Theatre – equipped numerous Black designers, technicians, managers, directors, and producers with the skills necessary to find work in the world of theater. The Signature Theater Company, an off-Broadway theater founded in 1991, has planned to dedicate its 2008–9 season to the writers of the Negro Ensemble Company, including Charles Fuller and Lonnie Elder.

Though the Black Power and Black Arts Movements were dominated by male voices, women were active nationally in founding and sustaining theater companies. In New York alone these included Barbara Ann Teer's National Black Theatre in Harlem, Hazel Bryant's Richard Allen Cultural Center, Rosetta Lenoire's AMAS Repertory, and Marjorie Moon's Billie Holiday Theatre in Brooklyn. Vinnette Carroll was the loudest voice among this sisterhood of cultural workers. As she said: "They told me that I had one-third less chance because I was a woman; they told me I had a third less chance again because I was black; but I tell you, I did one hell of a lot with that remaining one-third" (in Hill and Hatch, 401).

At the Zora Neale Hurston Festival in Eatonville, Florida. Left to right: Glenda Dicker/sun, George C. Wolfe, and Vinnette Carrol

During the 1960s Carroll applied to the New York State Council on the Arts for the establishment of a theater where "a black actor could have a place to learn his art and not have to rely on just being Black to get a job." Her Urban Arts Corps became remarkably successful in the production of several gospel musicals. She began with *Trumpets of the Lord* (1963), an adaptation of James Weldon Johnson's *God's Trombones* (see chapter 1). *Dont Bother Me, I Cant Cope* (1972) and *Your Arms too Short to Box with God* (1976) became Broadway hits, with Ms. Carroll becoming the first Black woman to direct on Broadway.

By the early 1960s Langston Hughes, like DuBois decades beforehand, felt himself to be an elder statesman to "the new generation." His *Black Nativity*, first performed on Broadway in 1961, is a version of the Christmas story that attempted to integrate gospel music into the story of the birth of Jesus. This paved the way for Vinnette Carroll and other musical revolutionaries. *The Believers* (1968), written by Josephine Jackson and Joseph A. Walker, is subtitled *The Black Experience in Soul*; its first act focuses almost entirely on the era before Reconstruction. The playwrights dramatized their belief that while in bondage, Blacks developed a new American culture (from their African background, as revealed by their musical heritage). The second half of the show brought the history up to date. The *New York Times* noted the great change in the Black musical on opening night:

> *The Believers* has something to say about being a Negro in the United States that its predecessors (How quickly they have dated!) did not say. Instead of ending with a whimper of pain, or a cheerful (or threatening) plea for racial togetherness, *The Believers* ends with the crisp, jaunty rattle of an African drum.
>
> (in Woll, 254)

In the years after Langston Hughes' death in 1967, the black musical was transformed from a marginal theatrical genre to a Broadway success story. A flood of awards greeted such new Black musicals as *Purlie* (based on Ossie Davis's *Purlie Victorious*), *Ain't Misbehavin'* (based on the music of Fats Waller), *Raisin* (based on Lorraine Hansberry's *Raisin in the Sun*), *Eubie!* (based on the music of Eubie Blake), *Bubbling Brown Sugar*, and *Dreamgirls*. This last was a fictionalized account of the female Soul trio the Supremes, a Motown group popular in the 1960s. In 2006 the show was made into a film with Beyonce Knowles, Eddie Murphy, Jamie Foxx, and Jennifer Hudson. Having been rejected from *American Idol*, in 2007 the gospel-trained Hudson won an Oscar for best supporting actress as Effie in *Dreamgirls*.

The younger generation of Black writers, directors, choreographers, and scenic designers working in the 1970s included Melvin Van Peebles (father of Mario), whose musical *Don't Play us Cheap* (1972; film 1973) received sparkling reviews. It is a joyous tale of a Saturday night rent party in Harlem and a mysterious encounter with two demons who assume human form in order to wreck the festivities. One demon ultimately relents when he falls in love with the lady of the house. The poet Nikki Giovanni, surprised by the similarity of the set to her own home, said:

> I take a certain pride that someone could put a set on Broadway of a Harlem apartment with a door that has five locks on it, a mirror in the living room that frames photographs of Martin Luther King, Malcolm X, Adam Clayton Powell and John Kennedy, with Aretha Franklin peeping through.
>
> (in Woll, 260)

In 1964 Adrienne Kennedy's *Funnyhouse of a Negro* was premiered at the East End theater and also won an Obie Award. It is a grimly imaginative and soul-searching play. The mind and spiritual conflicts of a young Black woman are painfully explored, both directly and indirectly, in terms of assimilation, integration, religion, black nationalism, the new African nationalism, and Pan-Africanism. The play gives expression to an hour of anguish in the mind of Sarah, whose dreams lead to madness and eventual suicide; her death can be seen as the result of her inability to accept her Blackness and all that it implies.

The playwright Ntozake Shange responded to Kennedy's evocation of a tortured soul in her choreopoem *for colored girls who have considered suicide/when the rainbow is enuf* (1975). Born as Paulette Williams in Trenton, New Jersey, in 1948, in 1971 she changed her name to Ntozake, which means "she who comes with her own things;" Shange means "she who walks like a lion." This work introduced the choreopoem to commercial audiences in a new kind of poetic approach to autobiography. Through her poems, in which she performed alongside an ensemble of women distinguished by the colors of their dresses, Shange explores heartache, heartbreak, her own suicide attempts, and the emancipatory thrill of coming to voice: "I found God in myself and I love her fiercely." The play moved from Woodie King's New Federal Theatre to the New York Shakespeare Company's Anspacher Theatre, and then to the Booth Theatre on Broadway (1976), the first work by a Black woman to reach Broadway since Lorraine Hansberry's *Raisin in the Sun* (1959). Freed by such playwrights as Adrienne Kennedy from the constraints of writing to uplift or to mobilize the race, Shange opened the door for hundreds of young women who had been silenced in the male-dominated Black Arts Movement. They began to use personal experience to create drama, believing that "I am enuf."

As the grants dried up, Black theaters began to close and the Black Arts Movement came slowly to its end. The next generation of BAM playwrights continued uncovering the Iwa of people of African descent by writing ever more complex plays. Their characters were often conflicted and contradictory, bringing into view a mature understanding of a people who were simultaneously heroic, humorous, humble, and hubristic. These writers had more complicated concerns than "burn, baby, burn" and/or uplifting the race. They experimented with form as well as content.

One of the plays by Charles Gordone (1925–95), *No Place to be Somebody: A Black Black Comedy in Three Acts*, for example, presents not only contradictory characters and subject matter but uses a form that is daringly original. It is written as a blend of realism, poetry, gangster movie melodrama, comedy, surrealism, and soul. The play is designed to function on two levels: on a physical level, the action takes place in a seedy West Village bar run by a Black man, Johnny Williams; but on another level, the action exists in the mind of Gabe Gabriel, a poetic and philosophical figure who is writing the play about Johnny Williams. Gabe serves as narrator, chorus, and spokesman for the author. Joseph Papp first accepted the play for a workshop presentation at the Other Stage of the New York Shakespeare Festival Public Theater. The critical acclaim accorded the play was such that it was moved to the Anspacher Theater, where it began its professional run on May 4, 1969.

Flyers for two productions of Euripides' *Trojan Women* that I directed, the first in 1972 and the second, set in Rwanda, in 1997

No Place to be Somebody won the Pulitzer Prize for drama in 1970. Gordone became the first Afro-American playwright to be so honored and the play was the first off-Broadway production to receive the prize.

The Actors' Equity Nontraditional Casting Project was founded in 1986, proposing the (then) revolutionary idea that the character "Lawyer" could be played by actors who weren't necessarily white or male. This encouraged the increasing practice of blind-casting Blacks in classical roles. Cultural workers began to think of themselves as writers who were Black rather than as Black

151

writers. A new generation of actors, writers, directors, and producers began to experiment with more complex ways of uncovering the richly embroiled inner life of Black people. The next chapter discusses some members of this generation who experienced the sea-change firsthand.

Food for Further Thought

For a variety of literary voices, read *Black Voices* (1968) and *New Black Voices* (1972), both edited by Abraham Chapman. The first gives examples of what the BAM artists were reading for inspiration and the second gives examples of what they themselves were writing. *Black Drama Anthology* (1971), edited by Woodie King and Ron Milner, contains a representative sampling of plays of the time. *Classic Plays from the Negro Ensemble Company* (1995), edited by Paul Carter Harrison and Gus Edwards, includes several plays produced by the NEC.

Write a simple poem that reflects your thoughts about questions of beauty, soul, and art, following the example of don l. lee (now Haki Madhubuti), quoted above.

Listen to Nina Simone sing "To Be Young, Gifted and Black" or "Mississippi Goddam." For a male voice, find James Brown's "Say it Loud: I'm Black and I'm Proud."

Start a discussion group to do further research on the 1960s and early 1970s. Calling on your research and reviewing the substance of this chapter, make a little scene wearing clothes and Afro wigs, using some of the "agit-prop" poetry and music of the time. Find a recording by the Last Poets, a group formed in 1968, and listen to their politically charged poetry. Are there similarities in the style and cadence to the way in which rap is performed?

8 Conversations
A Second Generation Takes Center Stage

Let a second generation full of courage issue forth.

(Margaret Walker, in Hayden, ed., 140)

Oh, Mother let's go down, let's go down,
Let's go down, let's go down.
As I went down in the valley to pray,
Studyin' about the good ole way,
Who shall wear that starry crown?

(Traditional)

How the actor, analogous to a musician with his piano on his back, his violin in his heart, and his trombone to his lips – in other words, his instruments within and on the surface of his skin – reaches out and manages to touch an audience of one or one thousand is the central question of the "living stage."

How the African actor – paper books destroyed by heat and humidity, carved wooden records eaten by termites – kept alive the myths, legends, historical practices, and dramatic expressions of a people scattered like thistledown in the wind is the central question of black theater.

What these two strands have in common is the spoken word. The spinning, stringing together, all but singing of the spoken word is how the actor touches her/his audience and how the African transmits the tale.

Considering these strands led me to conduct the interviews below. All nine actors are distinguished African Americans still active in film, television, and in the theater as this book goes to press. They are at the top of their form, at the peak of their careers; they are seasoned, experienced, and well trained. They are the generation just behind such groundbreakers as Sidney Poitier, Harry Belafonte, Diahann Carrol, James Earl Jones, Ruby Dee, and Ossie Davis – for my generation, those who come to mind immediately when we think of professional Black actors. They hold in their own minds memories of the American Negro Theatre; they carry in their own bodies the bridge to contemporary Black theater. They are heirs to a generation of performers remembered in tones of sepia, sterling, pewter, brass, and bronze – performers such as Dorothy Dandridge, the "sepia Marilyn Monroe;" Bert Williams and George Walker, the pewter court jesters; Josephine Baker, brassy home girl; Paul Robeson, sterling silver Renaissance

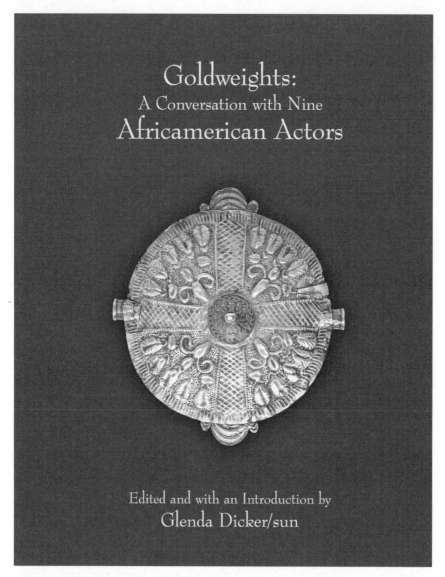

Goldweights:
A Conversation with Nine
Africamerican Actors

Edited and with an Introduction by
Glenda Dicker/sun

Cover of *Goldweights: A Conversation with Nine Africamerican Actors*, ed. Glenda Dicker/sun (2007)

man; and Lena Horne, the legendary, stormy bronze beauty. The actors I interviewed – Barbara Montgomery, Lynn Whitfield, S. Epatha Merkerson, Giancarlo Esposito, Vondie Curtis-Hall, Joe Morton, Clifton Powell, Debbie Allen, and Phylicia Rashad – have roots deeply buried in the legacy of theater veterans and in the tradition of Black culture.

There are other actors I would have liked to interview, but time constraints and scheduling conflicts prevented this. Morgan Freeman, Angela Bassett, Whoopi Goldberg, L. Scott Caldwell, Mary Alice, Denzel Washington, Denise Nichols, and Samuel L. Jackson, for example, would have been among many possible candidates for inclusion, as would Don Cheadle, Vanessa Williams, and Laurence Fishburne. But I also wanted to focus on those who had begun their careers in the theater, especially during the heyday of the 1980s, and only later moved to making films.

My nine interviewees began their careers in such venues as the Workshops for Careers in the Arts, Washington, DC, or in New York at Woodie King's New Federal Theatre, Hazel Bryant's RACCA (Richard Allen Cultural Center), the Negro Ensemble Company, and the New Lafayette Theatre; some of them have also appeared in Joseph Papp's New York Shakespeare Festival as well as on and off-Broadway.

When I interviewed them between 1998 and 2000 they were between the ages of 35 and 60. I found them full of history, both from the research they did for their depictions of bygone days and from their first-hand experiences of the days between Ntozake Shange's *for colored girls* (1975) and August Wilson's *Gem of the Ocean* (2003). They are now recognizable to a wide range of film and television audiences. They are characterized by staying power, integrity, and faith in their art. Their careers offer a playbook of carefully researched, well-realized roles, never dipping into stereotype and never betraying either their ancestors or their heirs. Each has carved out a body of work which stands as a beacon to the next generation of actors. It is to this generation that I wish to aim these nine voices.

Barbara Montgomery: Lady in A Red Dress

> "We just did the plays. We didn't do it to get a grant. We didn't do it to become stars. We did it because we loved doing it."

When Barbara Montgomery came dancing down MacBeth's table, draped sinuously in red, reading his letter, she insinuated herself into our consciousness like no Lady M has before or since. Plunging her beautiful fingers into Andrei Serban's pasteurized blood at LaMama ETC., Barbara showed us the sexy side of the infamous lady. Perhaps known best for her role in the sitcom *Amen*, she has a deep and rich background in theater and serves as something of a living reminder of what it was like in the "good old days." Her career provides a map from there to here. A leading actress with LaMama ETC. and the Negro Ensemble Company (NEC), Ms. Montgomery was once a barmaid at

Harlem's Top and Baby Grand cafés. As a young actor she traveled to Europe with the Cotton Club dancers, singing and dancing for her supper. We did the interview in her Harlem apartment – a place crowded with antique furniture, African art, and box upon box of theater memorabilia.

BM: To tell you the truth, I was about six years old; maybe seven. My father took me to the movie house in East Orange. He took me to see *Stormy Weather* (see chapter 6). And it wasn't until later on [. . .], like somewhere in the '80s, that it came to me. It came to me. I sat there. I saw Lena Horne. I saw the movie and I remember almost as if it were yesterday, I realized that I said I wanted to be a movie star. I didn't know I wanted to be an actor. I didn't know what an actor was. It happened like in a flashback that the little girl had that thought. I really feel like it was my destiny. I think it was my destiny and now what I'm doing is what that was all getting me to. And what is destiny but how far you go?

GD: How did you get started in NEC actually?

BM: So the NEC comes when, in '75 . . . it was '74 . . . I had done *My Sister, My Sister*. That's when I received the Obie. [In those days, I would] leave the Public Theater and walk around to LaMama after *The Wedding* and do *Thoughts*. I used to do two or three plays at one time. I'm telling you. I was standing by at *Raisin* and Trezania [Beverly] was covering me. I did *Raisin* a lot. I did *Raisin, My Sister, My Sister*, and work on a soap. I used to get three checks sometimes for live, not for residuals. There wasn't no residuals, honey. I didn't know what a residual was. I was just doing the work. But NEC was '75. We did *First Breeze of Summer*. Then we did *Eden*.

GD: Who were some of your early influences?

BM: My first teacher was Vinnette Carroll.

GD: Is this the Urban Arts School?

BM: Urban Arts, right. On 46th. And there it was. There we were. Rosalind Cash, Lex Munson, Della Lawrence, Duane Jones, a man by the name of Charles Martin. Well, Ellen Stewart definitely. I mean, Ellen Stewart, Ellen Stewart and um . . . [*thinking*] because that opened the doors to my instrument. You know, that kind of experiment. I was free to experiment. I mean, doing *The Wedding Band* with Ruby [Dee] . . . you know. That was good. We did *Five Black Visions* at the Public Theater Annex. Morgan [Freeman] Neil Harris and Richard Wesley. Gloria Foster did [Sonia Sanchez'] *Sister Sonji*. And then there was always, of course, Josephine Baker and Carmen DeLavillade.

GD: Looking back, Barbara, at the rich, rich, rich days that you talked about today, some of which we went through together, and all the excitement; the revolutionary fervor that was in the air; the new world order that was coming, can you talk about black theater today? Is there any such thing as black theater or a black theater movement?

BM: That there's a movement, I don't know. But as long as we are black artists, there has to be black theater. I want to make a theater of our history; historic theater. The Barbara Montgomery Theater of History and Culture or something like that.

Lynn Whitfield: Louisiana Belle de Jour

"Life for me was always rather theatrical. You know, I hailed from a true Southern family; a Louisiana family. Tennessee Williams had nothing on us."

Born in Baton Rouge, Louisiana, Lynn was raised in a house full of dramatic women scented with Chanel No. 5 – her glamorous mother and three aunts. Her father was a dentist who wrote music. As a little girl, she took private lessons in ballet and appeared in Passion plays as well as *Porgy and Bess*. She learned secrets from "across the river." The little ballerina sat with her grandmother watching the Million Dollar Movie each week, envisioning herself stepping into the shoes of Audrey Hepburn and Bette Davis as early as age five. In roles such as Roz Batiste in *Eve's Bayou* and Corinne Coles in *The Wedding*, she honors the women who raised her. Lynn started her acting career at the Black Repertory Company in Washington, DC. She soon moved to New York and in 1979–80 made her bones in the first international touring company of *for colored girls who have considered suicide/when the rainbow is enuf*. Having made her film debut in *Dr. Detroit* in 1983, three years later she played the title character in the television movie *Johnnie Mae Gibson: FBI*, the fact-based story of the first black female FBI agent. After gaining recognition for her work in a number of TV dramas, including *The Women of Brewster Place* (1990), she won an Emmy Award and international acclaim for her starring performance in *The Josephine Baker Story* in 1991. Whitfield subsequently split her efforts between TV and film, doing particularly strong work in Kasi Lemmons' *Eve's Bayou* (1997). In 1999 she was nominated for an NAACP Image Award for her work in *Oprah Winfrey Presents: The Wedding*. She has built a seemingly endless gallery of dramatic women, ranging from Brandi Web in *A Thin Line between Love and Hate* (1996) to her role in *The Women* (2008), a remake of George Cukor's film (1939) which was based on the play by Clare Booth Luce. She is a well-known presence on the Lifetime cable network and as a guest on many other television channels.

GD: Who were some of your early influences?

LW: I was always very happy whenever I could see Dorothy Dandridge in something. She was so beautiful; so effervescent. Diana Sands I loved. When I saw her in *Hospital*, which was a film, she was the only . . . she and Roscoe Brown were the only black people in this movie. She was just so incredibly wonderful. [. . .] I really related to her. And Ruby Dee was another. But kind of . . . that came a little bit later. But I really only had pretty much white people to watch. And I didn't think about like, "I'm watching white people." I just thought, "Oh, I could do this, too." It didn't occur to me until . . . Glenda, it didn't occur to me, even with all we were doing, honey . . . "Power to the People" stuff . . . It never occurred to me that when I went to Hollywood that I would be limited in what I could do.

GD: What role has race played in the evolution of your career? And has gender impacted on the types of roles you may have been offered or may not have been offered?

LW: Well, I come from a really interesting place, I think, because I think that the African diaspora, and more particularly African-American people, are the most fabulous people walking the earth. So I . . . it's hard for me to talk about this because so often we talk about it from the victim place; a place of not getting our 40 acres and a mule and all that. But the . . . out of necessity and need and misfortune, we have metamorphosed into a people that make the world more interesting to be in. We always add a little cayenne pepper to the circumstance, you know, the acid to the alkaline. And we're just beginning to explore African–American women now. So that is like a great advantage for me. What has for me been unpleasant about the play of race within the realm of my work is the limitations of other people's consciousness about who we are. I truly think sometimes it is a genuine like partial lobotomy about some things. It is a genuine misconception and misunderstanding of what is going on here. Even though this country would be so boring were we not here.

GD: What's the position of black theater in this country today? Is there anything like a black theater movement?

LW: No. Not that I know of. It is very, very, very sad.

S. Epatha Merkerson: Homegirl Keeping it Real

"When I moved to New York, I started making my living as an actor and that's what I have done. From that time on, I have done nothing else."

When Benjamin Bratt accepted his Emmy Award for best actor in a dramatic series (*Law & Order*), he thanked S. Epatha Merkerson by saying "She keeps it real." Epatha's personal approach to fashion puts comfort before style. Her hair is natural, her conversation is down to earth and her values are decidedly un-Hollywood. She maintains close ties with her friends from the early struggling days in the business and is still a Harlem homegirl in her heart.

Born in Saginaw, Michigan, Epatha started her theatrical training in children's theater and dance. She entered New York theater in the 1980s toward the end of the *for colored girls* tour and has not been out of work since. She has been nominated for numerous awards for her role as Lt. Anita Van Buren in *Law & Order*, including the Emmy, Image, and Screen Actor Guild Awards. In 2005 she was awarded the SAG, Golden Globe, Emmy, and NAACP Awards for her appearance in Reuben Santiago-Hudson's *Lackawanna Blues*, a coming-of-age story set in New York in the 1950s and 1960s with Merkerson in the role of Rachel "Nanny" Crosby, who runs a boarding house. In her colorful band of boarders, there are drylongso people, any one of whom could be said to embody the characters encountered in this book: Nanny herself is a migrant from a tobacco farm in Virginia; and the cast includes the war veteran, the radical race man, the Cab Calloway type musician played by Mos' Def, the numbers runner, the professional boxer, and the hairdresser, all of whom have their influence on the young storyteller. The plot examines the painful impact of integration on what had been a self-contained black community.

GD: Who were some of your early influences?

EM: Because when we were coming up, turning on the TV and seeing somebody black was a wonderful thing. And anytime Ruby . . . or you'd see a movie, Dorothy Dandridge or Hattie McDaniels . . . it was just a wonderful thing. Diahann Carroll when she had her TV show. Greg Morris on *Mission Impossible*. You know, anytime there were black folks on TV, especially when I was coming up . . . that's what we wanted to see. So I have to say that there's a group of those actors who were very influential and just making me feel good about being a Colored woman. And then years, years later I did *God's Trombones* with Ossie [Davis] and Theresa Merritt and Al Freeman, Jr. And Tremain Hawkins was our vocalist. And after the show every night, we would all congregate in the bar. And at the time, Brock Peters was there doing *Driving Miss Daisy* so he joined us. And there was me, with all of them. Just listening . . . and there was something that was so incredible about it all, too. Because there was Brock and there was Ossie and Al and Theresa. People I had known about for years and years and there I was sitting in their company; working on the very stage with them. And realizing how important they were to me being the person that I am; to my development as just a human being, and a prideful human being. I remember telling Ossie that walking to the elevator; how I had such a sense of accomplishment and pride that I could not only know who you are and have watched you for years, but then to be on the same stage with you and be able to sit and talk with you.

GD: What was New York like when you first arrived?

EM: [. . .] I don't have a problem with my blackness and I'm not going to allow anyone to make me think less of what our history is or who I am. So I looked forward to coming to New York because I knew there was a Negro Ensemble Company here. I knew there were small black theaters around. That if I'm going to do this, let me do this in the context where there is some honesty going on here. And that's what I found. You know, I did Zake's [Ntozake Shange's] play, Richard Wesley, and a lot of new plays, musicals and things, with mostly black folk. Very rare. I don't even remember if I had done any plays with white people.

So when I moved to New York, I really moved there to see if this was a career that would be feasible for me to do. And the most fortunate thing that happened to me was after my second month . . . third month there, I got cast in the last leg of the first national tour of *for colored girls*. So I was out with Barbara, Alston, Yvette Hawkins, Trazana Beverly. It was this whole group of sisters which I needed to be around. LaTonya was in that group. LaTonya Richardson. It was also an affirming moment because I was around a lot of black women . . . And so there was Hazel Bryant and somebody else and somebody . . . you know, everywhere you went . . . Frederick Douglass Center, Perry Street. I mean, people were just . . . Woodie . . . You know, I was telling someone now I really don't know what to tell young folks coming into New York. Because it's highly competitive now because there are so few opportunities . . . And that's why whenever anybody asks me, as a young person, what they should do, I say, "You should read." Because in books your mind will go anywhere with the stories. You are . . . it is you who are creating the visual . . . even though they've written it down, you see it. You see the color. You see the texture of the fabric that they're talking about. You see the height, even though they've given you the height. You know, "She was broad. She had nappy hair." You see the color, the deepness of the color. That is what, to me, makes an interesting actor on stage is you can see that they have imagined. And they continue to imagine.

Giancarlo Esposito: The Fecund Forest

"The movies are fun and make me money. The theater, however, is where I have my roots."

In 1980, playing the role of Zooman in Charles Fuller's *Zooman and the Sign*, Giancarlo Esposito burst onto the stage as beautiful as the sunrise and began to spew the most unbelievable invective. He held us captive for the next two hours. His portrayal of the sociopathic teen hoodlum won him rave reviews and both the Obie and Theater World Awards. Later roles include "Buggin Out," the motor-mouthed B-boy in Spike Lee's *Do the Right Thing*, and Esteban, the hypnotic sexy cobra of a pimp in the film *Fresh*. Over his long career – he made his Broadway debut at the age of 11 – the critics have adored Giancarlo Esposito. Listen to some things they say: his characters are often "the flashpoint for confrontation," "such a pro, he's often taken for granted;"

"He inhabits his characters so comfortably that we think he can't simply be creating a character – he must be drawing on himself, perhaps even leaning on himself;" "a character actor with leading man charisma." "Even in walk-ons he holds the screen by right;" "a persona glowing like burning coals;" he "seems to carry with him deep reserves of intensity that provide juice for the roles he plays." Born in Copenhagen to an Italian father and an African American mother, Giancarlo lived in Naples, Hamburg, and Rome with his parents and younger brother until the family settled in New York when he was five years old.

GC: But (one day) I saw this ad in *Show Business* and *Backstage*. And I saw the ad for Charles Fuller's *Soldier Story*, but what captured my attention was the Negro Ensemble Company. And all my life I've wanted a home and had never thought of an acting company. Then I thought, "This is perfect." So I went and auditioned for Douglas Turner Ward and I got very excited because I thought this play [*Zooman and the Sign*] was really special. I had to go back for at least five call backs for Douglas, and I knew that I was doing quite well in the process. I had a sense of it, but I had no idea. I remember Douglas saying to me, you know what really nailed the audition is that you have the face of an angel [*laughs*]. And I just went to work.

GD: What was New York like in those days?

GC: In those days, New York was a very interesting place. Of course, it had a little more edge around that 42nd, 43rd Street area; in that theater district. It was very, very edgy and very exciting at that time because you did have the smaller companies: NEC, Henry Street and Roger Furman who still had his theater, Hazel Bryant's RACCA [Richard Allen Cultural Center]. And you could always work. And it seemed like people were friendlier at that time. People really seemed to go to the theater. It was very much alive. I fell in love with New York and I just rode a bicycle from audition to audition, to the theater and back home and it was a very comfortable world for me. I didn't mind eating brown rice and soup and being poor. Not at all.

GD: Did you have a sense of a revolutionary change in the air in these times we're talking about . . . the late '70s, early '80s? Before Hazel Bryant died; before Roger Furman died or Doug lost his space?

GC: Yeah. You know . . . I did. And I was still young so I didn't really . . . I hadn't really yet investigated the history that went before me, but started to get very interested in the older actors and knowing where they came from and where they were going and also had a lot of jealousy because I realized that they were part of a world that was quickly being lost. Because, as I say, I always wanted a home. And one of the things that really destroyed me was at NEC. I'm thinking maybe they're still a company; maybe they'll come back to being a company. I wanted to be a part of that company. So all the older fellows,

Robert Hooks . . . .. all the guys who started all that Adolph Caesar, you know, who I got really close to. Rosalind Cash. You know, it's like these people did it because they loved it. It's really interesting because I never equated acting with being political until probably right around that time. And that was what really made me decide I didn't want to be the entertainment anymore. I really wanted to have to go into a deeper place and have a sense of who I was through my work, but have a sense that it moved people in a certain direction. And that was really important to me.

GD: Well, you talked a little bit about who your friends were in those days. Is there anybody else you would like to mention?

GC: You know, at that time I got kind of close to Charles Fuller. I thought that there was a big change happening with African American writers. And I felt like they were really coming into their own, and I felt like they were discovering a new way of expressing their stories that was so far out of the sort of commercial world that it had to be truth. You know, writers like Larry Neal and Amiri Baraka who just . . . They were really inspiring to me. And writers who you could actually talk to; who you could work with; who were not just saying, "Here, do my play." But they were there to solve the problems of the play. I love Charles Fuller for that reason.

GD: Were there other actors whose work you admire and were influenced by in terms of what I call the first generation, artists like Paul Robeson, Sidney Poitier, Harry Belafonte, and Ossie Davis. So if you could talk about that continuum a little bit?

GC: I was just going to mention Paul Robeson because he was such a brilliant, brilliant artist; really so committed to what he believed in and suffered for that as well. Of course, the person I love the most was Sidney because of what he . . . his characters were so full and had such meaning and such grace. I don't think there will ever be another. Sidney had that great silence; stillness that he allowed to come through his work. As well as Harry. Harry had . . . was a little more musical, he had a different kind of presence. Just the way he looked . . . that was sort of not allowed [*laughs*] for us. Ivan Dixon . . . another one. I don't know if it's the time that they came from, but it was a great sense of who they were. Absolutely uncompromised. And that to me translates as a great amount of strength in the society that we lived in at that time. I think we're so in danger of losing not only our oral history, but our written history through plays [because of] our fascination with the entertainment industry as it affects us in a commercial way. And I think for us as African Americans, we are dangerously close to losing . . . to losing our stories. And I'll tell you why I think it is. We have been so focused on assimilating; on being part of this whole machine and very uncomfortable with being able to see ourselves for who we are, that we're just doing what's mundane.

Vondie Curtis-Hall: Captain Prince Runs the Show

"I was always of the mind that one didn't have to be a starving artist to be a good artist."

I interviewed Vondie Curtis-Hall at the office of his production company, Motor City, on the Fox Studio lot in Los Angeles. Vondie arrives shattering the quiet. He seems to have been dropped from the sky via a *deus ex machina*, perhaps the helicopter from which he whipped Verona into shape as Captain Prince in Baz Luhrman's filmed version of *Romeo and Juliet* (1996). He swooped down from his successful Hollywood career, cell phone to his ear, spouting poetry which to my ear might as well have been in iambic pentameters: "I don't mean to come in here like Hollywood," he said, and then settled down for a calm, gracious interview. Born and raised in Detroit, Curtis-Hall trained as a musician at the Juilliard School, New York. His career has encompassed living theater (both musicals and dramas), television, and film. He plays the guitar, dances, and sings with the soulfulness of a Motown star. He was in the original cast of the Broadway hit *Dreamgirls*, and performed to rave reviews (with Ben Harney) in the American Place Theatre production of Vincent D. Smith's *Williams and Walker*. In film he has been seen in such diverse roles as Lloyd Price in *Don King: Only in America*, Miguel Montoya in *Mambo Kings*, and Sugar LeDoux in *Passion Fish*. In television he was nominated for an Emmy Award for outstanding guest actor on *ER*. Television audiences may be most familiar with him as Dr. Dennis Hancock on *Chicago Hope*. Married to Kasi Lemmons, director of *Eve's Bayou* and a star in *Silence of the Lambs*, he is now writing and directing his own films.

VCH: During that whole time . . . it's '86 or so like that . . . I saw *She's Got to Have it*. Spike's movie. And that really sort of inspired me to want to become a film maker. So the seed was sort of planted to become a film maker. But meanwhile, you know, my day job and what people knew me for was as an actor. So of course I kept acting and kept studying. That year I joined the Black Film Makers Foundation and I met Spike [Lee]. And Robert Townsend's picture had just come out, *Hollywood Shuffle*. And then Keenan [Ivory Wayans] made his movie [*I'm Gonna Git You Sucka*].

GD: Could we talk just a little bit more about the stage work? . . . about *Williams and Walker*? Any dramas that you might have done?

VCH: Yeah, let's see, I did the 25th anniversary of *A Raisin in the Sun* at the Roundabout Theater. I did some plays at the Negro Ensemble Company. I did *The War Party*, which was [a play] by Leslie Lee.

GD: But I wanted to ask you if you had a sense that there was a sense of revolutionary change in the air in the '80s? Or was it already a memory from the '70s?

VCH: Well, you know . . . I had a bunch of hope. I think early on in the '80s there was a bit of residue that stole momentum from the '70s. I think that was carrying over, though it was fading in the early '80s. And the success of the *Bubbling Brown Sugars* and The *Wizzes* and things like that, in terms of plays, and of course the Negro Ensemble Company you know, had a lot of success. And by the '80s the climate and Reagan and the whole thing really started chipping away at that. Though there was still some residual hope and feeling, the reality was that people really started getting into trouble. Really . . . the black musical started to fade to a point and, of course, cinema, there was a whole period there after the black exploitation period where there was nobody on screen. So I think there was an element of hope, but I think people were kind of clinging to the last vestiges of the '70s heyday.

GD: Okay. Now let's go back and look at the groundbreakers. Are you influenced by or do you especially admire first generation African Americans? I call the first generation Paul Robeson, Bert Williams, Lena Horne, Dorothy Dandridge, Ossie Davis, Diahann Carroll, Ruby Dee, Sidney Poitier, Harry Belafonte. I just want to know about your relationship to them.

VCH: Sidney Poitier was like a hero to me. He was like the guy. He was like a god. And I mean, just, *A Raisin in the Sun* and through his work with *In the Heat of the Night*, and just all his movies. I just thought he was the brother. So . . . but you know later in learning about Bert Williams and George Walker and [. . .] the Eubie Blakes and Paul Robesons . . . certainly the achievements and accomplishments that sort of paved the way for the Poitiers. It was just enormous. And the odds and the sort of crazy racism that they dealt with. Paul Robeson had to head to Europe. Like James Baldwin . . . everybody's got to bail. "I've got to get out of here." And everybody had their own struggle. I'm so happy now that in order to be . . . once you're a successful black person you can still marry and be and have black lovers and it's cool. I mean, it's okay now. I mean, just think about the days when, if you had any sort of notoriety, you were with a white person. When you married, you just didn't . . . it was like almost you couldn't move up in the system in Hollywood or something without like a white person on your arm. Yeah. I'm so happy that black folks can be movie stars and athletes or what have you and then the status symbol is not a white person. The status symbol is still having somebody of your own race with you as your partner.

Joe Morton: Morton the Magician Trades in Miracles

"The black community at large reacts to those roles [that I play] very strongly. It gives them pride, it gives them honor. They know I'm not going to do something that will make them ashamed."

Joe Morton is a magician, by avocation and in spirit. In *Honky Tonk Nights* (Broadway, 1986), about a black vaudeville company, he learned how to tap dance, how to do magic tricks, how to juggle, how to ride a unicycle, how to spin plates. In his life, he has taught himself illusionary magic for his pleasure. In his career, he trades in miracles for those of others. Like a wizard, he has sidestepped the landmines of stereotype and type-casting. Like an old-world alchemist, he has transformed the handsome, dignified asexual character after being portrayed by Sidney Poitier into a chameleon for the millennium. Joe walked into our consciousness on the three toes of the sweet, silent *Brother from another Planet* (1984), John Sayles's film about an escaped slave who lands up in fairly surreal circumstances in Harlem.

Joe was an only child and army brat who spent his early childhood on US bases in Europe and Asia. His wide-ranging roles have garnered him numerous awards, among them the Theatre World Award. He has also been nominated for the Tony Award (for *Raisin*), and for the NAACP Image Award, both for *Equal Justice* and for his role as a mounted policeman in *Tribeca*, Fox Television's anthology series, produced by Robert De Niro. Joe Morton, the magician, says: "If you want someone who is sort of still, has a bit of an edge, is older, you get Morgan Freeman. If you want someone who can carry a gun and still play a father, you get Danny Glover. My category is that guy who happens to be black" – witness his portrayal of the scientist Miles Dyson in *Terminator 2* (1991).

JM: I came to New York in 1968. In 1968, I was actually leaving school to come in to do what I thought was going to be this classical theater sojourn . . . to do Shakespeare and the Greeks. And as I found out, there wasn't a lot available for Black actors to do Shakespeare, other than the Public Theater because of Shakespeare in the Park. Then I think things changed around the '70s. Because I remember in the late '60s there were things like *Big Time Buck White, Jimmy Shine* . . . those kind of plays were beginning to happen . . . a lot of sort of agit-prop-type plays, but on kind of a really modern, contemporary scale. You know, Richard Wesley . . . all these playwrights . . . Charles Gordone and all these guys were writing these incredibly wonderful plays, and it was the favorite flavor for several years. So New York theater was sort of flourishing. There were any number of different choices in terms of what you could do, which sort of came to a rapid end, interestingly enough, in the '80s, when you're then dealing with, "How much money can I make?" At that point, Black theater was no longer the thing and the English theater, especially the Stoppard plays and those things became the thing. And even at the Public Theater, which was always sort of representational of the cutting edge, was sort of then beginning to shift. Joe [Papp] was becoming more of a showman and less of an entrepreneur. Joe was sort of becoming more of, "It's my show," kind of thing. It was sort of an interesting shift. Now that's just in terms of Black theater.

GD: Are you influenced by or do you especially admire any of the first generation of African American performers?

JM: Well, Charles Gilpin. And Robeson as well. In both those cases, you have two gentlemen who, especially Paul Robeson, you have a man who is not only looked on as this quintessential performer, actor, singer, but his politics as well are things that young African Americans sort of need to pay attention to in terms of what he was willing to give up in order to hold onto what was important to him. You know, the one man I've been trying for the last several years to work with is Harry Belafonte. I think Harry Belafonte is an incredible actor as well as the performer that he is as a singer. But whenever I've seen him act, and this goes back to that movie where he's one of two people on the planet after a nuclear holocaust. He also did a film called *An Angel Named Levine* with Zero Mostel. I mean, he's done some incredible acting work. And his history actually was that when he and Sidney went to school, it was Harry who was the actor, and not Sidney. And the way that worked is, Harry was doing a play. His father got ill. Sidney was the standby. Harry couldn't go on. Sidney went on. Boom! And not only is the rest history. But Harry was so disillusioned with Hollywood, he would get scripts first, be disgusted with them and hand them to Sidney, one of which was *Lilies of the Field.* But he did not want to do a movie where he was this Black man working for these white nuns. He just couldn't figure it. And I just have always admired that about him and admired who he is as a political person. Who he is as a singer. I mean, he and I have had several wonderful conversations. He's someone that I really, really look up to and hope to direct one day.

Clifton Powell: Black is Beautiful

"Yo, I want to be in a f***king play."

Clifton Powell's role as Chauncy in John Singleton's *Menace II Society* (1993) has made it impossible for him to walk anywhere in public without being hailed by the character's name. People of all ages know him and love to stop and shoot the breeze. He credits his experience with Workshops for Careers in the Arts in Washington, DC, for having saved his life and starting him down the long path to a successful career. Though he had no clear idea of what acting entailed, one day he walked into Workshops and announced "Yo, I want to be in a f***king play." It was there at the age of 16 that he first learned the meaning behind the phrase "Black is beautiful." A teacher showed him a photograph of an African warrior and told him that the man looked like him – ebony of skin and fierce of stance. It was a revolutionary notion for the young gang banger (then called "block boys"). It transformed his view of himself and guides the way in which he has continued to live his life. Threatened with being pigeon-holed as the angry Black man in film after film, he purposefully seeks out opportunities which will showcase his broad range as an actor. His efforts have paid off: He was cast as Martin Luther King, Jr., in *Selma, Lord, Selma* (1999), and has also appeared in such blockbusters as *Phantoms* (1998) and in such diverse showcases as *Buffalo Soldiers* (1997), *Why Do Fools Fall in Love* (1998), and in Eddie Murphy's *Norbit* (2007). His high cheekbones and flashing eyes invariably rivet the viewer. Powell played the role of Ray Charles' manager in the Oscar-nominated biopic, *Ray* (2004). During our interview he recalled his first meeting with Douglas Turner Ward, artistic director of the NEC.

CP: Auditioning for Doug is really very tough because he never looks up at you. He has his cue cards and he's listening. And at first, I was thrown off. I was like, "Who is this guy? Who does he think he is?" You know. But from the days of Workshops and going up to New York and seeing *The River Niger* on Broadway with Charlie Brown, I just said, "You've got to go to NEC."

GD: What year was that that you did *Zooman* at Crossroads [Theatre Company in New Brunswick, New Jersey]?

CP: I think it was . . . it had to be around 1984 or '85. And then after *Zooman*, I did *Langston*, and I did . . . right in there *The Hooch* with Kevin Hooks; Kevin Hooks' first stage piece. It was an army piece. Yeah. Down at the Henry Street Settlement House. And so all those plays, *Zooman, Langston, The Hooch*, and then finally going out on the road with [Richard Wesley's] *The Mighty Gents* and played "Braxton" against Ving Raimes . . . Ving played "Frankie." It was just brilliant, you know? And Braxton, as you know, was this cold-blooded businessman who was a killer, who had graduated from the neighborhood. So I came out and he was very seductive and he was very sharp. And what I try to do every night in anything that I've done is try to find new things every night, because I think the lazy actor falls into a trap of not working hard every night. So by the time I got to The *Mighty Gents*, I felt like I was really an actor; really in tune to my instrument. And I had made a complete transition.

GD: So that was when you kind of hit your stride as an actor. Did you make a conscious decision to work only in films rather than theater? Of course, you still do both. Let's talk about that transition and maybe *House Party* or *Menace to Society*, talk about that a little bit.

CP: Okay. Well, I think what happened in New York, in the late '80s, was everything dried up. NEC dried up. The money dried up. And everybody began to look toward California to come out and just really make a living. And we didn't come out here to be stars. Sam[uel L. Jackson], Angela [Basset], Vondie, Ving, myself; any of us. We came out here to really just continue to do our work, you know. Because in New York we did it because we loved it. I mean, we didn't make a lot of money. I mean, my first play at Crossroads, I made $80 a week. And *Langston* was such a big piece and we were changing it every day, and I was playing a lead, and I had anxiety. So I said, "Instead of going home tonight, I'd better stay here all night long and study." So I spent the night in the theater. You know, that's because you love it. And so when we got out here, you come out here and you realize in the early years out here I had no clue what I was doing. All I knew is what I knew from back East. So if they asked for a fireman or army guy or gangster, I came in in full dress. So for *A Tour of Duty*, I came in in full army dress. And the guy said, "You're not from here, are you?" I said, "No, sir." He said, "Thank you for being so prepared." So, being prepared was just my calling card. So when I first got out here, I saw the Hughes Brothers, who I worked with their uncle back at NYU. So I saw them at a beach party when I first got out here and I was like, "Man! I just saw you guys a couple of weeks ago!" They said, "Well, what are you doing?" I said, "I'm an actor, man. I'm an actor." They said, "Well, what do you want to do?" I said, "Put me in a movie . . . whatever." They said, "Well, we're shooting a movie called *House Party*." And these guys put me in *House Party* sight unseen; never seen my work. And gave me a week . . . I made like $400 a day. I was like, "Man, this is a lot of money." So again, it wasn't thinking of stardom. It was just, "How can I make a living and keep doing my work?" And after that . . . and I think the biggest thing is nobody really explained to me what Hollywood protocol was. So I didn't come out thinking of what kind of image I should have or how I should address people, or how I should dress, or how I should act at this party. We just didn't know any of that. We just came with the same spirit that we had from DC; from New York, of helping each other.

Debbie Allen: Redbird Flies by the Light of the Moon

"We'd drag my mother's dirty clothes out into the back and jump right into the clothes. So I was back there flying and everything."

Debbie Allen and her sister Phylicia Ayers-Allen Rashad (interviewed next) seem to live enchanted lives. They grew up in Houston, Texas, raised by a dentist and a poet. They each credit their mother, Vivian Ayers-Allen, for their talent and success, and also bask in the glowing admiration of their father, Dr. Andrew Allen. They have a production company to develop new work which they call Dr. Allen's Daughters (DAD). Their mother surrounded them with books, music, and art. She instilled in them a love for art, culture, and learning from an early age. Both sisters speak of the year they spent with their mother in Mexico as a defining experience. Both have achieved enormous success: Phylicia as a respected, even beloved, actor of television and the stage; and Debbie as a force of nature. They are uncommonly close and congenial rivals.

Debbie Allen does it all and has it all. She acts, dances, directs, choreographs, writes, and produces. She has a high profile that almost defies description. Her tasks have ranged from starring as Charity in *Sweet Charity* and Beneatha in *Raisin* (both on Broadway), choreographing not only the Academy Awards but the breakthrough television show *Fame*, to producing and directing the *Cosby Show* spin-off *A Different World*. Having finally succeeded in getting the film version of Steven Spielberg's *Amistad* produced in 1977 (after years of effort), she went on to perform in a box-office-breaking show by Karen Jones, *Harriet's Reno* (about Harriet Tubman). Her current plans include directing the all-African American version of Tennessee Williams's *Cat on a Hot Tin Roof* for Broadway. On any given day, she has at least 15 balls in the air. You never see her out of breath and she certainly never drops one of those balls. For the interview, I met Debbie in her dressing room at the Kennedy Center in Washington, DC, during a break from rehearsal of her annual children's show.

GD: What took you from Washington to New York?

DA: Louis Johnson had an opening in *Purlie* [1981]. This was a musical that had starred Melba Moore and was soon to close on Broadway and go on the road. So I went up there, auditioned and sang with my little tambourine and got the part. And I met George Faison the first week I came there. George Faison was the hottest young choreographer in all of New York City. He had just recently left Alvin Ailey and he choreographed a piece called *Suite Otis*, which was about Otis Redding. And he had choreographed a piece called *Slaves*, where he went all the way back through the middle passage. You know, we're just catching up to that now. This was what? [more than] 25 years ago. And then I performed with George. I quit *Purlie* and joined his company and became a true gypsy in the dance world. And this was great because I had learned a lot at Howard University how to do it for ourselves. We knew how to paint the theater, clean the seats, sell the tickets, make the costumes, do the lighting. And so with George that's what we did. He could sew like nobody . . . I've never seen a man who could sew like him. He made those dance costumes and we'd stay up all night and oohh . . . one week we'd perform at Lincoln Center. The next week we'd be somewhere in a church basement. You know, one week we'd make $50 and the next week we'd make $250. The next week could make nothing. But we just stayed together. But we were supposedly on our own and Phylicia started getting work on Broadway. She was in that show, *Ain't Supposed to Die* [Melvin Van Peebles, 1971]. She was part of the Negro Ensemble, which was great. But we weren't making any money. So I had to go . . . I had to leave the dance company and go back to Broadway and I joined a show called *Raisin*, a musical of *Raisin in the Sun*. So that was the beginning. And then Broadway, I just stayed . . . I kept working in the Broadway theater and musical theater. I played Beneatha for two years, I think. Yes. I took a lot of slapping from Virginia Capers. She tried to take my head off! Yeah, we had come out of the incredible early '70s where Black is Beautiful and Black Power became the cornerstone of all of our communities, whether you wanted it to be or not; whether you were bougie and very upper middle class and you were threatened by that, everybody was affected. All of us; all the young kids who had been anywhere near a school or anywhere living and breathing, joined this movement. And it was kind of like self-indoctrination into self-esteem and self-empowerment. So coming out of that was a lot of poetry. It was a Renaissance. No one's ever talked about it . . . I mean, we talk about the Harlem Renaissance. But there was a Renaissance in the '70s. It was an awakening of black consciousness, which was not only just historic, but it was also futuristic. Sun Ra catapulting us into ourselves and who we are to become, and waken up. It was like a big, old wake-up call. So by the time I got to New York, and there was so much black theater going on . . . LaMama, Woodie King, Hazel Bryant, Billie Holiday Theatre in Brooklyn. Stuff in Jersey that I didn't even . . . I didn't quite get to Jersey, but I spent a lot of time at Woodie King and the Billie Holiday. We were doing wonderful theater; theater that was cutting edge kind of revisionism, revival . . . I played Anna Lucasta. That was great. I did the first salsa/soul musical that still has yet to be repeated. I did this with Joe Papp in his summer festival. We did a show called *Mondongo*, which is called the intestine of the pig and what it is basically [is] that oneness of the black people in America and the black people in Latin American countries. They were the same. The drum was the unifying force. That's when we got into the Yemanya and Yaweh . . . We started hearing . . . we didn't know all of these religions. We started getting a sense of what that was and Yoruba. What was all of that? And what was the voodoo? It was the vodoun, which was really what was left of our purest African religions. And some of it . . . the purest was out of Cuba. I wanted so badly to go to Cuba, but this was not a politically correct time; still not. So we did some fascinating work. I remember doing a piece with Derek Walcott called *Ti-jean and his Brothers*. And this was like reinventing folklore. It was out of the Caribbean. But you know, black people in America . . . at this point we had kind of gone around a full circle with not embracing our folklore. You know, dispelling ourselves from Aunt Jemima and Uncle Remus and Brer Rabbit. You know, and those should have been our heroes. You know, Little Black Sambo. They should have been our heroes. So we were empowered. I had the biggest Afro, child. My Daddy was like, "Oh, God no! Jesus, please have mercy!" It was a wonderful time.

GD: I want to talk about if race and gender have played a role in the evolution of your career.

DA: Absolutely. Being a black person and a woman, two very challenging and empowering facts of my life. As a black person certainly denial of certain opportunities for such a long time. But at the same time, knowing that . . . learning early on that I had to reach beyond those obvious routes to get to wherever I wanted to go, which makes me more of an explorer, which has made me more of an adventurer, which has made me try to get higher on the mountain so I can see farther away where I might want to go. Being a woman has been actually very tricky because there is a side of being a woman that allows you to do things, as a black person, that men are not. It allows you to challenge people in ways that black men are not even getting close to be able to; to raise those issues. But at the same time, being a woman, I have learned, has been I guess what some people would call a handicap. For me, it is probably the most empowering part of myself, the woman part. Yes. Women have pockets. That's something I learned from my mother.

GD: Do you have any advice for the up and coming?

DA: Up and coming? Honey, stay up and stay coming! Come and stay up. Run. Work hard. Sweat. Study. Study. Study. Study. Read. Read. Educate yourself. Find out what pushes your buttons. And go with that because when you're passionate about something, you can really make it happen. That's the only way to really make it happen.

Phylicia Rashad: Holy Actor

"And I felt totally comfortable, just talking to the light all night long; just talking to the light."

As the sister of Debbie Allen (see above), Phylicia Rashad shared the same childhood background. Between 1984 and 1992, she played a character who transformed the image of the African American mother on television: most people think Phylicia really is Claire Huxtable of *Cosby Show* fame. She was an attractive, smart, working professional who balanced her career with the challenges of presiding over a large brood (Dr. Huxtable included). When talking to her, however, I realized at once that she is not Claire Huxtable at all. She is all that Claire is, but much, much more. She seems younger in person than even the Claire of 1984. She glows from an inner light. Having worked as a singer/dancer on Broadway as early as *The Wiz* (1978), she went on to perform in many other shows. She attributes her success and focus as an actor to her discovery of the practice of meditation around the mid-1980s. She speaks about the power of spirituality with an eloquence that almost approaches rapture. I went to Atlanta to see Phylicia in the title role of Euripides' *Medea* at the Alliance Theater. I interviewed her the next day on the front porch of her borrowed, beige brick, white-columned house. As we talked, eating watermelon, we seemed to be in a world apart from the busy street outside. Phylicia can't stand dirt. She cleaned the large round table thoroughly before we ate, all the while mesmerizing me with tales of her search for Medea.

GD: Can we focus on how you prepared for Medea, the role in which you're currently appearing the Alliance Theater here in Atlanta?

PR: For one, you know as a drama student, when you read Euripides; when you read *Medea*, there's not really a real background on her. You understand that she lived in the land of the Golden Fleece; that she betrayed her country and her father to come with Jason to help him obtain the Fleece. [. . .] She's responsible for the killing of her brother and she has cut his body up in many pieces and thrown it into the ocean so that the soldiers who were following them in pursuit had to stop to gather the body parts to bury them properly. All right? All of this is Medea. And then you understand that she has killed King Pelias, but you don't understand how she did it. Then we see, in the course of the play at the end of the play, that she kills her sons . . . in Euripides' play. Well, see, the thing about Euripides' play is that we're coming in at the end of the action. By the time we get there, the love affair is over. All that is done. All that is a thing of the past. And we don't quite understand the fullness of the personalities involved because it is not inherent in the text. So when I began to read books and essays about Medea, the first thing that was coming up in my mind and for me to see was, first of all, it was a big deal not to be Greek. The Greeks were the original cultural snobs. And when you look at that Greek culture, you can understand Eurocentricity in its fullness. It began right there. So when I started reading about Medea . . . She is a descendant of the Sun. She is the Sun's granddaughter. Well now, that's a deep thing because when we speak of the Sun, we are speaking of radiant energy that is burning all the time; that is giving life and energy and force and light all the time on the ignorant as well as the wise. On the good as well as the bad . . . we are talking about the giver and sustainer of life. As a young girl, Medea was schooled in the Temple of Hecate. Hecate is the goddess. And they're calling her a sorceress and they're calling her a witch. And as I kept digging and digging and digging, what it turns out is that Hecate, they call her "the goddess of magic and sorcery," that's what the Europeans . . . the Greeks say. She was the goddess of healing arts. Medea was a high priestess in the Temple of Hecate. When Jason came to Kolchis, Medea was virgin high priestess in the Temple of Hecate. She had spent her life in the temple and her attainment was such that people in her country did not dare look her in the face. Not because she was evil, but for the same reason you don't go looking the Sun in the face, because of that power. So I was reading about these things and I said, "Oh, I begin to see," because we're coming in at the end of the play. So I have to see what happened before. Okay, now let me look at who Jason was. Let me find out about him. Jason was reared by Kylem. Now who was Kylem? A centaur . . . half man and half horse . . . This is who reared Jason; half man and half horse. Now can you imagine what that was like? Here he comes with muscles . . . I have it in my mind . . . He's a stallion, baby! With hair streaming and skin gleaming . . . she had never seen nothing like that! She thought, when she looked at him, she thought she was seeing a god. And when he came and she looked at him and saw him, desire arose within her. Well, yoga tells you that desire [can be] the enemy of the soul, because desire brings about the downfall because when you desire something and you don't get it, anger comes. And when anger comes you are blinded. You can't see the truth anymore. Desire is the thing that must be watched. So I was using things that I had to learn from the practice of meditation. How could you attempt this role without this research?

Food for Further Thought

When I interviewed the actors in this chapter, I was especially interested in how they approached acting as a craft with an identifiable set of skills. Some of the questions I asked them are:

What was your training as an actor?
Can acting be taught?
What are the primary skills an actor needs?
Do you work for objectives? To overcome obstacles?
Do you find value in improvisation?
How do you use your own personal experience to draw a character?
Do you adhere to any one method in preparing for a character?
Do you prepare by putting anything down on paper?
How do you work when you're rehearsing?
Do you ever employ emotional memory?
How do you find the truth, the reality of characters who are not sympathetic, such as (for example) Zooman in Charles Fuller's *Zooman and the Sign?*
What are the differences you found in acting for stage and movies?
What do you seek or admire in a director?

How would you answer these questions yourself?

Read newspapers and magazines to find out the range of roles the actors you most admire are now choosing.

Among the many books that could be highly recommended further reading, I would point you toward Donald Bogle's *Brown Sugar (1980)* and *Blacks in American Films and Television* (1988); *Black Magic* (1967) by Langston Hughes and Milton Meltzer. There are also countless biographies and autobiographies by artists ranging from Sidney Poitier, Ethel Waters, Eartha Kitt, and Dorothy Dandridge, to Ruby Dee and Ossie Davis. Choose the ones that appeal to you most.

9 A Presence of Ancestry
I Believe I Can Fly

I believe I can fly
I believe I can touch the sky.

(Traditional)

Your crown has already been purchased. All you have to do is put it on and wear it.

(Black folk saying)

In his book *The Past as Present in the Drama of August Wilson* (2004), Harry Elam quotes James Baldwin: "If history were past, history wouldn't matter. History is the present . . . You and I are history. We carry our history. We act our history (Elam, xi)." This final chapter looks at some of the ways the cultural history explored in this book is playing out in the present landscape of black theater. Fifty years after Emancipation, the younger generations were eager to distance themselves from the shame and humiliation of slavery, going so far as to challenge their ethnic designation. Articles in the press argued whether they should call themselves Colored, Ethiopian, Black, African, or Negro. In this book, depending on the context, I have called the people who could not fly the enslaved, Colored, Negro, Aframerican, New Negro, Afro-American, and Black. Many people now use the terms African American and Black interchangeably. What is important here is not what names to use, but to understand that the changing designations have described a search for Iwa, a way to express an ever-evolving inner life.

Toward the end of the 1950s a young playwright named Lorraine Hansberry came to prominence. In her own way, Lorraine Hansberry, before Angela Davis, was a young soldier for the revolution. Ms. Hansberry walked through a door opened for her by Alice Childress and wielded a sword-like intelligence to slay segregation, shame, and self-loathing. In her plays, articles, essays, and commentary, she proved herself to be a singular voice of Iwa. She was like Amos Tutuola's brave African huntress, who picked up her father's spear to fight for her family; she also bears comparison with Maxine Hong Kingston's woman warrior, who had her lineage carved into her back so she would never forget from where she came. She was a herald, a trumpet, a clarion call to honor the unquenchable Iwa that carried the people who could not fly out of slavery and into the modern era. She was deeply involved in the fight for civil rights and believed that the movement had its roots in the black protest and revolt of enslaved people, such as Gabriel Prosser and Hannibal in *The Drinking Gourd* (discussed in chapter 2). As an artist she believed that all people had stature and that there were no dramatically uninteresting people. Like Alice Childress, she searched for the extraordinary in the ordinary. She was a visionary who followed in the tradition of the "Mother Playwrights," though – unlike them – she enjoyed commercial success. (Langston Hughes's *Mulatto* of 1935 and Lorraine Hansberry's *A Raisin in the Sun* of 1959 are the only two plays by Afro-American authors that ran for more than a year on Broadway.) This was the play with which the 28-year-old Hansberry made her Broadway debut. The legacy of that success was to open doors for her dramatic daughters, Anna Deveare Smith, Suzan-Lori Parks, and others.

Hansberry's title *A Raisin in the Sun* is derived from a phrase in Langston Hughes's "Lenox Avenue Mural": "What happens to a dream deferred/Does it dry up/Like a raisin in the sun?" (in Woll, 229). Lorraine Hansberry was the first Black woman to have a play produced on Broadway. She was the first Black playwright and the youngest playwright to win the New York Drama Critics Circle Award. Claudia McNeil, Sidney Poitier, Ruby Dee, and Diana Sands came together in 1959 to become part of a groundbreaking ensemble: not only was the playwright Black, but so were the cast (except for one), the director (Lloyd Richards), and some of the investors.

Lorraine Hansberry wrote *A Raisin in the Sun* with the struggle for Black equality in mind. The play also explored a number of other important themes, notably abortion – Ruth Younger must make a difficult choice; feminism – Beneatha creates a central conflict of the play because her brother thinks she is getting above herself by wanting to be a doctor; pretentiousness among the rising black bourgeoisie, represented by George Murchison; and the call by DuBois and Malcolm X for Pan-Africanism, represented by Asagai. During the play's three acts, Walter Lee struggles both with his internal challenges (selfishness) and with his external ones (racism). At the play's climax, he comes into his manhood by accessing the Iwa instilled in him by his parents. He stands before the audience as a fully Emancipated Interlocutor.

The play has been translated into over 30 languages and has been produced internationally. In 1961 it was released as a film, starring Ruby Dee and Sidney Poiter. In 1973 a Tony Award-winning musical based on the play was mounted at the Arena Stage in Washington, DC, followed by a season on Broadway with Joe Morton in the role of Walter Lee and Debbie Allen as Beneatha. Lorraine Hansberry died of cancer on January 12, 1965, aged only 34. In San Francisco, the Lorraine Hansberry Theatre, which specializes in original stagings and revivals of African-American theater, is named in her honor.

Sidney Poitier originated the role of Walter Lee on stage and screen. Poitier became the first African American man to receive the Academy Award in a leading role for his portrayal of an itinerant carpenter in *Lilies of the Field* (1962). His career defines and documents the modern history of blacks in American film. His depiction of blacks on the stage, in the movies, and on television was and remains revolutionary. Mr. Poitier nearly single-handedly dignified and demolished the brutal black buck stereotype. His pantheon of characters is distinguished by unflinching dignity. He was electrifying in Norman Jewison's *In the Heat of the Night* (1967) as Virgil Tibbs, a black detective from the North trying to solve a murder in a southern town. When Rod Steiger's character asks him "What do they call a fancy nigger like you up north?," Virgil declares, "They call me Mr. Tibbs!" This response turned him into an Emancipated Interlocutor speaking on behalf of every maligned black man in the movies and on stage. Sidney Poitier wore a mantle, a cape-like coat of protection, that had passed through the hands of Ira Aldridge, James Hewlett, and Paul Robeson on the wings of High John.

On an April night in 2002, in what seemed like an appropriate gesture of continuity, Poitier passed his mantle on to Denzel Washington, whose career has similarly embraced a range of complex characters. He was Malcolm X on stage in the 1980s in Kirk Kirksey's *When Chickens Come Home to Roost* and went on to appear in the title role in Spike Lee's film *Malcolm X* (1992). He was Pfc. Melvin Peterson in the NEC production of Charles Fuller's *A Soldier's Play* (1981). In 1988 he received the best supporting actor award for his portrayal of a soldier fighting in the Civil War as a member of the 365th US Army Regiment (see chapter 5). When Denzel Washington was eventually recognized as best actor for his role in *Training Day* (2001), Sidney Poitier was there to receive an honorary Oscar for lifetime achievement – hence the "appropriate gesture of continuity" on that night in April 2002.

Would you say Denzel's character in *Training Day* is an Emancipated Interlocutor?

Ossie Davis (1917–2005) and Ruby Dee became "national treasures" when they received the National Medal of the Arts in 1995. They are like royalty in American theater and are also highly respected civil rights activists. Like Ella

Jo Baker before her, Dee is a member of CORE, NAACP, SNCC, and SCLC. Dee and Davis were personal friends of both Martin Luther King and Malcolm X. Ossie Davis is author of the most successful of the civil rights plays, *Purlie Victorius*, which reached Broadway in 1961. A satire of southern plantation stereotypes, the play is a trickster tale of monumental proportions. Davis starred as Purlie, who returns to his plantation home with the hope of buying an old house and converting it into a church. When his funds for the project disappear, he attempts to outwit the staunch segregationist Cap'n Cotchipee and obtain the money. *Purlie Victorious* was clearly a comedy, but in 1964 Howard Taubman noted in the *New York Times* that "it unrelentingly forces you to feel how it is to inhabit a dark skin in a hostile, or at best, grudgingly benevolent world" (Taubman, online). Some ten years later, it was adapted into the musical *Purlie,* which swept Broadway's major awards that season. Leads Cleavon Little and Melba Moore both won Tony and Drama Desk Awards for their performances. Moore also won a Theatre World Award, and Little received a New York Drama Critics Circle Award.

On November 28, 2000, in an interview for Black History Month, Ossie Davis spoke about the play and his politics:

> It – the arts, for the black community, were always a form of our politics, our protests. And, when I came into the theater, the people who were most important to me were the heroes of the theater at that time – Paul Robeson and Canada Lee and Lena Horne. And they were all a part of the struggle. So, I came in at that level and sort of joined the theater and joined in the struggle. And they were always, and still are, in my mind, intertwined in my experience.
>
> Well, all right, let's say, for example, that in 1959, a young lady named Lorraine Hansberry wrote a play called *A Raisin in the Sun.* First young black lady to do such a thing. And Lloyd Richards, a black director, directed that play. And it was about our struggle. And then, spurred on by that, I wrote a play – a comedy – took it to the same producer. And in 1961, he put my play on Broadway. Oh, that was a tremendous triumph. On opening night, we found that in the audience was Dr. W. E. B. DuBois, who was 90 years old at the time. And he came backstage and climbed some steps to tell us how much he appreciated the play. And then one matinée day, I looked down in the first row, and there's another shiny young man looking straight up at me named Martin Luther King. I really went up [on his lines] and had to get myself together. And previous to that, at another matinée, Malcolm X had come to see the play. And he said, "You're trying to do with laughter, you know, what I'm trying to do with, with protests and all of that." So, their blessing and their appreciation and their acceptance of Ruby and me as a kind of part of the inner circle was – oh, my God. There's nothing that could beat that.
>
> (O. Davis, 2000, online)

Ruby Dee. Courtesy of Ms. Dee

Ossie Davis is survived by his wife, Race Woman Ruby Dee, who has appeared with Denzel Washington in the film *American Gangster* (2007) and with Alicia Keys in the Sundance Channel series, "Iconoclasts." She is an actor of such iridescent power that she transforms whatever role she accepts. As she once put it, *"The kind of beauty I want most is the hard-to-get kind that comes from within — strength, courage, dignity."*

After *A Raisin in the Sun*, Dee appeared on Broadway with her husband in *Purlie Victorious*. She later repeated that role in the film version, *Gone Are the Days* (1963). Recognized for her nuance and sensitivity, she garnered some of the best roles for black women in the 1950s and 1960s. On stage, she was the first black woman to play lead roles at the American Shakespeare Festival, and won an Obie Award for her portrayal of the infinitely suffering but never defeated Colored woman Lena in Athol Fugard's *Boesman and Lena,* a play written in 1974, before South Africa's apartheid regime had ended. She also won a Drama Desk Award for her role in Alice Childress's *Wedding Band* and an Ace Award for her performance in Eugene O'Neil's *Long Day's Journey into Night.* Dee has appeared in over 50 movies. She has been nominated for eight Emmy Awards, winning twice for her role in *Decoration Day* and for her guest appearance in the China Beach episode, "Skylark." She is particularly proud of her one-woman show *Zora Is My Name*, about pioneering novelist, folk-lorist, and anthropologist Zora Neale Hurston. Ruby Dee opened doors for Gloria Foster, Barbara Montgomery, and Phylicia Rashad to shine in classical roles.

Sidney Poitier, Ruby Dee, and Harry Belafonte can all properly be called black persons of the blacks, brothers and sister in black, race men, and race woman. As elder ambassadors of Iwa inspiration, they are wearing the crowns purchased for them by Paul Robeson and Florence Mills. When Ossie Davis died in 2005, Riverside Church was filled to overflowing. Lines snaked around the block formed by the unfortunate who could not get in. Those attending the solemn ceremony were standing in the presence of ancestry. George C. Wolfe and Suzan-Lori Parks, among many others, have found original ways to uncover and express Iwa inspiration in their plays – and they too stand in the presence of ancestry.

Lloyd Richards (original director of *A Raisin in the Sun*) became Dean of the Yale University School of Drama and Artistic Director of the Yale Repertory Theatre in 1979, a post he held until 1991. Throughout his career, Richards sought to discover and develop new plays and playwrights. His search for a major new American playwright bore fruit with the Broadway production of August Wilson's *Ma Rainey's Black Bottom* in 1984. This is part of Wilson's ten-part chronicle of African American life, *The Pittsburgh Cycle* or *Century Cycle* (1982–2005), including *Fences, Joe Turner's Come and Gone, The Piano Lesson, Two Trains Running* and *Seven Guitars*, of which Richards directed successive installments.

A tribute after Wilson's death in 2005 made the following comment: "August Wilson had the blues. He got them as a young man, listening to Bessie Smith records in a ramshackle Pittsburgh boarding house, and he spent the rest of his life unleashing that wail on the stage" (A&E Interactive, online).

A presence of ancestry

An obituary notice in the *New York Times* stated:

> The playwright's voice in American culture is perceived as having been usurped by television and film, but he [Wilson] reasserted the power of drama to describe large social forces, to explore the meaning of an entire people's experience in American history. [. . .] He was reclaiming ground for the theater that most people thought had been abandoned.
>
> (Tony Kushner, in Isherwood, 2005)

Wilson was always aware that he was standing in the powerful presence of ancestry. He was influenced by what he called the "four Bs" – Blues, Baraka, Bearden, and Borges: as he said in a radio interview in 2004, when he saw Romare Bearden's paintings, "it was the first time that I had seen black life presented in all its richness, and I said, I want to do that – I want my plays to be the equal of his canvases" (National Public Radio, online).

Wilson's *Pittsburgh Cycle* echoes the African American experience in the whole of the 20th century, one decade covered in each of the ten plays. As he put it:

> Somewhere along the way it dawned on me that I was writing one play for each decade. Once I became conscious of that, I realized I was trying to focus on what I felt were the important issues confronting Black Americans for that decade, so ultimately they could stand as a record of Black experience over the past hundred years presented in the form of dramatic literature.
>
> (Wilson, 2006, online)

The series examines not only such major themes as slavery, migration, urbanization, and discrimination, but the spirituality of ordinary folk. I now go on to focus on four of these plays (in chronological order of event, though that is not the order in which they were written): *Gem of the Ocean, Joe Turner, Ma Rainey* and *Fences*. To start with *Gem*: Phylicia Rashad, who played as Aunt Ester, was interviewed about the play, which is set in 1904. As she said:

> What August Wilson was, has done with this century, this ten-cycle canon of plays, is he captured, through the lives of people who were normally disregarded – he is showing us the development and history of a people in the 20th century in this country. And he's also telling us a lot about the history of this country and the development of this country with the lives of these people.

Aunt Ester is 285 years old and embodies the history and wisdom of her race. Her improbable age suggests that she arrived with one of the first shipments slaves to America. Aunt Ester probably remembers how to fly.

In his review of the play, Ben Brantley considered that "Wilson immerses himself densely here in the influences of the period: the Bible and Voodoo, the fear and fierce disappointment of African-Americans at the failed promises of the Civil War, the struggle to advance. This rich and varied tapestry is laced with Wilson's mischievous humor, as well as poetry and music" (Brantley, online). *Gem of the Ocean* also introduces the Underground Railroad Conductor in dramatic form: Solly Two Kings, a former slave and pilot on the Underground Railroad, is never without the chain he once wore; it reminds him of where he was and what he must do. He has the authority of a king in the shabby clothes of a homeless person. Revealing the influence of writings by Jorge Luis Borges, Wilson ventures deep into the realm of magical realism. Citizen Barlow, another character in the play, is led by the incantatory speech and song of those around him into the collective memory of his people. He hears cries and whispers from centuries earlier and from the hush arbors of slavery days. And the soft words, as he repeats them, rumble like thunder: "Remember me." Mr. Wilson has placed Citizen Barlow and the audience in the powerful presence of ancestry. Like James Baldwin, he suggests that for Black Americans to forget their past is to be without a compass in the present and a clear road to the future.

Wilson's play *Joe Turner's Come and Gone*, first produced in 1986 by the Yale Repertory Theatre, was inspired by the blues song of the same title. Recorded by the legendary W. C. Handy, the song was primarily associated with many estranged black women who had lost their husbands, fathers, and sons to Joe Turner – a plantation owner who illegally enslaved blacks in the early 20th century. The third play in Wilson's cycle, it is set in a Pittsburgh boarding house in 1911 and examines African Americans' struggles to define their Iwa following the repression of slavery. For the character Herald Loomis, this struggle involves the physical migration from the South to Pittsburgh in an attempt to find his wife. Pittsburgh was one of the many urban areas in the North to which blacks migrated in the first decade of the 20th century. In no other play does Wilson address the power of the African American past more directly than in *Joe Turner*.

Ma Rainey's Black Bottom, Wilson's first play to reach Broadway (1984), is about the blues, jazz, and vaudeville artist Gertrude "Ma" Rainey (1886–1939) and her fellow musicians. The play, which introduced Charles Dutton to the theater-going public, is set in a recording studio in 1927. The music evokes the atmosphere of one of the rent parties we visited with Zora (see chapter 5). In the studio, imperious Ma Rainey presents herself as an important musical figure. Much of the play is also set in a rehearsal room, where Ma Rainey's musicians discuss the hardships of life in Jim Crow America. Eventually, it emerges that everyone present has experienced various degrees of racist treatment. Wilson paints Ma Rainey as an abusive employer, with undeserved grandiose notions of her own importance. For a different portrait of Ma Rainey, see Angela Davis's *Blues Legacies and Black Feminism: Gertrude "Ma" Rainey, Bessie Smith, and Billie Holiday*. Davis's book also contributes to an understanding of such former sharecroppers as KoKo Taylor, who brought the blues north over an invisible bridge. Davis quotes veteran New Orleans jazz musician Danny Barker:

> Ma Rainey was Ma Rainey. When you said "Ma," that means Mother, "Ma," that means the tops. That's the boss, the shack bully of the house, Ma Rainey. She'd take charge, "Ma". Ma Rainey's coming to town, the boss blues singer. And you respect Ma. Grand "Ma", my "Ma", and ma "Ma". That's "Ma". That's something you respect. You say Mother. That's the boss of the shack. Not papa, mama.
> (Davis, 1999, 121)

In 1990 Wilson claimed his second Pulitzer Prize for drama, as well as a Drama Desk Award, for *The Piano Lesson*. Set during the Great Depression of the

1930s, this play pits brother against sister in a contest to decide the future of a treasured heirloom – a piano, carved with African portraits by their grandfather, an enslaved plantation carpenter. The brother wants to sell it to buy land, while the sister adamantly insists that the instrument carries too much family history to part with. *The Piano Lesson* opens as Boy Willie arrives at the home of his sister, Bernice. Willie dreams of buying the same Mississippi land that his ancestors had once worked as slaves, but in order to raise the capital for this purchase, he must convince his sister to part with the family heirloom that is both a reminder of the family's enslaved past and a tribute to their survival. Bernice is an exoduster. She left Mississippi and moved north to Pittsburgh, bringing her roots with her as represented by the piano. The setting is resonant with the declining years of the Harlem Renaissance and the Federal Theatre Project (FTP, 1935–9), which was formed to offer work to out of work actors and writers. Inspired by Bearden's collage of the same name, *The Piano Lesson* demonstrates that the past is not past; rather, the legacy of slavery still burdens, and the ancestors still inspire. As James Earl Jones put it in 2001:

> It's hard for an actor to go wrong if he's true to the words August Wilson has written. When I played Troy Maxson in *Fences* on Broadway in 1987, the speeches simply guided themselves, they're so well constructed. August was a poet before he became a playwright, and poetry is still part of the language his characters speak. You don't always hear people talk like that in real life, but you wish you could.
>
> (Jones, online)

The second play in Wilson's cycle is called *Fences*. Set in the 1950s, it is about a former athlete, Troy Maxon, who forbids his son to accept an athletic scholarship. Now an illiterate garbage collector, Troy has become embittered by a white-controlled system that has denied him the baseball stardom he feels he deserves. *Fences* opened on Broadway in spring 1987 to enormous critical acclaim and earned Wilson his first Pulitzer Prize. It starred James Earl Jones, who won one of his two Tony Awards for that performance, and introduced Courtney B. Vance to theater audiences. Troy's character is reminiscent of the young T. O. Jones, an eighth-grade dropout, who organized the Sanitation Workers' Union in Memphis and led the Sanitation Workers' Strike in 1968. Martin Luther King went to Memphis to show support for the strikers, one of the gestures that provoked his assassination. In 1993 Charles (OyamO) Gordon wrote his play *I Am a Man* to celebrate the memory of T. O. Jones:

> Jones was buffeted on all sides by the city's racist mayor; by national union representatives from AFSCME [American Federation of State, County, Municipal Employees, who opposed Jones' untutored, improvisational leadership style]; by upper class Negroes who looked down on him due to his lack of a higher education; by the local police; by the white power structure which simply

didn't want to see a black workers union powerful enough to disrupt life in Memphis; and by the demands of his family. Jones weathered them all at great personal cost.

(Gordon, personal communication)

Though Troy Maxon is not an activist in the sense that Jones was, he clearly represents the frustration and bitterness of "ordinary" people living under Jim Crow in the 1950s and of soldiers recently returned from World War II.

The final play in Wilson's cycle, *Radio Golf,* received its premiere at the Yale Repertory Theatre in April 2005. The following October, just an hour after Wilson announced to the press that he was ill and had been given only a few months to live, he was interviewed by Suzan-Lori Parks: "When we spoke, my heart and mind were clouded with sadness. I could hardly keep from crying, but Mr. Wilson was clear, focused, funny and, as always, brilliant as hell. And on October 2, 2005, August Wilson passed away at the age of 60" (Parks, 2005 online).

George C. Wolfe, an African American playwright and director of theater and film, took a new look at both Lorraine Hansberry and Ntozake Shange. In his *Colored Museum,* he stood the stereotypes on their heads while coaxing humor out of the foibles of the race. The play had its world premiere on March 26, 1986, at the Crossroads Theatre, New Brunswick, New Jersey. Later that year it was produced by the New York Shakespeare Festival Public Theater and won Wolfe the 1986 Dramatists Guild Award. The work consists of 11 vignettes that satirize various elements of African American culture. The one that received most praise is titled "The Last Mama on the Couch Play." It attacks the traditional style of black realism in Lorraine Hansberry's drama, and the plot and style of Shange's choreopoem. Wolfe himself said of *The Colored Museum*: "Black American culture is a very fragmented thing. We're all trying to come up with some definition of what we are. My absolute definition of me is the schizophrenia, the contradiction . . . 'I can't live inside yesterday's pain,' says Topsy, 'but I can't live without it' " (Wolfe, online).

In 1989 Wolfe won an Obie Award for best off-Broadway director for his play *Spunk*, an adaptation of three stories by Zora Neale Hurston. His musical *Jelly's Last Jam,* based on the life of jazz artist Jelly Roll Morton, dates from 1991. After a Los Angeles opening, it moved to Broadway, where it received 11 Tony nominations. In 1993 Wolfe was appointed artistic director of the New York Shakespeare Festival Public Theatre, where he produced Anna Deveare Smith's *Fires in the Mirror,* and *Twilight.* Among other notable works he went on to direct are Tony Kushner's *Angels in America* (1993) and *Perestroika* (1994). In 1996 (with star and choreographer Savion Glover) Wolfe created *Bring in 'Da Noise, Bring in 'Da Funk,* a dance musical which tells the story, through tap, of black history from slavery to the last decade of the 20th century. This play reimagined Bill "Bojangles" Robinson's tap dancing feats for the rap generation. The work won both Wolfe and Glover Tony Awards. In 2005 Wolfe directed *Lackawanna Blues* for HBO television, starring S. Epatha Merkerson. It is based on the one-man show originally written and performed at the Public by Reuben Santiago-Hudson. It is a coming-of-age story for the author set in New York in the 1950s and '60s.

How would you compare the following comments by George C. Wolfe with Askia Toure's statement from chapter 7 (repeated below) about the role of the revolutionary black artist?

> I think, by and large, people in the theater are liberal. But liberal intentions or not, they don't want to share the power. There has been a long history of white artists extolling the cultures of non-whites. But, ultimately, when you strip it down, it's cultural colonization. Until the people from those cultures are involved in making decisions as directors, writers, producers, artistic directors – and there are very few of them – there will be no substantial change. As a person of color with power in the American theater, I am a rare creature. I've been successful, I've been applauded. (Though I still can't get a cab in New York.) The fact that I am a rare thing is a reflection of how rigid the systems are and how much more rigid they are becoming. Ultimately, it's all about sharing the power. And for a large number of white Americans, this is a very frightening prospect. But in the end, they will have to give it up because the opening of the doors is not noble – it's inevitable.
>
> (Wolfe, online)

During a discussion at the New Lafayette, Askia Muhammad Toure rose to read the following:

> The role of the revolutionary Black artist is that of a liberator, freeing the collective consciousness of his people by countering the reactionary cultural images of the oppressor with strong, positive affirmative cultural images of revolutionary Blackness, inspiring the people with hope for a better day, of victory and total liberation. [...] He is the racial and cultural historian, sharpening and informing the racial or group memory, rebuilding the damaged psyche of the Black nation – a kind of nation builder of the Black mind. Yes. Art for people's sake, rather than art for art's sake is the motto of the revolutionary Black artist.
>
> (in Bullins, 1969, 16)

Could the two statements be framed as a dialogue between two characters from different time periods who agree on goals but differ on tactics? For inspiration in staging such a scene, read Jeff Stetson's play *The Meeting* (1984), which concerns an imaginary meeting between Martin Luther King and Malcolm X. It takes place on February 14, 1964, in a hotel room in Harlem. There are many scenes suitable for two actors, as well as a monologue for King, describing the first march he ever led, and one for Malcolm, a passionate account of why his philosophy differs from King's nonviolent policy.

In 2002 Halle Berry became the first African American to receive the Academy Award for best actress, having played the role of Leticia Musgrove in the film *Monster's Ball* (2001). Coincidentally, Berry had previously both starred in and produced the made-for-television movie, *Introducing Dorothy Dandridge* (1999). Dandridge was the first African American to be nominated for the Academy Award in the best actress category. She was a supremely talented artist who was haunted by her inability to find first-class work. According to Donald Bogle, "Dorothy Dandridge was a Black film star in a Hollywood that worshiped her, yet at the same time, clearly made no place for her" (Bogle, 1997, repr. 1999, 2). Born in Cleveland on November 9, 1922, she received little formal education, instead touring with her sister Vivian in a show by their mother titled *The Wonder Children*. Dorothy appeared on the cover of *Life* magazine in 1954, the first African American to do so. That same year she played the much-coveted role of Carmen Jones in the all-black adaptation of Bizet's *Carmen* (with Harry Belafonte), a film directed by Otto Preminger based on the Broadway show. She was nominated for a Golden Globe Award for her starring role in *Porgy and Bess* (1959) alongside Sidney Poitier.

Halle Berry, bearing a striking resemblance to Dandridge, told a new generation about the incandescent beauty (Berry won the Miss USA world contest in 1986). *Introducing Dorothy Dandridge*, a labor of love for the fellow Clevelander, dramatizes the toll that Jim Crow took on Dandridge and such contemporaries as Lena Horne. She sang in fine hotels, but couldn't stay in any of their rooms. As the movie shows, one hotel drained its swimming pool to keep her from enjoying a swim. On September 8, 1965, she was discovered dead on her bathroom floor; whether it was a suicide or an accident was never clearly determined. Berry was awarded both the Emmy and SAG Awards for her portrayal of Dandridge. In her Academy Award acceptance speech for *Monster's Ball*, Berry acknowledged a presence of ancestry by paying tribute to Dorothy Dandridge.

Dorothy Dandridge

If she had lived to be a witness that night (as Sidney Poitier was for Denzel Washington), what do you think Dorothy Dandridge might say to Halle Berry? How would you characterize Berry's role in *Monster's Ball*? Do any of the old-time stereotypes apply?

Just as 1964 was once described as the "year of [LeRoi] Jones," 2004 might be described as the year of the woman in the black dramatic arts. *A Raisin in the*

187

Revival of Lorraine Hansberry's *A Raisin in the Sun*, with Phylicia Rashad, Audra McDonald, and Sean Combs, 2004

Sun received a Broadway revival with Sean Combs, earning Tony Awards for Phylicia Rashad and Audra McDonald, while playwright Suzan-Lori Parks was the first black woman playwright to be awarded a Pulitzer Prize for drama for her play *Topdog/Underdog*. On that occasion she declared, "As the first African-American woman to win the Pulitzer Prize [for drama], I have to say I wish I was the 101st." She is wearing the crown purchased for her by Lorraine Hansberry. Along with many Obie Awards for playwriting, in 2001 Parks also received a MacArthur Genius Award.

Topdog/Underdog tells the story of two brothers. The first is named Lincoln. He has a job at an arcade impersonating Abraham Lincoln sitting at Ford's Theater. The arcade's patrons pay to shoot Lincoln with blanks. His roommate and brother, Booth, is a master shoplifter. Booth desires to become as adept as Lincoln once was at the common street-scam, three-card monte. *Topdog/Underdog* is performed as a cross between a hip-hop riff and a Greek tragedy – as entertaining as the former and as gripping as the latter. The play opened at the Public Theatre under the direction of George C. Wolfe with Don Cheadle and Jeffrey Wright. When it moved to Broadway, the rapper Mos Def replaced Mr. Cheadle.

Topdog is the only play by a black woman, aside from one-woman shows (perhaps most memorably *Lena Horne: the Lady and her Music*, 1981), to make it to

Broadway since Ntozake Shange's *for colored girls,* which opened there in 1976. Moreover, it is an extremely rare example of a drama written by a woman and featuring a male-only cast. After the off-Broadway premiere, Mos Def could barely contain his excitement. Ms. Parks recalls: "[he] ran backstage and told one of the actors, 'Ah, man, what a great play. The guy who wrote this . . .' And the actor laughed. [Because] a woman was the playwright" (in Fanger, online).

Parks's plays have been hailed for their creative mix of fantasy, myth, and history, expressed in metaphoric language that captures the explosive patois heard on the inner-city streets and in the rural backwaters of America. With their unsettling and unconventional ways of prodding audiences to consider the heritage of race relations in US society, they have been traveling the regional theater circuit since the mid-1990s. Parks was urged to pursue writing plays by no less a crown-purchaser than James Baldwin, who was her teacher at Mt. Holyoke College and found her to be an "an utterly astounding and beautiful creature who may become one of the most valuable artists of our time." When asked what was it like to be a pupil of James Baldwin, Parks responded:

> He had faith in me long before I even had faith in me. That's the great gift that a writing teacher can give a young writer. You can't overestimate the value of hearing, "Hey, you're good." He was encouraging in a scary way, not a soft mushy way. He teaches you to be tough on yourself."
>
> (Parks, 2003, online)

Among Parks's inventive catalogue of characters are another African American man who works as an impersonator of President Abraham Lincoln (*The America Play,* 1994); a Hottentot woman kept in a cage as a sideshow curiosity (*Venus,* 1996); and a homeless mother with five children by five different fathers (*In the Blood,* 1999). Parks wrote the screenplay (2005) for ABC television's adaptation of Zora Neale Hurston's *Their Eyes were Watching God,* starring Halle Berry. In 2002 she decided to write a play a day for a year. This ambitious project was initiated with simultaneous premieres across the US on November 13, 2006, and will involve nearly 700 theaters in more than 30 cities. Parks is planning to write the book accompanying a musical based on the life and music of Ray Charles and is also working on an adaptation of Toni Morrison's novel *Paradise.*

What do you think of these remarks?

> We should now demand that we must reach back into our pockets, bank accounts, date books and palm pilots and exert efforts to read, stage and mount these timeless works. The black theater canon serves as our present day griot, storyteller, keeper of the culture and connector to the past. This past informs the present, which necessarily prepares us, culturally, spiritually and politically for tomorrow."
>
> (Demetria McCain, online)

For a final exercise, do some research to help you form an answer to the following questions:

What is happening in black theater today? Are you familiar with any of the following:
Pearl Cleage, Charles Smith, Kenny Leon, Larry Leon Hamlin (deceased), Ricardo Kahn, Tazwell Thompson, Lydia Diamond, Javon Johnson, Aisa Davis, Tanya Barfield, Roslyn Ruff, Katori Hall? What can you find out about them?

Do you agree that black theater has been replaced in part by the multi-million dollar music industry, whether in the form of hip-hop, gangsta rap, or any other style?

How does the innovative but controversial work of people like Tyler Perry impact the legacy of black theater?

Look again at Douglas Turner Ward's *New York Times* article of August 8, 1966, which led to the formation of the Negro Ensemble Company (chapter 7). Taking all your research into consideration, can you write a similar essay in which you summarize the current state of black theater and propose a new way "to read, stage and mount" what McCain calls the timeless works of the black theater canon?

As this book goes to press, most of you will remember the night of December 31, 1999. It was not only the end of a decade, the 1990s, but the end of a century, a *fin de siècle* that saw tremendous change in the United States and the world. For more than half of the 20th century Black Americans lived under Jim Crow. In the waning days of that century Stokely Carmichael died from cancer and Betty Shabazz perished in a house fire. Within the first decade of the 21st century countless others have died, not least Coretta Scott King, Rosa Parks, August Wilson, Lloyd Richards, and Ossie Davis. These pivotal figures were living witnesses to turbulent events from the mid-1950s onward. Stokely Carmichael is credited with coining the phrase "Black Power." Betty Shabazz was the widow of Malcolm X. She went on to live a life of service as she emerged from his shadow to create her own identity. Coretta Scott King

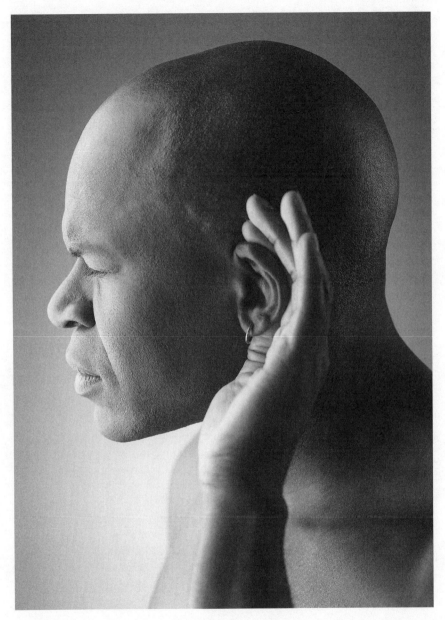

"Alexanduh say he can fly. Say all his people in Africa could Fly"

walked with her husband through the transformational history of his life. Her own funeral was attended by all the surviving giants of the Civil Rights Movement (although Harry Belafonte's invitation was rescinded at the request of George W. Bush). The funeral of Rosa Parks was treated as an affair of state. Before her burial in Detroit, her body lay in the Capitol Rotunda, an honor never before accorded a woman. Lloyd Richards died on his 87th birthday June 30, 2006. The previous year, August Wilson succeeded in finishing this *Pittsburg Cycle* before his death at the age of 60.

When we invoke their names, we are standing in the presence of ancestry. With the passing of these men and women the memories they held in their bodies might be forgotten. But because of the power of black theater and other forms of cultural expression explored in this book, these memories can remain alive. The past still moves among us on the mysterious wings of High John the Conqueror.

I hope that now you can trace your cultural ancestors all the way back to the people who could fly. And to the people left behind because they could not fly. And to their children who strained and struggled to create a new identity out of necessity. Who ran so fast from the patty rollers that they nearly flew; who crept toward freedom in the still of the night; who walked and rode north for better opportunities; who sat down to stand up; who fought in the wars; who wrote their unnaturally suppressed inner lives into visibility with narratives, novels, plays, poems, and songs. All of this celebrates their inextinguishable life essence, their Iwa. Their legacy is not only rich, but vital. I hope that you will want to continue this rich, vital legacy in your own Black Life Book.

References

A&E Interactive, 2005. "In Memory of AUGUST WILSON." Thursday, October 06: online at http://www.typepad.com/t/trackback/3318641.

Andrews, William L., ed., 1988. *Six Women's Slave Narratives*. New York: Oxford University Press.

Arnesen, Eric, 2003. *Black Protest and the Great Migration: A Brief History with Documents*. Boston and New York: Bedford/St. Martin's.

Arsenault, Raymond, 2006. *Freedom Riders: 1961 and the Struggle for Racial Justice*. New York: Oxford University Press.

Baraka, Amiri, and Amina Baraka, 1983. *Confirmation: An Anthology of African American Women*. New York: Quill.

Bascom, Lionel, ed., 1999. *A Renaissance in Harlem: Lost Essays of the WPA*. New York: HarperCollins Publishers.

Bass, George Houston, and Henry Louis Gates, Jr., 1991. *Mule Bone: A Comedy of Negro Life*. New York: HarperCollins Publishers.

Bates, Daisy, 1962, repr. 1986. *The Long Shadow of Little Rock*. Fayetteville: University of Arkansas Press.

Beals, Melba Pattillo, 1994. *Warriors Don't Cry: A Searing Memoir of the Battle to Integrate Little Rock's Central High*. New York: Washington Square Press.

Berlin, Ira, and Leslie M. Harris, eds., 2005. *Slavery in New York*. New York: New Press.

Bial, Raymond, 1995. *The Underground Railroad*. Boston: Houghton Mifflin Company.

Blight, David W., ed., 2004. *Passages to Freedom: The Underground Railroad in History and Memory*. Washington: Smithsonian Books.

Bogle, Donald, 1980. *Brown Sugar: Eighty Years of America's Black Female Superstars*. New York: Harmony Books.

Bogle, Donald, 1988. *Blacks in American Films and Television: An Encyclopedia*. New York and London: Garland Publishing.

Bogle, Donald, 1997, repr. 1999. *Dorothy Dandridge: A Biography*. New York: Berkley Trade.

Bogle, Donald, 2004. *Toms, Coons, Mulattoes, Mammies, and Bucks: An Interpretive History of Blacks in American Films*. New York and London: Continuum.

Bolcolm, William, and Robert Kimball, 1983. *Reminiscing with Sissle and Blake*. New York: Viking Press.

Bonner, Marita, 1925. "On Being Young – a Woman – and Colored." *The Crisis*, December.

Bontemps, Arna, 1936. *Black Thunder: Gabriel's Revolt Virginia, 1800.* Boston: Beacon Press.

Botkin, B. A., 1973. *Lay my Burden Down: A Folk History of Slavery.* New York: Dell Publishing.

Bradford, Sarah H., 1886, repr. 1993. *Harriet Tubman: The Moses of her People.* Carlisle, Massachusetts: Applewood Books.

Branch, William, 1989. *Parting the Waters: America in the King Years, 1954–63.* New York: Simon & Schuster.

Brantley, Ben, 2004. "Sailing into Collective Memory." *New York Times,* 7 December: online at http://theater2.nytimes.com/2004/12/07/theater/reviews/07 ocea.html?n=Top/Reference/Times%20Topics/People/R/Rashad,%20Phylicia.

Brown, William Wells, 1847. *Narrative of William W. Brown, a Fugitive Slave, Written by Himself.* Boston: Anti-Slavery Office: online at http://docsouth. unc.edu/neh/brown47/menu.html.

Brown-Guillory, Elizabeth, 1990. *Their Place on the Stage.* New York: Praeger Publishers.

Bruckner, D. J. R., 1987. "Stage: 'Mississippi Delta'." *New York Times,* September 30, Section C, p. 24, col. 5.

Bullins, Ed, 1969. *Black Theatre: A Periodical of the Black Theatre Movement.* New York: New Lafayette Theatre Publications.

Bullins, Ed, ed., 1969. *New Plays from the Black Theatre.* New York: Bantam Books.

Bullins, Ed, ed., 1974. *The New Lafayette Theatre Presents: Plays with Aesthetic Comments by 6 Black Playwrights.* Garden City, New York: Anchor Press/Doubleday.

Burns, Ken, 2003."Harlem's Hell Fighters," online at http://www.stephenlharris. com/harlems_hell_fighters.htm.

Busby, Margaret, ed., 1992. *Daughters of Africa: An International Anthology of Words and Writings by Women of African Descent.* New York: Ballantine Books.

Cantor, George, 1991. *Historic Landmarks of Black America.* Detroit: Gale Research.

Carson, Clayborne, D. Garrow, G. Gill, V. Harding, and D. Hines, eds., 1991. *Eyes on the Prize Civil Rights Reader: Documents, Speeches, and Firsthand Accounts from the Black Freedom Struggle, 1954–1990.* New York: Penguin Books.

Chapman, Abraham, ed., 1968. *Black Voices: An Anthology of Contemporary Afro-American Literature.* New York and Toronto: New American Library.

Chapman, Abraham, ed., 1972. *New Black Voices: An Anthology of Contemporary Afro-American Literature.* New York and Toronto: New American Library.

Cooper, Anna Julia, 1892. "A Voice from the South." In Lemert, Charles, and Esme Bhan, eds., 1998. *The Voice of Anna Julia Cooper.* Lanham: Rowman & Littlefield Publishers.

Courlander, Harold, 1976. *A Treasury of Afro-American Folklore: The Oral Literature, Traditions, Recollections, Legends, Tales, Songs, Religious Beliefs, Customs, Sayings and Humor of Peoples of African Descent in the Americas.* New York: Crown Publishers.

Craig, E. Quita, 1980. *Black Drama of the Federal Theatre Era.* Amherst: University of Massachusetts Press.

Davis, Angela Y., 1999. *Blues Legacies and Black Feminism: Gertrude "Ma" Rainey, Bessie Smith, and Billie Holiday.* New York: Vintage Books.

Davis, Michael D., and Hunter R. Clark, 1992. *Thurgood Marshall: Warrior at the Bar, Rebel on the Bench.* New York: Birch Lane Press.

Davis, Ossie, 1965. "Malcolm X's Eulogy." Delivered at Faith Temple Church of God, February 27: online at official Malcolm X at website, © 2003, http://www.cmgww.com/historic/malcolm/about/eulogy.htm.

Davis, Ossie, 2000. "Black History Month 'Speaking Freely' Transcript" First Amendment Center: online at http://www.firstamendmentcenter.org/about.aspx?id=12774.

Davis, Thulani, 1993. *Malcolm X: The Great Photographs.* New York: Steward, Tabori & Chang.

Dicker/sun, Glenda, ed., 2007. *Goldweights: A Conversation with Nine Africamerican Actors.* Self-published.

Dodson, Howard, and Sylviane A. Diouf, eds., 2004. *In Motion: The African-American Migration Experience.* Washington, DC: National Geographic.

Dodson, Jualynne E., 2002. *Engendering Church: Women, Power and the AME Church.* Lanham: Rowman & Littlefield Publishers.

Douglass, Frederick, 1845. *The Narrative of Frederick Douglass.* In Gates, Henry Louis, Jr., ed., 1987. *The Classic Slave Narratives.* New York: Signet Classic.

Duberman, Martin B., 1963. *In White America: A Documentary Play.* From Mississippi Freedom School Curriculum: online at http://www.educationand-democracy.org/FSCfiles/C_CC3b_InWhiteAmericaExpt.htm.

Dubois, W. E. B., 3rd edn., 1903. *The Souls of Black Folk: Essays and Sketches* Chicago: A.C. McClurg & Co.: online at http://docsouth.unc.edu/church/duboissouls/dubois.html.

DuBois, W. E. B., 1919. "Returning Soldiers." *The Crisis,* XVIII, May: online at http://www.vale.edu/glc/archive/1127.htm.

Dunbar, Paul Laurence, 1913. *The Complete Poems of Paul Laurence Dunbar.* New York: Dodd, Mead & Company.

Elam Jr., Harry J., 2004. *The Past as Present in the Drama of August Wilson.* Ann Arbor: University of Michigan Press.

Elam Jr., Harry J., and Robert Alexander, eds., 1996. *Colored Contradictions.* New York: Penguin Books.

Electronic New Jersey Project, 2004. "A Digital Archive of New Jersey History: Paul Robeson Biography": online at http://www2.scc.rutgers.edu/njh/PaulRobeson/PRBio.htm.

Emanuel, J., and Gross, T., eds., 1968. *Dark Symphony: Negro Literature in America.* New York: Free Press.

Engle, Gary D., 1978. *This Grotesque Essence: Plays from the American Minstrel Stage.* Baton Rouge and London: Louisiana State University Press.

Fanger, Iris, 2002. "Pulitzer Prize Winner Shakes off Labels." *Christian Science Monitor,* April 12: online at http://www.csmonitor.com/2002/0412/p19s01-alip.html.

Ferguson, Blanche E., 1966. *Countée Cullen and the Negro Renaissance.* New York: Dodd, Mead & Company.

Foster, Frances Smith, ed., 1990. *A Brighter Coming Day: A Frances Ellen Watkins Harper Reader.* New York: Feminist Press at City University of New York.

Fraden, Rena, 1996. *Blueprints for a Black Federal Theatre, 1935–1939.* Cambridge: Cambridge University Press.

Fry, Gladys-Marie, 1990. *Stitched from the Soul: Slave Quilts from the Ante-Bellum South.* New York: Dutton Studio Books.

Gallen, David, 1992. *Malcolm X: As They Knew Him.* New York: Carroll & Graf Publishers.

Garrow, David J., ed., 1987. *The Montgomery Bus Boycott and the Women who Started it: The Memoir of Jo Ann Gibson Robinson.* Knoxville: University of Tennessee Press.

Gates, Henry Louis, Jr., ed., 1987. *The Classic Slave Narratives.* New York: Signet Classic.

Gates, Henry Louis, Jr., 1988, repr. 1989. *The Signifying Monkey: A Theory of African-American Literary Criticism.* New York: Oxford University Press.

Gay, Joseph R., 1913. *Progress and Achievements of the 20th Century Negro: A Handbook for self-improvement which leads to Greater Success.* Philadelphia, New York, and Chicago: various imprints.

Gwaltney, John Langston, 1980. *Drylongso: A Self-Portrait of Black America.* New York: Random House.

Hamalian, Leo, and James V. Hatch, 1991. *The Roots of African-American Drama: An Anthology of Early Plays, 1858–1938.* Detroit: Wayne State University Press.

Hamer, Fannie Lou, 1965. "Montgomery County." *Mississippi Black Paper: Fifty-Seven Negro and White Citizens' Testimony of Police Brutality.* New York: Random House.

Hamilton, Virginia, 1985, repr. with illustrations by Leo and Diane Dillon, © 2004. *The People Could Fly.* New York: Alfred A. Knopf.

Hansberry, Lorraine, 1972. *Les Blancs: The Collected Last Plays of Lorraine Hansberry.* New York: Random House.

Harris, Middleton, ed., with Morris Levitt, Roger Furman, and Ernest Smith, 1974. *The Black Book.* New York: Random House.

Harris, Stephen L., 2003. *Harlem's Hell Fighters: The African-American 369th Infantry in World War I.* Dulles, Virginia: Potomac Books.

Harrison, Paul Carter, and Gus Edwards, eds., 1995. *Classic Plays from the Negro Ensemble Company.* Pittsburgh and London: University of Pittsburgh Press.

Hatch, James V., and Ted Shine, eds., 1974. *Black Theatre USA: Forty-Five Plays by Black Americans, 1847–1974.* New York: Free Press.

Hatch, James V., and Ted Shine, eds., 1996. *Black Theatre USA: Plays by African Americans 1847 – Today.* New York: Simon & Schuster.

Hayden, Robert, ed., 1967. *Kaleidoscope: Poems by American Negro Poets.* New York: Harcourt, Brace and World.

Henson, S., 2006. "Suzan-Lori Parks, or Why I Have Fiction-writer Envy." *Grits for Breakfast,* 16 May: online at http://gritsforbreakfast.blogspot.com/2006/05/suzan-lori-parks-or-why-i-have-fiction.html.

Hill, Errol, ed., 1980. *The Theater of Black Americans.* 2 vols. Englewood Cliffs, New Jersey: Prentice-Hall.

Hill, Errol G., and James V. Hatch, 2003. *A History of African American Theatre.* Cambridge: Cambridge University Press.

Hine, Darlene Clark, ed., 1993. *Black Women in America: An Historical Encyclopedia.* New York: Carlson Publishing.

hooks, bell, 1989. *Talking Back: Thinking Feminist, Thinking Black.* Boston: South End Press.

Horton, James Oliver, and Lois E. Horton, eds., 2001. *Hard Road to Freedom: The Story of African America,* Vol. 1. New Brunswick, New Jersey, and London: Rutgers University Press.

Hoyt, Robert G., 1970. *Martin Luther King, Jr.* Waukesha, Wisconsin: Country Beautiful Foundation.

Huggins, Nathan Irvin, 1971. *Harlem Renaissance.* New York: Oxford University Press.

Huggins, Nathan Irvin, 1976. *Voices from the Harlem Renaissance.* New York: Oxford University Press.

Hughes, Langston, and Arna Bontemps, eds., 1949. *The Poetry of the Negro 1746–1949.* Garden City, New York: Doubleday & Co.

Hughes, Langston, and Milton Meltzer, 1967. *Black Magic: A Pictorial History of the Negro in American Entertainment.* New Jersey: Prentice-Hall.

Hurmence, Belinda, 1984. *My Folks don't Want me to Talk about Slavery.* Winston-Salem, North Carolina: John F. Blair.

Hurmence, Belinda, 1989. *Before Freedom.* Winston-Salem, North Carolina: John F. Blair.

Hurmence, Belinda, 1994. *We Lived in a Little Cabin in the Yard.* Winston-Salem, North Carolina: John F. Blair.

Hurston, Zora Neale, 1935. *Mules and Men.* Philadelphia: J. B. Lippincott.

Isherwood, Charles, 2005. "August Wilson, Theater's Poet of Black America, is Dead at 60." *New York Times,* 3 October: online at http://www.nytimes.com/2005/10/03/theater/newsandfeatures/03wilson.html?_r=1&oref=slogin.

Jacobs, Harriet, 1861, repr. 2001. *Incidents in the Life of a Slave Girl.* Mineola, New York: Dover Publications.

James, Joy, ed., 1998. *The Angela Y. Davis Reader.* Massachusetts: Blackwell Publishers.

Johnson, James Weldon, ed., 1922, repr. 2002. *The Book of American Negro Poetry.* New York: Bartleby.

Johnson, James Weldon, 1927, repr. 1990. *God's Trombones: Seven Negro Sermons in Verse.* New York: Penguin Books.

Jones, James Earl, 2001. "Playwright, August Wilson:, His Poetic Plays about African-American Life offer plainspoken truths that transcend race": online at http://www.cnn.com/SPECIALS/2001/americasbest/pro.awilson.html.

Jones, LeRoi, and Larry Neal, eds., 1971. *Black Fire: An Anthology of Afro-American Writing.* New York: William Morrow & Company.

Joseph, Peniel, ed., 2006. *The Black Power Movement: Rethinking the Civil Rights–Black Power Era*. New York and London: Routledge.

Kalman, Bobbie, 1997. *Life on a Plantation*. New York: Crabtree Publishing Company.

Keckley, Elizabeth, 1868, repr. 1988. *Behind the Scenes or Thirty Years a Slave and Four Years in the White House*. New York and Oxford: Oxford University Press.

King, Woodie, Jr., and Ron Milner, eds., 1971. *Black Drama Anthology*. New York: New American Library.

King, Woodie, Jr., ed., 1995. *The National Black Drama Anthology: Eleven Plays from America's Leading African-American Theaters*. New York and London: Applause.

Krasner, David, 2002. *A Beautiful Pageant: African American Theatre, Drama, and Performance in the Harlem Renaissance, 1910–1927*. New York: Palgrave Macmillan.

Lemann, Nichola, 1991. *The Promised Land: The Great Migration and how it Changed America*. New York: Alfred A. Knopf.

Lemert, Charles, and Esme Bhan, eds., 1998. *The Voice of Anna Julia Cooper*. Lanham: Rowman & Littlefield Publishers.

Levine, Lawrence, 1977. *Black Culture and Black Consciousness: Afro-American Folk Thought from Slavery to Freedom*. New York: Oxford University Press.

Lewis, David Levering, 1981. *When Harlem was in Vogue*. New York: Alfred A. Knopf.

Lhamon, W. T., Jr., 1998. *Raising Cain: Blackface Performance from Jim Crow to Hip Hop*. Cambridge: Harvard University Press.

Litwack, Leon F., 1979. *Been in the Storm so Long: The Aftermath of Slavery*. New York: Alfred A. Knopf.

Locke, Alain, 1925. "The New Negro". Preface to Locke's edition of African American writings, in Emanuel, J., and T. Gross, eds., 1968. *Dark Symphony: Negro Literature in America*. New York: Free Press.

Major, Clarence, ed., 1969. *The New Black Poetry*. New York: International Publishers.

Malcolm X, 1964. "The Ballot or the Bullet": online at http://www.edchange.org/ multicultural/speeches/malcolm_x_ballot.html.

Marks, Carole, 1989. *Farewell – We're Good and Gone: The Great Black Migration*. Bloomington and Indianapolis: Indiana University Press.

Marsh, Carole, ed., 1990, repr. 2003. *Out of the Mouths of Slaves*. Gallopade International: Peachtree City, Georgia.

Maxwell, William J., 1999. *New Negro, Old Left:* African-American Writing and Communism between the Wars. New York: Columbia University Press.

McCain, Demetria, 2004. © dmccain13@aol.com.

McWhorter, Diane, 2002. *Carry me Home: Birmingham, Alabama, the Climactic Battle of the Civil Rights Revolution*. New York: Simon & Schuster.

McWhorter, D., 2004. *A Dream of Freedom: The Civil Rights Movement from 1954 to 1968*. New York: Scholastic Nonfiction.

Mellon, J., ed., 1988. *Bullwhip Days, The Slaves Remember: An Oral History*. New York: Avon Books.

Meltzer, Milton, ed., 1964. *In their Own Words*. New York: Thomas Y. Crowell.

Meltzer, Milton, 1984. *The Black Americans*. New York: HarperCollins.

Mindich, David T. Z., 1998. *Just the Facts: How "Objectivity" Came to Define American Journalism*. New York: New York University Press.

Mitchell, Loften, 1967. *Black Drama: The Story of the American Negro in the Theatre*. New York: Hawthorn Books.

Morehouse, Maggi M., 2000. *Fighting in the Jim Crow Army: Black Men and Women Remember World War II*. Lanham, Boulder, New York, and Oxford: Towman & Littlefield Publishers.

Morgan, Thomas L., 1992, 1997. © "Bert Williams & George Walker": online at http://jass.comw&w.html.

Museum of the Confederacy, 1991. *Before Freedom Came: African-American Life in the Antebellum South*. Virginia: University of Virginia Press and the Museum of the Confederacy.

National Public Radio, 2004. "Intersections: August Wilson, Writing the Blues." 1 March: online at http://www.npr.org/templates/story/story.php?storyId=1700922.

Neal, Larry, 1968. "The Black Arts Movement." *Drama Review*, 12/4.

O'Connor, John, and Lorraine Brown, eds., 1978. *Free, Adult, Uncensored: The Living History of the Federal Theatre Project*. Washington, DC: New Republic Books.

Oliver, Clinton F., and Stephanie Sills, eds., 1971. *Contemporary Black Drama: From A Raisin in the Sun to No Place to be Somebody*. New York: Charles Scribner's Sons.

O'Meally, Robert G., 1998. *The Jazz Cadence of American Culture*. New York: Columbia University Press.

Parks, Suzan-Lori 2003. Interview. "A Moment with Suzan-Lori Parks, Playwright." *Seattle Post Intelligencer*, May 26: online at http://seattlepi.nwsource.com/books/123373_moment26.html.

Parks, Suzan-Lori, 2005. Interview. "The Light in August: An African spiritual strength born of adversity undergirds August Wilson's 10-play cycle": Theatre Communications Group, online at http://www.tcg.org/publications/at/Nov05/wilson.cfm.

Patterson, Vivian, 2000. *Carrie Mae Weems: The Hampton Project*. Williamstown, Massachusetts: Aperture.

Pearson Education, 2007. "African-American Quotations: From Muhammad Ali to Andrew Young": online at http://www.infoplease.com/spot/bhmquotes1.html.

Perkins, Kathy A., and Judith A. Stephens, eds., 1996. *Strange Fruit: Plays on Lynching by American Women*. Bloomington and Indianapolis: Indiana University Press.

Pitts, Jr., Leonard, 2008. "Unsung Heroes Deserve Credit for Victories." *Miami Herald*, January 20: online at http://www.miamiherald.com/540/story/385097.html.

Prince, Bryan, 2004. *I Came as a Stranger: The Underground Railroad*. Toronto, Ontario: Tundra Books.

Randall, Dudley. "Booker T. and W. E. B." In Robert Hayden, ed., 1967. *Kaleidoscope: Poems by American Negro Poets.* New York: Harcourt, Brace and World.

Ransby, Barbara, 2003. *Ella Baker & the Black Freedom Movement: A Radical Democratic Vision.* Chapel Hill and London: University of North Carolina Press.

Reagon B., 1986. Interview with Bernice Reagon. In Clayborne Carson et al., eds., 1991. *Eyes on the Prize Civil Rights Reader: Documents, Speeches, and Firsthand Accounts from the Black Freedom Struggle, 1954–1990.* New York: Penguin Books.

Reardon, William R., and Thomas D. Pawley, eds., 1970. *The Black Teacher and the Dramatic Arts: A Dialogue, Bibliography, and Anthology.* Westport, Connecticut: Negro Universities Press.

Redkey, Edwin S., ed., 1992. *A Grand Army of Black Men: Letters from African American Soldiers in the Union Army, 1861–1865.* New York: Cambridge University Press.

Rhyne, Nancy, 1999. *Voices of Carolina Slave Children.* Orangeburg, South Carolina: Sandlapper Publishing Company.

Schoener, Allon, ed., 1968. *Harlem on my Mind: Cultural Capital of Black America, 1900–1968.* New York: Random House.

Sotiropoulos, Karen. 2006. *Staging Race: Black Performers in Turn of the Century America.* Cambridge: Harvard University Press.

Stephens, Judith A., ed., 2006. *The Plays of Georgia Douglas Johnson: From the New Negro Renaissance to the Civil Rights Movement.* Urbana and Chicago: University of Illinois Press.

Sterling, Dorothy, ed., 1994. *The Trouble they Seen: The Story of Reconstruction in the Words of African Americans.* New York: Da Capo Press.

Stowe, Harriet Beecher, 1981. *Uncle Tom's Cabin.* New York: Penguin Books.

Sweet, Frank W., 2000. *A History of the Minstrel Show.* Palm Coast, Florida: Backintyme.

Taubman, Howard, 1964. "Common Burden: Baldwin Points Duty of Negro and White." *New York Times,* May 3: online at http://www.nytimes.com/books/98/03/29/specials/baldwin-burden.html.

Taylor, Jr., Quintero, 1998. *The Colored Cadet at West Point.* Lincoln, NE: University of Nebraska Press.

Terry, Wallace, 1984. *Bloods: An Oral History of the Vietnam War by Black Veterans.* New York: Ballantine Books.

Till-Mobley, Mamie, and Christopher Benson, 2003. *Death of Innocence: The Story of the Hate Crime that Changed America.* New York: Random House.

Toll, Robert C., 1974. *Blacking Up: The Minstrel Show in Nineteenth Century America.* New York: Oxford University Press.

Traylor, Eleanor W., 1980. "Two Afro-American Contributions to Dramatic Form". In Erroll Hill, ed., *The Theater of Black Americans*, vol. 1. Englewood Cliffs, New Jersey: Prentice-Hall.

Urban League, 1998. "The Opportunity Reader: Stories, Poetry, and Essays from the Urban League's Opportunity Magazine": online at http:www.randomhouse.com/catalog/display.pperi/isbn=9780375753794&view=excerpt.

Van Deburg, William L., 1992. *New Day in Babylon: The Black Power Movement and American Culture, 1965–1975*. Chicago and London: University of Chicago Press.

Vaughan, Marcia, 2001. *The Secret to Freedom*. New York: Lee and Low Books.

Ward, Douglas Turner, 1966. "American Theatre: For Whites Only?" *New York Times*, August 14, Section H, pp. D1, 03.

Washington, Booker T., 1963. *Up from Slavery*. Garden City, New York: Doubleday and Company.

Watkins, Mel, 1994. *On the Real Side*. New York: Simon & Schuster.

White, Floyd, 1940. *In Drums and Shadows: Survival Studies among the Georgia Coastal Negroes. Savannah Unit, Georgia Writers' Project, Work Projects Administration*. Athens; Georgia: University of Georgia Press.

Williams, Linda, 2001. *Playing the Race Card: Melodramas of Black and White from Uncle Tom to O J. Simpson*. Princeton and Oxford: Princeton University Press.

Willis-Braithwaite, Deborah, and Rodger C. Birt, 1993. *Van der Zee: Photographer, 1886–1983*. New York: Harry N. Abrams.

Wilson, August, 1991. *Three Plays*. Pittsburgh: University of Pittsburgh Press.

Wilson, August, 2005. Interview [with Suzan-Lori Parks]. "The Light in August: An African spiritual strength born of adversity undergirds August Wilson's 10-play cycle": Theatre Communications Group, online at http://www.tcg.org/publications/at/Nov05/wilson.cfm.

Wilson, August, 2006. Kansas City Repertory Theatre Play Guide: online at http://www.kcrep.org/box_office/documents/PlayGuide_001.pdf.

Wolfe, George C., 1992–6. "From New Traditions Compendium Forums & Commentaries": online at http://ntcp.org/compendium/artists/GEORGEC.html.

Woll, Allen, 1989. *Black Musical Theatre: From Coontown to Dreamgirls*. Baton Rouge and London: Louisiana State University Press.

Women in History, updated 2008. "Rebecca Jackson Biography. Lakewood Public Library": online at http://www.lkwdpl.org/wihohio/jack-reb.htm.

Woodward, C. Vann, 1957. *The Strange Career of Jim Crow*. New York: Oxford University Press.

Yetman, Norman R., ed., 1970, repr. 2000. *Voices from Slavery*. Mineola, New York: Dover Publications.

Yetman, Norman R., ed., 1970, repr. 2002. *When I was a Slave: Memoirs from the Slave Narrative Collection*. Mineola, New York: Dover Publications.

Index

O'Connor, John, 111
Old-Time Negro Preacher, 17, 18, 20–1,
    60, 83
O'Neal, Frederick, 96
O'Neill, Eugene, 92, 179
oral history, 11
Orman, Roscoe, 14

Pan-Africanism, 129, 175
Papp, Joseph, 150, 155, 165
Parks, Rosa, 115, 116, 135, 190, 191–2
Parks, Suzan-Lori, 1, 4–5, 175, 179, 188–9
Patterson, Chuck, 14
Pattillo, Melba, 116–17
patty rollers, 14, 18, 34, 67
Peake, Mary, 54
Perkins, Kathy, 69
Peters, Brock, 159
Picaninny, 22, 23
Pickens, James, 107
Plessy vs. Ferguson, 57
Poitier, Sidney, 96, 153, 162, 164, 166,
    175, 176, 179
Pollard, Mother, 116
Powell, Adam Clayton, 83, 94, 149
Powell, Clifton, 166–8
Preminger, Otto, 186
Progressive Era, 58–9
prohibition, 83
Prosser, Gabriel, 29, 30–1, 175
Pryor, Richard, 18, 26
Pullman Porters, 72–3
Purvis, Robert, 41

Quakers, 29, 41
quilts, 35–7, 42

Race Men, 59-60
Race Women, 62–5, 67–9
radio, 76–7
Raimes, Ving, 167
Randall, Dudley, 60–1
Randolph, Asa Philip, 73
Randolph, Philip, 134
Ransby, Barbara, 135, 136
rape, 14
Rashad, Phylicia, 147, 168, 169, 171–3,
    179, 181, 188

Ray, Gloria, 117
Reagon, Bernice Johnson, 4, 135
Reconstruction era, 2, 51, 65, 66, 71
Redding, Otis, 169
Redemption, 66, 69–70
Rice, Thomas "Daddy," 21
Richard Allen Cultural Center, 147, 155,
    161
Richards, Lloyd, 175, 177, 179, 190,
    192
Richardson, Latonya, 160
Richmond, David, 119–20
Rick, Willie, 131, 132
Riley, Larry, 107
Ringgold, Faith, 42
Roberts, Terrance, 116–17
Robertson, Carol, 128
Robeson, Paul, 89, 91–3, 153–6, 162,
    164, 166, 176, 177, 179
Robinson, Bill Bojangles, 82, 112, 185
Rochelle, Nicolle, 91
Rock, Chris, 18
Roger, Alex, 26
Roosevelt, Eleanor, 126
Roosevelt, Teddy, 99
Roots, 15–16, 52
Rowe, Katie, 50
Rudd, John, 14
Ruff, Roslyn, 190
Rutledge, Sabe, 50

Sanchez, Sonia, 93
Sanders, Pharaoh, 107
Sands, Diana, 114, 157–8, 175
Sanitation Workers' Strike (Memphis,
    1968), 183–4
Savary, Jerome, 91
Sayles, John, 165
Schoener, Allon, 95
Schomburg, Arturo Alfonso, 87
Schuyler, George, 134
Schwerner, Andrew, 123, 126
Seaton, Sandra, 68
segregation, 57, 97, 113–23
Sellers, Cleveland, 131–2
separate but equal, 57, 113
Serban, Andrei, 155
Shabazz, Betty, 129, 190